Just War and Ordered Liberty

When is war just? What does justice require? If we lack a commonly-accepted understanding of justice – and thus of just war – what answers can we find in the intellectual history of just war? Miller argues that just war thinking should be understood as unfolding in three traditions: the Augustinian, the Westphalian, and the Liberal, each resting on distinct understandings of natural law, justice, and sovereignty. The central ideas of the Augustinian tradition (sovereignty as responsibility for the common good) can and should be recovered and worked into the Liberal tradition, for which human rights serves the same function. In this reconstructed Augustinian Liberal vision, the violent disruption of ordered liberty is the injury in response to which force may be used and war may be justly waged. Justice requires the vindication and restoration of ordered liberty in, through, and after warfare.

Paul D. Miller is a professor of the practice of international affairs at Georgetown University, a senior nonresident fellow with the Atlantic Council, and a research fellow with the Ethics and Religious Liberty Commission. He served as director for Afghanistan and Pakistan on the National Security Council staff in the White House for Presidents George W. Bush and Barack Obama. He previously served in the Central Intelligence Agency and is a veteran of the war in Afghanistan with the US Army.

T0381700

Just War and Ordered Liberty

Paul D. Miller

Georgetown University

CAMBRIDGE
UNIVERSITY PRESS

CAMBRIDGE
UNIVERSITY PRESS

University Printing House, Cambridge CB2 8BS, United Kingdom

One Liberty Plaza, 20th Floor, New York, NY 10006, USA

477 Williamstown Road, Port Melbourne, VIC 3207, Australia

314–321, 3rd Floor, Plot 3, Splendor Forum, Jasola District Centre, New Delhi – 110025, India

79 Anson Road, #06–04/06, Singapore 079906

Cambridge University Press is part of the University of Cambridge.

It furthers the University's mission by disseminating knowledge in the pursuit of education, learning, and research at the highest international levels of excellence.

www.cambridge.org
Information on this title: www.cambridge.org/9781108834681
DOI: 10.1017/9781108876544

First published 2021

A catalogue record for this publication is available from the British Library.

Library of Congress Cataloging-in-Publication Data
Names: Miller, Paul David, author.
Title: Just war and ordered liberty / Paul David Miller.
Description: Cambridge, United Kingdom ; New York, NY : Cambridge University Press, 2021. | Includes bibliographical references and index.
Identifiers: LCCN 2020028704 (print) | LCCN 2020028705 (ebook) | ISBN 9781108834681 (hardback) | ISBN 9781108876544 (epub)
Subjects: LCSH: Just war doctrine. | War (Philosophy) | War – Moral an ethical aspects. | United States – Military policy – 21st century – Case studies.
Classification: LCC U21.2 .M5624 2021 (print) | LCC U21.2 (ebook) | DDC 172/.42–dc23
LC record available at https://lccn.loc.gov/2020028704
LC ebook record available at https://lccn.loc.gov/2020028705

ISBN 978-1-108-83468-1 Hardback
ISBN 978-1-108-81971-8 Paperback

This book is dedicated to my grandfather, Harold E. Miller (1913–88), and my father, David H. Miller (1944–). Coming from the Mennonite tradition, both were pacifists and conscientious objectors during World War II and the Vietnam War, respectively. My father challenged me to justify my decision to serve in the United States Army. Though this book is a not a direct response to pacifism, it is, with love, the fruit of a lifetime of reflection on justice and war inspired by our debates.

As long as the empire of the Roman People maintained itself by acts of service, not of oppression, wars were waged in the interest of our allies or to safeguard our supremacy; the end of our wars was marked by acts of clemency or by only a necessary degree of severity; the Senate was a haven of refuge for kings, tribes, and nations; and the highest ambition of our magistrates and generals was to defend our provinces and allies with justice and honor. And so our government could be called more accurately a protectorate of the world than a dominion.

—Marcus Tullius Cicero, *On Duties,* book II, chapter VIII

Contents

Acknowledgments

I concluded my first book, *Armed State Building*, by briefly speculating about what it might look like to apply just war to the problem of state failure and state building. In my second book, *American Power and Liberal Order*, I acknowledged a debt to the just war framework and asserted that the grand strategy I proposed was inspired by and consistent with it – without specifying exactly how. This book is an overdue explication of how I understand just war and how it fits with my body of work. With my call, in Chapters 6 and 7, for a marriage between the Augustinian and Liberal traditions, this book also sets the table for a subsequent work of political theory exploring Augustinian Liberalism and its application at home and abroad.

I have quoted at length from a number of ancient, medieval, and early modern texts, most of which are available only in older translations. Like many scholars before me, I benefited from the Carnegie Institution's Classics of International Law, published between 1911 and 1950. I want to acknowledge the Liberty Fund and especially its Liberty Library, which has republished or made available online many of the texts in the Carnegie series and much else besides. There is a crying need for newer translations, critical editions, accessible versions, and (for the sake of my students) abridgments of many of these works (especially those by Gentili and Grotius). For ease of reading, I have standardized and Americanized spelling and capitalization in all quotations.

This manuscript has been reviewed by the CIA's Prepublications Classification Review Board to prevent the disclosure of classified information.

Portions of this book borrow from previously published material. These articles are used with permission of the publishers: "The Lessons of Iraq," *The City*, Winter 2011, Houston Baptist University; "Reassessing Obama's Legacy of Restraint," *War on the Rocks*, March 6, 2017; "Afghanistan, Justice, and War," *First Things*, February 2013; "Augustinian Liberalism: A Symposium," and "Augustine of Hippo, Christian Democrat," *Providence Magazine*, Spring/Summer 2018;

"The Price of Cheap Order: Afghanistan, America, and Endless War," *Providence Magazine*, December 2018.

I would like to thank the participants of the 2019 Just War Symposium hosted by the McDonald Centre for Theology, Ethics, and Public Life at Christ Church, Oxford University, who critiqued an earlier draft of this manuscript. Special thanks to Marc LiVecche, Nigel Biggar, James Turner Johnson, Daniel Strand, Debra Erickson, J. Daryl Charles, Joe Capizzi, Steven Firmin, and Jessica Gliserman. Thanks as well to *Providence Magazine* for funding the symposium. Thank you to Bessie Blackburn and, again, James Turner Johnson, for volunteering to review the completed manuscript.

I would also like to thank the students of "Just War and International Relations," an undergraduate seminar at the University of Texas at Austin in the spring of 2018: Brandon Bengston, Taner Mauro, Charlie Bell, Drew Williams, Jon Murphy, Mariam Soufi, Chase Underwood, Garrett Thomas, Jon Roberts, Harrison Scott, Nolan McCarthy, Siara Shoemaker, Brandon Brown, Zeyi Lin, Jacob Ali, Anna Muy, Matthew Noriega, and Annalisa Stoll. Our discussions shaped this book and I deeply appreciate the honesty, respect, and thoughtfulness of our semester-long dialogue. Thanks as well to Dr. Luke Perez for pushing me to teach the seminar and begin work on this book.

Finally, thank you to my children, Liam, Lily, and Lydia, for pulling me back to real life when I became too preoccupied with this book; and to my wife, Jennilee, for your infinite patience and boundless love.

1   Thinking about War

I did not begin by thinking about war in general but about a particular war, above all about the American intervention in Afghanistan.[1] This may sound odd because the war was quickly overshadowed by wars in Iraq, against ISIS, in Syria, by Russia, and much else besides. Most observers long ago turned their attention elsewhere. But having served in Afghanistan with the US Army; as an analyst for the Central Intelligence Agency in the Office of South Asian Analysis; and as director for Afghanistan and Pakistan on the National Security Council staff in the White House for presidents George W. Bush and Barack Obama, I did not have that luxury. I have also chosen to focus much of my scholarship on Afghanistan in the years since. Having given a decade of my life to the war, it was deeply personal to me – even before Humam Khalil Abu-Mulal al-Balawi murdered a friend of mine with a suicide bomb in Khowst in 2009.

My thinking about justice and war largely took shape during my involvement in the Afghan war. I continually asked myself not merely whether we had just cause to go to war in Afghanistan, which seemed so obviously true as to need little argument, but *what does justice require?* What did it mean to accomplish justice through the instrument of war in Afghanistan and against jihadists worldwide? What would a just outcome look like? How do we justly win and conclude such a war? These questions, more than the simple question of the immediate triggering cause of the war, seemed to need answers. I found little discussion of these issues in the emerging literature on just war in Afghanistan. As with many students, among the works I consulted was Michael Walzer's *Just and Unjust Wars*; as I discuss in Chapter 5, I found his examination of intervention unsatisfying. Jean Bethke Elshtain's *Just War against Terror*,

---

[1] Interestingly, almost none of the major authors under consideration in this book bear the same relationship to a specific conflict in their day. The closest is Walzer and his opposition to the war in Vietnam, which inspired *Just and Unjust Wars*. Readers of Walzer will recognize the homage I have paid to him here.

written in response to the terrorist attacks of 2001, was little better: a polemic against pacifism and a defense of American leadership against the enemies of civilization. I felt her argument was true but rudimentary: I agreed with it so far as it went, but I felt and still feel that there is much more to be said about justice and war.

In my first contact with just war scholarship, I was dissatisfied by the notion that war must always be justified as an act of self-defense. The United States' initial military operations against al-Qaida in 2001–2 were clearly justified acts of self-defense, removing the threat of future al-Qaida attacks. But on a gut level, I felt that self-defense was morally unsatisfying as a full explanation for what the war was supposed to be about. Even in 2001 and 2002, it seemed to me *unjust* to simply kill or capture as many al-Qaida operatives as possible and retire from the battlefield. Such a war would be a war of vengeance and bloodlust – emotionally satisfying in the moment but not something that would hold up under later theological or historical scrutiny. War is not about making sure the right people are dead. War is – as I learned from Augustine – about building a better peace. War is not intrinsically good; it may be instrumentally good, but only if it serves the ends of peace and justice – otherwise it is simply wicked. What was the peace and justice we were seeking in the fight against jihadists and in the war in Afghanistan? *When is war just? What does justice require?* These questions led me to read deeply in the just war literature, and they were the seeds that grew, over the course of twenty years, into this book.

The Problems

Just war scholarship is a body of thought about restrictions that should be placed on the occasion and conduct of war. It seeks to answer some of the most consequential questions of politics and philosophy: When is war just? What does justice require? Just war stands in distinction to pacifism, according to which it is never just to kill, and realism, according to which killing needs no justification other than raison d'état. Just warriors believe that killing is a morally serious act that needs special justification – but that such justification is nonetheless possible.

Unfortunately, public discussion about the justice or injustice of war faces the same challenge that all public discussion has faced in the postmodern era: a lack of agreed-upon foundations. Because of the religious and philosophical pluralism of contemporary democratic society, we lack a commonly accepted understanding of justice. As a result, the just war discourse often seems to be little more than a ritualized intellectual game, one in which contestants use the same words – words like "justice," "just war," and even "right" and "wrong" – to mean different things. As one scholar has noted, there are "many diverse views on which assumptions, conditions, and commitments are key to, and definitive of, this tradition."[2]

Additionally, much of just war scholarship through the twentieth century was concerned with World War II, the Cold War, the advent of nuclear weapons, and the Vietnam War. These concerns are decreasingly relevant in the post-Cold War era. Interstate war has been on a long-term decline since World War II, war between great powers has vanished (so far), and international borders enjoy a high level of integrity compared to earlier centuries. Nuclear war – especially a devastating global nuclear exchange – seems far less likely now than at any time since the dawn of the nuclear age. These developments could plausibly be interpreted as the triumph of just war thinking: changing norms about the acceptability of war as an instrument of national policy may have contributed, in part, to the decline in interstate war. If so, just war's triumph was also its undoing: the animating concerns of much of twentieth-century just war thinking are not as prominent today.[3]

But in place of interstate war, great power war, and nuclear war, the twenty-first century has brought a host of new security challenges (or old challenges under new guises), including transnational organized criminal networks, terrorist groups, slavers, pirates, and drug traffickers – phenomena rarely addressed in just war thought prior to the end of the Cold War. Other transnational phenomena, including humanitarian crises, refugee flows, natural disasters, pandemic disease, and environmental emergencies, have prompted calls for states to use military force to contain or mitigate the effects of such events, again without much guidance from just war thinking until the end of the Cold War.

Political leaders still need ethical guidelines for the use of force in changing circumstances and normative pluralism. Offering realistic and prudent recommendations about the ethics of military force that are relevant to the security challenges of the contemporary world and that can command an overlapping consensus in the public square is an extraordinarily difficult task. How can the just war framework be reshaped to address these contemporary security concerns and speak to the broadest audience possible?

Since the end of the Cold War, many scholars have tried to make the just war framework relevant. There is a burgeoning literature that applies

---

[2] O'Driscoll, *Renegotiation of the Just War Tradition*, 92.
[3] See Murray, "Remarks on the Moral Problem of War," for an example of just war thinking in the early Cold War. On the post-Cold War evolution, see Hehir, "Just War Theory in a Post-Cold War World." See also Walzer, *Arguing about War*, chapter 1.

just war categories to individual questions of the contemporary security environment. But their efforts have been piecemeal. There is a wide-ranging discussion focused on the justice of humanitarian interventions,[4] culminating in the development of the "Responsibility to Protect."[5] After the terrorist attacks of 2001, another discussion focused on just war against nonstate actors, the justice of targeted killings, and war against (or by) nonuniformed combatants.[6] Others have tried to adapt just war thinking to the problem of cyberwar,[7] robots,[8] torture,[9] drones,[10] and private security companies.[11] Scholars are trying to answer a range of questions: Is intervening to help a failed state a new form of imperialism, or is it the moral duty of great powers? What rules should govern the use of force against nonstate actors? What are the implications of fighting ter-rorists or other nonstate actors abroad, in another state incapable or unwilling to fight them? What is the justice of stability and peacebuilding operations? What are the ethics of drone warfare, cyber warfare, and covert action?

These are helpful efforts, but these debates have been muddied by the tendency to discuss a variety of different problems without reference to each other. There is one debate over humanitarian intervention, another one over post-conflict reconstruction, another one over the Responsibility to Protect, and others over counterinsurgency, counterterrorism, military occupation, and nation building. And scholars have made little progress offering a foundation for just war that can win broad agreement in our pluralistic societies.

Part of the reason just war scholarship has been unable to address these questions adequately is because it has been cut off from its own roots. A final problem this book grapples with is the problem of the intellectual history of just war inquiry.[12] While it may seem that this is only a problem for scholars and academic specialists, I argue that the ahistorical nature of some contemporary just war thinking is directly linked to its unfocused and unsatisfying nature. Much of contemporary just war thinking tends to be secular, legal, and ahistorical compared to the rich theological world-view from which the language of just war originally sprang. Just war

---

[4] Boyle, "Traditional Just War Theory." Elshtain, "Third Annual Grotius Lecture." Fixdal and Smith, "Humanitarian Intervention and Just War."

[5] Weiss, et al., *Responsibility to Protect.*

[6] Bellamy, *Fighting Terror.* Boyle, "Just War Doctrine." Elshtain, *Just War against Terror.* Flint and Falah, "How the United States Justified Its War." Totten, *First Strike.*

[7] Eberle, "Just War and Cyberwar."

[8] Simpson and Müller, "Just War and Robots' Killings."

[9] Cole, "Torture and Just War."   [10] Williams, "Distant Intimacy."

[11] Fitzsimmons, "Just War Theory and Private Security Companies."

[12] O'Driscoll, "Divisions within the Ranks?"

thinking was, for centuries, a branch of Christian political theology. But just war thinkers gradually substituted legal for theological reasoning during the early modern era: just war migrated from a branch of theology to a subset of international law. The result has been to turn a holistic worldview that tied love to public justice and human flourishing into a narrow, procedural version of justice, and to turn a doctrine of the use of force into a checklist for international lawyers. As Nicholas Rengger argues, just war thinking "has been forced into an intellectual framework ill suited to its intellectual style and most effective mode of being."[13] That is why modern just war thought has tended to lack adequate foundations for its claims and to reduce a complex body of thought to one overriding rule: do not cross international borders with armed force.

But the historical foundations of just war thinking do not provide easy answers either. For example, part of this book is motivated by a simple question: what is a just cause for war? There is an alarming diversity of answers to that question among just war thinkers. Augustine's standard is vague: war is a response to an injury received. What kind of injury? At what scale? By whom, against whom? Is the injured party the only one who can respond, or can others respond on his or her behalf? Does the injury have to take place across international borders? Augustine gives no answers. Later thinkers would provide specific, diverging, and sometimes expansive lists of just causes, including: to defend the true faith, to enforce the right of free passage, to enforce the right to proselytize, to defend against invasion, to recover stolen property, to exact recompense for damages, to deter future wrongdoing, to vindicate honor, to preserve the balance of power, to defend the innocent, to defend one's rights, to defend human rights generally, to punish the wicked, to punish crimes against nature, to stop genocide, and more. There is no consensus, no satisfying answer to the most important questions of just war inquiry. When is war just? What does justice require?

Interestingly, virtually no work has appeared addressing the implications for just war of the most significant change in international politics since 1945, the one I argue provides the umbrella concept under which the rest can be set in relation to one another and that can center the debate in widely accepted norms: the system of ordered liberty among nations. The existence of the liberal international order is itself the primary reason states even contemplate undertaking humanitarian interventions because liberal ideals drive states to alleviate human suffering. Similarly, the existence of the international liberal order is why the response to the terrorist attacks of 2001 was, for the most part, a coordinated, global,

---

[13] Rengger, "On the Just War Tradition," 361.

internationalized response rather than the response of a single state. Finally, the language of classical liberalism that undergirds the liberal international order is still used and respected broadly enough to enjoy consensus in a pluralistic society and to root our deliberations about war in democratic legitimacy.

The Arguments of This Work

In this work I advance several interwoven arguments to reformulate just war thinking and address the challenges of the contemporary security environment. First, I advance a historical argument. I argue the intellectual history of just war thinking should be understood as unfolding in three traditions, which I call the Augustinian, the Westphalian, and the Liberal. Cian O'Driscoll is right that "In place of a unified or coherent just war tradition, we are greeted by a cluster of rival theories and competing visions …. We must acknowledge the possibility that there is no such thing as the just war tradition, singularly conceived."[14] Or as Anthony Coates judged, "The unity that is the just war tradition embraces many formulations that contend one with another and that defy uniform classification."[15] The multiplicity of just war traditions accounts for the unfocused nature of just war debates in the post-Cold War era. "There are significant differences, not only in the conclusions reached, but in the conceptions of just war theory employed to reach those conclusions,"[16] according to James Turner Johnson.

Just war thinking is best understood as a kind of applied political theory. Each just war tradition is an application of a different set of deeper philosophical commitments. The difference between traditions is seen at the level of fundamental concepts, in how they treat the issues of natural law, justice, and sovereignty; and at the level of application, in how they treat the issues of civil war and humanitarian intervention.[17] The Augustinian just war tradition is an application of the political theory of medieval Christendom; the Westphalian, of the early modern Enlightenment; and the Liberal, of the broader commitments of classical liberalism. (The three traditions are roughly, but not strictly, chronological. They overlap in time during transitional eras where concepts were evolving slowly, as I trace in Chapter 3.) This way of understanding the

---

[14] O'Driscoll, *Renegotiation of the Just War Tradition*, 92, 110. O'Driscoll ultimately concludes there is such a thing as the just war tradition: as a shared moral language and an interpretive community with plural meanings. It is the plural meanings I focus on here.
[15] Coates, "Humanitarian Intervention," 59.
[16] Johnson, *Ethics and the Use of Force*, 2.
[17] Boyle, "Traditional Just War Theory." Coates, "Humanitarian Intervention," 59.

history of just war thinking helps better frame its evolution: instead of a dichotomy between "classic" and "modern" just war, or between "religious" and "secular," both of which carry implicit judgments about which version of just war is "right," this framework aims to be more descriptive and, thus, gives us more latitude to draw the best from each tradition.[18]

The Augustinian tradition of just war thinking was an application of medieval political theory with roots in antiquity that matured into its classic expression during the Wars of Religion. This pre-Enlightenment political theory rested on the idea that natural law exists and should guide human social and political order to fulfill natural human moral aspirations; that sovereignty means responsibility for the common good; and that justice should guide states to use force to defend and uphold the common good. In that context, just cause for war was understood to include not merely self-defense, but the defense of justice and peace, defense of the innocent, and punishment of the wicked – as defined by the commonly accepted, teleological standards of natural law. Statesmen in turn were expected to wage war to defend the common good and, broadly, uphold peace and justice. And statesmen were to fight war with the right intention: out of love for one's neighbor and one's enemies, not for glory, honor, revenge, or profit. Fighting to uphold justice and to prevent the wicked from perpetrating justice was understood as the duty Christian love required of statesmen.

The Westphalian tradition arose after the Thirty Years War and the Peace of Westphalia (1648). It moved away from the Augustinian tradition in three respects. It was a tradition of legal reasoning, not political theology; its conception of natural law was descriptive, not teleological; and it tended to focus on procedural justice, not substantive justice. Together these innovations amounted to a change in the fundamental orientation of just war thinking, which is why I characterize it as a change of tradition, not a change within the tradition. The Westphalian tradition left behind much of the theological background that had given the medieval tradition its content and meaning. The vestigial language of "just cause" and "right authority" remained, for example, but with transformed meanings. Because natural law jettisoned its teleological aspect, Westphalian thinkers also had a different notion of justice, and therefore of just cause and sovereignty: sovereignty evolved from defense of the

---

[18] On the downsides of Johnson's usage of the term "classic" just war, see Zehr, "James Turner Johnson and the 'Classic' Just War Tradition." By recognizing the plurality of just war traditions, I also sidestep the question of whether Christian churches or theologians are in a position of special authority over a singular tradition. They might claim such a status over the Augustinian tradition, but not the later traditions. See Lang, "Just War Tradition and the Question of Authority."

common good to defense of international borders and just cause consequently shrank to encompass only territorial self-defense. The right authority for the use of force was understood unproblematically to rest with the state, regardless of how the state chose to use it or for what purpose.

The embryonic Liberal tradition has arisen since World War II in an effort to rectify the weaknesses of the Westphalian tradition and, since the end of the Cold War, address new and emerging security concerns, often by borrowing and reinterpreting Augustinian concepts shorn of their theological commitments. Concepts such as human rights and accountable governance do the work that natural law and justice did in the Augustinian tradition: external standards outside and above the state, used to judge the state's legitimacy. War is just when it vindicates rights, including the rights of states whose security has been violated, of course, but also the rights of individuals. The Liberal just war tradition allows war to vindicate the rights of individuals suffering under a humanitarian emergency, insists on respecting individual rights in how war is fought, and understands the vindication of individual rights as a crucial part of ending wars justly. The Liberal school is still developing and there is no consensus on its boundaries yet, so my characterization of it inevitably involves my own choices and preferences.

But my purpose is not merely descriptive and historical. I am a participant and partisan in the ongoing conversation about just war. The second main argument of this book is that the emerging Liberal tradition is right to highlight weaknesses of the Westphalian tradition, and that there is a fundamental compatibility between the Augustinian and Liberal traditions. The central organizing concepts of the Augustinian tradition (love and the common good as external standards outside and above the state) can and should be recovered and worked into the Liberal tradition, for which human rights serves the same function. The Augustinian tradition of just war thinking argued that the right intention of warfare was love for our neighbors and for our enemies. It further argued that the defense not of self, but of the common good was the lived embodiment of such love. Much the same can be said with the idiom of human rights: the right intention in war is to vindicate rights, and just cause in war is to defend and uphold a system of ordered liberty for allies and enemies alike. As Johnson rightly argues, "There are striking similarities between the assumptions basic to classic just war thinking and certain features of contemporary armed conflict."[19] This approach promises to make just war relevant to the contemporary security environment

---

[19] Johnson, *Ethics and the Use of Force*, 89. See also Coates, "Humanitarian Intervention."

and to do so on moral foundations – those of classical liberalism – that can command an overlapping consensus in the contemporary, pluralistic public square.

Just war was never an isolated exercise in military ethics; it was originally an argument about the rights and purposes of the state, about natural law, and about justice. Even in its Westphalian guise, just war was an argument against theocracy and universal empire. The early modern Augustinians argued that wars for religion were utopian, inconsistent with humanity's sinful nature, doomed to achieve the opposite of the justice they professed, and that they violated the state's God-given jurisdiction. But other thinkers reached the same conclusions by different routes. The same body of political theory – the theory of secularized Christendom – gave birth to classical liberalism and, eventually, to what we today call the liberal international order. Even the Westphalian tradition was animated by a desire to thwart utopian and universal imperial ambitions. The similarity between just war in all its guises and classical liberalism is why a reconstituted Liberal just war approach can command a consensus in liberal democratic societies. Like the just war traditions, classical liberalism also argues that there are limits on the state's jurisdiction; that sovereignty is not unlimited; that there should be no coercion in matters of belief; and that universal empire is a dangerous ambition. If we are to be faithful to the political theory of the just war traditions, we should by the same logic be faithful to the political theology of classical liberalism and its progeny, the liberal international order. Similar principles animate both. Indeed, the kinship goes so far that, if it is a just cause to oppose universal empire, we might just as well say that the defense of liberalism is a just cause. It is a just cause to defend a system designed to prevent universal empire, to guard against theocracy or ideological totalism, and to enforce limits on government's jurisdiction: that system is what we today call the liberal international order. This view draws on the Augustinian tradition's surprisingly expansive view of the self, whose defense justifies war. War is just when fought in the defense of our individual selves, our states, our allies, our neighbors, but also of innocent victims of oppression, and even the commonwealth of all humanity when it is threatened by grievous crimes against nature. Building on the Augustinians' view of the corporate self, I argue that the defense of the liberal international order is a just cause.[20] The liberal international order

---

[20] Implicit within my argument is a methodological point. I lean on a historical and theological approach to just war thinking because this approach corrects for the limitations of the Westphalian tradition and early attempts at formulating the Liberal tradition. In this I broadly concur with Johnson's approach, though Johnson may occasionally go too far in stressing the normative authority of what he calls the "classic" tradition. For

is the contemporary manifestation of the global common good whose defense is just for its members and the preservation of which reflects love for our neighbors and for our enemies.

I apply this Augustinian Liberal framework to the two questions animating this book. First, when is war just? The violent disruption of ordered liberty is the "injury" in response to which force may be used and war may be justly waged. This obviously covers cases of defense against invasion, but it also covers humanitarian intervention. The Augustinian tradition at its zenith (from the early sixteenth to the mid-seventeenth century) explicitly addressed the problems of what today we call state failure, armed nonstate actors, and humanitarian intervention. These thinkers argued that the sovereign had just cause to wield force against nonstate actors and, even, to redress conditions of state failure, although typically with strong qualifications. These writers rested their arguments on an underlying philosophical framework: war, they believed, was an extension of the sovereign responsibility to defend the common good (itself an extension of a prior and more fundamental duty to love all humanity), and under extreme conditions love demands intervention to punish the wicked and defend the innocent, even when that involves crossing international boundaries. As Johnson has argued about humanitarian intervention, "This is a fundamental just war idea, but one which has been obscured by the Westphalian system's focus on sovereignty as tied to territorial boundaries."[21]

Second, what does justice require? Justice requires the vindication and restoration of ordered liberty in, through, and after warfare. From the Augustinian Liberal framework, I argue for a strong and expansive understanding of *jus post bellum*: war requires victors to make right the wrongs that prompted the war, make right the wrongs *of* war (the destruction of combat), and prevent the recurrence of such wrongs in the future. The upshot of my argument is that while just cause is more expansive than is conventionally understood, the responsibilities of post-conflict restoration are commensurably far higher. Taken together, this Augustinian Liberal approach to just war thinking permits intervention but *increases international responsibility for what intervention entails*, and thus should dampen any enthusiasm for intervention that might otherwise exist.

---

a discussion of Johnson's approach, and its critics, see O'Driscoll, "Hedgehog or Fox?" and "James Turner Johnson's Just War Idea."

[21] Johnson, *Ethics and the Use of Force*, 92. See also O'Driscoll, *Renegotiation of the Just War Tradition*, chapter 4.

Methodology

The first main argument of this book is a historical argument. Much of this book is thus a work of intellectual history. I tell a story about the development of just war thinking and argue that we should understand that story as unfolding in three distinct traditions. I am building on an uncontested and universal recognition in the scholarly literature that just war thinking has evolved and changed over centuries. Scholars have offered different ways of categorizing the differences evident in just war thought. For example, Johnson distinguishes between the "classic" and "modern" just war doctrines, Richard Tuck between the "scholastic" and "humanistic" just war traditions, Coates between "traditional" and "modern," and Daniel M. Bell Jr. between just war as a component of Christian discipleship and just war as a public policy checklist.[22]

My original contribution to this historical debate is twofold. First, I make explicit the criteria by which I distinguish one tradition from another: changing notions of natural law, justice, and sovereignty, because these are the foundational concepts to which thinkers appeal to justify their arguments about the justice of war. Why these concepts? I came on these foundational concepts in the course of research for this book. Quentin Skinner counsels that to do intellectual history we must "trace the relations between the given utterance" – in my case, utterances about just cause – "and this wider linguistic context as a means of decoding the actual intention of the given writer."[23] I originally set out to write a history of the concept of *just cause* but found I could not do so without also tracing the concepts of natural law, justice, and sovereignty, which comprise the "wider linguistic context" of discussions about just cause.

By using this criteria I offer my second contribution to the historical debate: clarifying that there are three traditions, not two, defined by the

---

[22] See Bell, *Just War as Christian Discipleship*; Coates, "Humanitarian Intervention"; Johnson, *Ideology, Reason, and the Limitation of War*; Tuck, *Rights of War and Peace*. Biggar calls the tradition from Augustine to Grotius the "early Christian" just war tradition in Biggar, *In Defence of War*, chapter 5. The *Stanford Encyclopedia of Philosophy* distinguishes between "traditionalists" and "revisionists," which is roughly parallel to the difference between the Westphalian and Liberal traditions. See https://plato.stanford.edu/entries/war/. One of the earlier attempts to chart the history of this conversation was Van Vollenhoven's classic discussion in *The Three Stages in the Evolution of the Law of Nations*. His three stages –1570–1770, 1770–1914, and the post-World War I era – suffer from their omission of anything before the early modern era and subsequent to the Great War. His later two stages can map roughly onto what I have called the Westphalian and Liberal traditions, though his liberal tradition was more an aspiration than a reality in his day. On the history of just war thinking, see also Begby et al., "Ethics of War. Part I"; Nardin, "Moral Basis for Humanitarian Intervention"; von Elbe, "Evolution of the Concept of the Just War."

[23] Skinner, "Meaning and Understanding in the History of Ideas," 49.

major shifts in western intellectual currents, which I call the Augustinian, the Westphalian, and the Liberal. Defining and describing the history of just war thought this way is original to the literature and (what might be considered a third contribution of this book) helps highlight the distinctive aspects of each just war tradition and each thinker, as shown throughout the subsequent chapters.

I am drawing here on the idea that an intellectual tradition is an ongoing cross-generational conversation with shared parameters and meanings in which later discussants take up, interrogate, evolve, and comment on the words of their predecessors. Traditions can evolve, but they have a hard core of consistent and shared concepts and interpretations; any change to them amounts not to a change within a tradition but to a change of tradition. In tracing the evolution of the concepts of justice, sovereignty, and natural law, I am attempting a similar task, on a small scale, as what Alasdair MacIntyre did in his groundbreaking work. His argument about the change in the meaning of words, such as *rationality* and *virtue*, and thus in the moral traditions they infuse, is similar to what I am suggesting here.[24]

What is a tradition? "Tradition was the name given to those cultural features which, in situations of change, were to be continued to be handed on, thought about, preserved and not lost," according to one anthropologist.[25] Tradition is "the symbols, stories, and memories which gave one both identity and status," or a "reservoir," a collection of "selected aspects of a past" worth preserving against change.[26] An intellectual tradition is a continuous epistemic community that appeals to a recognized source of authority and legitimacy, a standard or canon that distinguishes what is deemed worth passing on from what can be cast aside.

In that sense, a tradition can be recognized when certain ideas, words, texts, or authors are "marked" as special by being repeated, quoted, or literally transcribed by subsequent generations. These "marked" texts are not slavishly followed but often reinterpreted to serve the needs of the present. "Tradition resorts to a 'consensual mode of theorizing', 'a situation in which all members of a community ... share a single over-arching framework of secondary-theoretical assumptions and carry out intellectual innovation within that framework,'" according to another scholar.[27] Such innovation is carried out with an eye to what is relevant for the needs of one's day: "The re-arrangements and adaptations undergone by

---

[24] MacIntyre, *After Virtue* and *Whose Justice? Which Rationality?*
[25] Graburn, "What Is Tradition?," 6.   [26] Graburn, "What Is Tradition?," 7, 9.
[27] R. Horton, quoted in Boyer, "Stuff 'Traditions' Are Made Of," 51.

traditional stories are a consequence of their pertinence. People must 'process' them in order to remember them, as a material that cannot be connected to previous knowledge is very likely to be abandoned."[28] That is why traditions show internal variance and change; indeed, a tradition that does not change quickly dies because it becomes disconnected from the felt needs of its originating culture. "The study of tradition must deal with what is actually treated as 'relevant', 'repeated' and 'authoritative' in people's minds."[29]

In studying just war traditions, we are studying the repetition and evolution of key ideas, concepts, words, and texts over the course of centuries. Some scholars have criticized this way of reconstructing just war thinking, arguing that we cannot treat it as a sort of "relay race" in which the baton of concepts and ideas are handed off seamlessly from one thinker to the next. This critique, if true, would cast doubt on the integrity of the narrative I relate below. The criticism applies best to the pre-Thomistic era, and I acknowledge in the narrative below how Augustine's legacy was recognized and appropriated retroactively. From Thomas Aquinas onward, there is a traceable "relay race" of ideas, at least through the eighteenth century, evidenced by thinkers' regular citations of and responses to one another.[30] The traditions I trace are not about the narrow use of a few technical terms, such as *iustum bellum*, but are a broad stream of political theory, including concepts of natural law and sovereignty. This broader array of concepts means there are more points of contact between generations, which thus makes them more traceable across time. Indeed, the very fact that Francisco de Vitoria quotes Aquinas, and Francisco Suárez quotes Vitoria, and they all quote Augustine is strong evidence that there is an intellectual tradition worth tracing. The fact that Samuel von Pufendorf chooses to quote different authorities (Thomas Hobbes above all), and that Christian von Wolff then takes his cue from Pufendorf, is again strong evidence that we are looking at a new tradition. (A note on terminology: I use the phrases *just war thinking, inquiry, scholarship,* or *framework* as all-inclusive terms to refer to any reflection on justice and war. I reserve *just war tradition* to refer to one of the three traditions I describe in this book.)

---

[28] Pascal, "Stuff 'Traditions' Are Made Of," 62.
[29] Pascal, "Stuff 'Traditions' Are Made Of," 64.
[30] See Wynn, *Augustine on War and Military Service*, 131. In a second line of criticism, Wynn emphasizes (rightly) that just war ideas are embedded in the "ongoing *practice of political culture*," (131, emphasis in original), which he implies (wrongly) limits their applicability and influence outside of their context. Just war thinkers, like Cicero, were engaged precisely in reflecting abstractly on the practice of their particular political culture to extract general principles, principles which later thinkers then reflected upon and reinterpreted for their times. That ongoing conversation constitutes an intellectual tradition.

Is the historical schematic I describe a reconstruction or a reinterpretation? Am I uncovering a schematic that was already there in the primary sources or am I imputing an artificial schematic to a material that lacked any internally organizing framework? Is this historical schematic endogenous or exogenous to the material? The answer, of course, is a little bit of both. In some sense, all reconstruction is also an act of reinterpretation. No twenty-first-century scholar can perfectly reconstruct fifth-century thinking. Even were I to claim that I was merely summarizing past thinkers' work, I would inevitably be bringing my own interpretation to bear in the selection of works and quotations. In the case of this book, it is even more a reinterpretation insofar as I have focused narrowly on the concepts of natural law, justice, sovereignty, and just cause, and insofar as I have deliberately looked for evidence of continuity and change between thinkers and traditions. That said, for any work on scholarship to have intellectual integrity, it must stick as close to the primary sources as possible. My interpretations rest on extensive engagement with – and quotation from – the primary sources to demonstrate that my interpretations are rooted in the historical material. Finally, while the historical schematic is of my own devising, it is at least partly endogenous to the object of study insofar as the Westphalian thinkers seem to have had some degree of self-consciousness about breaking from the past and embarking on a new and distinct intellectual project. Twentieth and twenty-first-century scholars, of course, show even more historical self-consciousness.

I describe the different just war traditions through engagement with a representative (not exhaustive) selection of thinkers from each tradition. I focus on major, well-known figures in hopes of casting fresh interpretive light on how they relate to one another and to the broader traditions in which they stand. Regrettably, because I aim to describe the major sources of influence from one generation to the next, I focus on "canonical" figures, rather than less-well-researched or marginalized figures whose work may be interesting but who were less influential, such as Christine de Pisan (1364–1430).[31] An advantage to focusing on a few individual thinkers is that I avoid a weakness common to some intellectual history, that of ascribing agency to abstractions or concepts. I deal concretely with what a specific person thought, said, and wrote, and thus can assess more confidently about his meaning, impact, and legacy.[32] The

---

[31] See O'Driscoll, "Keeping Tradition Alive," for a discussion of non-"canonical" figures. Pisan was influential in synthesizing the chivalric code with just war thinking, which incorporated *jus in bello* into the tradition; but *jus in bello* lies outside the scope of this book.
[32] Dunn, "The Identity of the History of Ideas."

tradeoff is that by focusing on a few individuals, I do not aspire to write a comprehensive intellectual history of the just war traditions.

I make another trade-off, that between replicating a thinker's thought as faithfully as possible, yet also forcing it into the uniform analytical structure used throughout most of this book so as to better compare thinkers across time. I attempt to heed the unique questions and problems each thinker confronted (without which intellectual history becomes detached from reality and emptied of meaning) yet also zero in on the abstract principles they argued for (without which intellectual history has nothing to do).[33] Finally, I do not offer much detail on just war thinkers' life and times except for sparse details relevant to the development of their thought – not because I think biographical and political circumstances are irrelevant, but because the political backdrop of European history is well known and does not need detailed treatment here.[34]

How do I recognize some figures as "canonical" and others not? Largely by observing which thinkers have been treated most extensively by other just war scholars. A critic might argue this is tautological, or at least self-reinforcing: thinkers are canonical if they have been studied in the past, but the scholars who studied them were the ones who constructed and defined the canon. That is true but misses the purpose of this book: I am not seeking an external standard of canonicity. My point is rather to study the traditions as received, and their relations to each other, not challenge how they came about, which means I accept the general scholarly consensus on who the major influential figures are. My task is not to demonstrate that these thinkers were influential, which has been amply demonstrated by other scholars, but to observe the course of the traditions they embodied and, especially, to observe the transitions from one tradition to the next.

The story I tell is, in one sense, a familiar one: historians have universally recognized that the shift from the medieval world to the early modern one included a shift in intellectual currents. I follow the intellectual history of the transition from medieval cosmology to early Enlightenment philosophy and thence to the contemporary era through one particular instance of it: how thinkers thought of natural law, sovereignty, justice, and war, especially on the criteria of just cause for war. I offer a selective engagement with a handful of the traditions' most important thinkers, narrowly focused on their understanding of natural

---

[33] Dunn, "Identity of the History of Ideas."

[34] Bellamy, *Just Wars* is probably the best single-volume intellectual history of the just war traditions, though his choice to include "realist" strands of thought in his history is regrettable. For biographical details on just war thinkers, see Brunstetter and O'Driscoll, *Just War Thinkers*.

law, sovereignty, just cause, and intervention (I do not engage with *jus in bello*, or with *jus post bellum* until the concluding chapters), showing how these concepts evolved from century to century.

It is important to acknowledge that the division I outline between traditions is, of course, not as stark as these chapters might suggest. Some earlier thinkers who otherwise held most theological views in common with the Augustinians anticipated the Westphalians' conclusions about intervention, including Bartolomeo Las Casas (1484–1566), Balthazar Ayala (1548–84), and Luis de Molina (1535–1600), largely out of concern for how the argument for intervention could be abused. And some who broadly shared the Westphalians' views on natural law and justice, such as Hugo Grotius and Alberico Gentili, nonetheless sided with the Augustinians in their views of the purposes of sovereignty and the right of intervention. Any schematic designed to organize a broad sweep of intellectual history is necessarily an exercise in simplification. The one I adopt here is deliberately designed to emphasize discontinuities. There are, of course, continuities among the just war scholars and traditions, but they are less interesting for my purposes. This schematic is a useful organizing framework for understanding what was, in reality, a millennia-long argument about some of the most complex and consequential questions in politics, philosophy, and theology.

Outline

The bulk of this book is a work of intellectual history, demonstrating that there are three just war traditions. I reconstruct the Augustinian tradition (Chapter 2), the transition between it and its successor (Chapter 3), the Westphalian tradition (Chapter 4), and competing visions for the emerging Liberal tradition (Chapter 5). I focus specifically on changing notions of natural law, justice, sovereignty, and just cause. Several issues, including right authority, the right to rebel, sedition, and the permissibility of humanitarian intervention, hinge crucially on how natural law and just cause are understood.

In Chapter 6 I lay sound groundwork for my own contribution to just war thinking, which I lay out in full in Chapter 7. I argue that the Liberal tradition's critique of Westphalia is sound. I argue that there is a fundamental compatibility between the Augustinian and Liberal traditions, and I seek to incorporate insights from the former into the latter. I argue that the defense of ordered liberty is a just cause for war. I apply that insight to the institutions of liberalism today, including the liberal international order. I argue that the liberal international order is the contemporary manifestation of the common good, whose defense is just for its members, the preservation of which reflects love for our neighbors and for our enemies. In this Augustinian Liberal perspective, the violent disruption of ordered liberty is the injury in response to which war may be justly waged. In turn, just wars result in the vindication and restoration of ordered liberty.

In Chapter 8 I apply this new Augustinian–Liberal hybrid to a series of contemporary cases, including the wars in Iraq, Afghanistan, and Syria; the possibility of war with North Korea; and the novel cases of "cyberwar" and autonomous weapons. These cases illustrate in more concrete terms the implications of my argument about just war and ordered liberty.

2   The Augustinian Tradition

The Augustinian just war tradition took shape against the backdrop of Christendom, from antiquity through the late medieval period. Augustine of Hippo (354–430) was the first (or most influential) to fuse together crucial concepts inherited from pagan antiquity with Christian thought on natural law, justice, the state, and war. He did not, however, leave us a formalized just war doctrine. Later thinkers within the same tradition would further develop Augustine's thought, especially during the Wars of Religion.

The Augustinian tradition's distinctive features begin with a teleological conception of natural law, in contrast to the Enlightenment's descriptive conception. Natural law, in the Augustinian and Thomist sense, reflects not merely man's nature as it is but as it should be, accounting for the moral aspirations and moral instincts they believed were natural to man's being. Because human nature is best understood as social, not individual, and as spiritual, not (solely) animal, natural law stipulates that we act in accordance with our social, spiritual, and moral natures to fulfill our moral aspirations and achieve our full flourishing. (Post-Grotian and post-Hobbesian thinkers conceive of natural law in very different terms.) Another way of putting it is that we should act in accordance with justice, which Aquinas argues is the summation of virtue or the virtue of the whole. Justice is the virtue of living well in society, with love towards one another, towards the community of one's fellow men and women, and even towards the kinship of all humanity. Justice, in fact, requires charity, a point Aquinas brings out quite clearly.

What does it mean to love our neighbors politically? In Augustine's language, it means to live in accordance with the "tranquility of order." As we will see, the "tranquility of order" is a key concept that is akin to what we mean when we talk about the "public good" or the "common good"; it may be best captured by the idea of a "just and lasting peace" within and among nations. In the Augustinian tradition, "the peace to be aimed at was that of Augustine's *tranquilitas ordinis*, the peace of a society ordered so as to serve justice."[1] Responsibility for upholding this kind of peace is what "sovereignty" meant in the pre-Westphalian era. Peace is not merely the absence of violence but the presence of the conditions that enable flourishing, the preservation of which was the raison d'être of the state. For statesmen and decision makers, their duty is to protect, uphold, and defend the tranquility of order. Protecting the tranquility of order is how we love our neighbors in the political realm.

This is the foundational political theology underneath the Augustinian just war doctrine. In this sense, the Augustinian tradition is unique in understanding war as an act of love insofar as the prince shows love by bringing the blessing of justice and order to his commonwealth and to his enemy alike.[2] Just war is war that accords with justice: it is authorized political violence required to uphold love-directed justice. War is an instrument for defending and sustaining the tranquility of order, under-stood as an act of love for our neighbors and our enemies alike. We can see the distinctive aspects of this approach most easily by examining how it deals with humanitarian intervention, revolt and rebellion, crimes against nature, and state building. Thinkers in the Augustinian tradition – espe-cially the later thinkers, who were more specific on these points – consist-ently prioritized the protection of the innocent, the pursuit of justice, and the preservation of just order. Sovereignty was understood to be a tool for achieving the tranquility of order, but when a sovereign became an obstacle or threat to that order rather than its servant and guardian, war against such a sovereign by rebels or other sovereigns was justified. The later Augustinian thinkers generally favored what we would call humani-tarian and state-building interventions: military operations to stop war crimes or crimes against humanity, protect civilians, punish tyrants and war criminals, and foster conditions of lasting peace and stability. As such, they stand in contrast to their Westphalian successors, for whom the norm of mutual noninterference among states assumed paramount importance.

In this chapter I reconstitute the Augustinian just war tradition. I focus on key texts in the just war canon, emphasizing natural law, justice, and sovereignty. I start my discussion of the Augustinian tradition, not with Augustine but with Marcus Tullius Cicero. Augustine's thought owes much to classical antiquity, particularly to Cicero, the most influential Latin man of letters, the literary tradition in which Augustine stood. Augustine credits part of his spiritual formation to one of Cicero's lost

---

[1] Johnson, *Ethics and the Use of Force*, 19.
[2] Johnson downplays the role of charity in the medieval or "classic" just war tradition. See for example Johnson, "Just War in the Thought of Paul Ramsey," 189. Contrary to his reading, I find charity or love present in Augustine, Aquinas, and Suárez at least.

works, and references to Cicero are replete throughout Augustine's corpus. And for our purposes, it will be helpful to see how some elements of the Augustinian tradition are not distinctively Christian. That will be an important point when I later argue for reincorporating elements of the Augustinian tradition into the embryonic Liberal tradition of the twentieth and twenty-first centuries. After Augustine, I engage with a representative (not exhaustive) selection of key thinkers: Aquinas and Vitoria; and, in the following chapter, Suárez in the Catholic tradition, and Gentili and Grotius in the Protestant tradition. The latter are pivotal figures who laid the groundwork for the subsequent emergence of the Westphalian just war tradition.

Marcus Tullius Cicero (103–43 BC)

Cicero was a Roman senator, philosopher, and one-time consul during the waning days of the Roman Republic. Cicero was not initially part of the Roman elite; he was a *novus homo*, a self-made man whose superior talents gained him entry into the political elite. As such, Cicero was both near to and separate from the center of power, giving him enough proximity to speak intelligibly about its use but enough distance to be capable of critique (a common feature among just war thinkers' biographies). He analyzes war as part of a broader discussion of justice, itself part of an examination of the many virtues that make up a man's duties in life. Cicero's positioning of war as part of justice sets him apart from some later Christian thinkers who discuss war under the heading of charity: they saw the obligation to wage just war as a function of our obligation to love our neighbors and love our enemies. There are parallels, however: Cicero, whose ethics and political theory were influenced by Stoicism, emphasized the importance of personal and public virtue as among the final goods of human life, an approach later Christian thinkers harmonized with the Christian virtues of faith, hope, and love.

Cicero on Natural Law and Justice

Cicero's starting point is the same as other thinkers in the Augustinian tradition: he begins with an appeal to nature and to common reason. Cicero is following a path well-trodden by his Greek and Roman predecessors, who assumed the existence of a natural law: rules of right and wrong evident in nature, inscribed into the created order of the universe, readily accessible to the rightly formed intellect, binding upon all humanity across differences of time and culture. The character Marcus in Cicero's dialogue *On the Laws* denies that written law (what we would call positive law) creates justice; on the contrary, "the origin of justice is to be sought in the divine law of eternal and immutable morality."[3] Natural law is an essential part of the just war idea: only if there is a commonly accessible standard of justice separate from revealed religion can we have an intelligible discussion about justice that is applicable among nations with different cultures, values, and religions. The idea of natural law grew organically from the pagan philosophy of the pre-Christian era, but, as we will see, Christian thinkers (and post-Christian thinkers) had no trouble adapting it and making it a cornerstone of their philosophical theology.[4]

The content of Cicero's natural law, and that of his medieval Christian followers, differs from later Enlightenment thinkers. To Cicero, as to Aristotle, nature teaches that man is a social and political animal, not the disembodied, atomized individual of John Locke's or Hobbes' "state of nature." Nature, to Cicero, "prompts men to meet in companies, to form public assemblies and to take part in them themselves .... We are not born for ourselves alone, but our country claims a share of our being, and our friends a share," echoing Aristotle's notion that man is a social and political animal. This leads to a natural kind of patriotism. "The bonds of common blood hold men fast through good-will and affection; for it means much to share in common the same family traditions, the same forms of domestic worship, and the same ancestral tombs." But in a typically Ciceronian move, he balances this with a concession to the kinship of all humanity. "To debar foreigners from enjoying the advantages of the city is altogether contrary to the laws of humanity," the beginning of the idea that humanity is, or ought to be, a single family, an idea that will play an important role in later Christian thought.[5]

The character Marcus expands on this idea in *On the Laws*, describing law and justice as "the common rule of immortals and mortals," from which idea he concludes that "This universe, therefore, forms one immeasurable Commonwealth and city, common alike to gods and mortals."[6] Marcus is at pains to stress that this law is not founded on custom but on an objective and external standard of nature outside and above the nations. "If then in the majority of nations, many pernicious and mischievous enactments are made, as far removed from the law of justice we have defined as the mutual engagements of robbers, are we bound to call them laws? ... [W]e cannot call that the true law of the people, whatever be its name, if it enjoins what is injurious."[7] Cicero is

---

[3] Cicero, *Political Works*, 37.
[4] Rommen, "Natural Law." Sigmund, *Natural Law in Political Thought*. Simon, *Tradition of Natural Law*.
[5] Cicero, *On Duties*, 12, 55, 47. See also section I.XVI for his further reflections on Nature.
[6] Cicero, *On the Laws*, 26.   [7] Cicero, *On the Laws*, 47.

rejecting what will later be called the law of nations (received custom) in favor of natural law, or principles of reason derived independently of practice.

Nature, then, encourages sociability, love for one's country, benevolence to all humanity, and fellowship with the gods. The influence of Cicero's political situation is clear: writing during the waning days of his republic, he was concerned to reinforce social solidarity amid conditions of fragmentation, social unrest, and civil war. But his philosophical conclusions transcended his narrow purpose. That natural law includes sociability and obligations to humanity will be crucial for Augustinian just war thinkers, especially in the hands of later Christian thinkers.

From this natural social inclination, Cicero derives the virtues, including justice, "in which consists the greatest luster of virtue," and which is part of "the principle which constitutes the bond of human society." The characters in his dialogue *On the Laws* agree that they should "derive the principles of justice from the principles of nature," for "nature herself is the foundation of justice," established by the "law" of "right reason."[8] They agree that the "virtues proceed from our natural inclination to love and cherish our associates," and this natural inclination "is the true basis of justice."[9] Cicero, in his other work, writes that since "men ... are born for the sake of men, that they may be able mutually to help one another; in this direction we ought to follow Nature as our guide, to contribute to the general good [and] cement human society more closely together." This goal is the animating purpose of social and political life.[10] Cicero's belief that nature should be our "guide" and that it leads us to work for the "general good" illustrates that his understanding of natural law is teleological (something Aquinas will bring out much more clearly). Human beings have a natural moral inclination; natural law tells us to follow those inclinations for the good of ourselves and the society of which we are a part.

Cicero on War

Cicero's understanding of justice has clear implications for his understanding of war. "The first office of justice is to keep one man from doing harm to another, unless provoked by wrong." The state enforces justice; it apportions to each his or her due, including punishment to the wrongdoer. War is a response to wrongdoing by another state. This is straightforward and, to us, obvious; but Cicero was unlike most of his Greek and

---

[8] Cicero, *On the Laws*, 25, 30, 32.   [9] Cicero, *On the Laws*, 33.
[10] Cicero, *On Duties*, 22.

Roman predecessors in making it explicit and treating it as a standard by which to judge his own people's wars. Cicero insists on the formalities being observed: "no war is just, unless it is entered upon after an official demand for satisfaction has been submitted or warning has been given and a formal declaration made." In passing, Cicero endorses an early version of the last resort principle: "We must resort to force only in case we may not avail ourselves of discussion."[11]

That does not mean Cicero believes self-defense is the only just cause for war. He suggests that wars can also be fought for honor or "supremacy," so long as they are a response to a slight or to danger. But when that is the case, Cicero argues, such wars should change how we fight. "When a war is fought out for supremacy and when glory is the object of war, it must still not fail to start from the same motives which I said a moment ago were the only righteous grounds for going to war. But those wars which have glory for their end must be carried on with less bitterness."[12] Later Christian thinkers would disallow wars for glory or honor altogether.

Interestingly, this is typical of Cicero's remarks on war: he focuses much of his attention on what we would call "right intention," and with *jus post bellum*. He spends comparatively little time talking about what sort of wrongs justify a belligerent response and much more time exhorting his readers to ensure that when they wage war, they wage it with restraint, exercise magnanimity in victory, and avoid vengeance. "There are certain duties that we owe even to those who have wronged us," he argues, in a passage that sounds more Augustinian than pagan. "For there is a limit to retribution and to punishment; or rather, I am inclined to think, it is sufficient that the aggressor should be brought to repent of his wrong-doing." The goal of war is the reconciliation of the enemy.[13]

Cicero's concern for peace and reconciliation is evident throughout his discussion of war. "We should always strive to secure a peace that shall not admit of guile," he writes. "The only excuse, therefore, for going to war is that we may live in peace unharmed; and when the victory is won, we should spare those who have not been blood-thirsty and barbarous in their warfare." "The achievements of peace" are more important than "the achievements of war," and this concern should shape and limit how a war is fought and the way a war is concluded. War "should be under-taken in such a way as to make it evident that it has no other object than to secure peace." He gets more specific: "As to destroying and plundering cities, let me say that great care should be taken that nothing be done in reckless cruelty or wantonness."[14] Again, Cicero is likely responding to

---

[11] Cicero, *On Duties*, 36.   [12] Cicero, *On Duties*, 38.   [13] Cicero, *On Duties*, 33.
[14] Cicero, *On Duties*, 35, 74, 80, 82.

the bitterness and, to him, apparently senseless destruction of Rome's civil wars. The wars between Marius and Sulla, between Caesar and Pompey, and between Brutus and Augustus (in which Cicero himself was caught up and eventually executed) lasted for half a century and included purges of the aristocracy, the confiscation of property, Roman armies marching on the capital city, and repeated interruptions of the republican constitution. Cicero was acutely aware of the need not just for military victory, but for peace and reconciliation in the aftermath. The notion of post-conflict reconciliation is not an invention of Christian or Liberal thinkers and does not depend on their broader philosophical or theological commitments.

Remarkably for his day, Cicero uses his moral criterion to judge his own state and finds it wanting. He repeatedly condemns his predecessors for the infamous destruction of Corinth, which took place in 146 BC, a century before Cicero's time. The Roman Republic had provoked and won a conflict with the Achaean League to consolidate its hegemony over the Mediterranean. Upon its victory, the Roman army sacked and destroyed Corinth, a major commercial and cultural center in Greece, to prevent the league from regaining its strength. The destruction of Corinth was a departure from past Roman practice and was controversial even in its day. Cicero, building on his concern for magnanimity in victory, agrees. "Not only must we show consideration for those whom we have conquered by force of arms but we must also ensure protection to those who lay down their arms and throw themselves upon the mercy of our generals," he writes. "I wish they had not destroyed Corinth."[15] In criticizing the sack of Corinth, Cicero was also establishing a standard by which he could condemn his contemporaries' lack of restraint in the prosecution of their wars.

Cicero's understanding of justice and his concern for reconciliation and magnanimity culminate in his endorsement of the Romans' past benevolent imperium. He counsels the wise and just person to win the favor of others through love, not fear, and then directly uses this counsel to appraise the acts of statesmen. We can see here a just war argument being used to justify a very early version of what we would today call the liberal international order:

As long as the empire of the Roman People maintained itself by acts of service, not of oppression, wars were waged in the interest of our allies or to safeguard our supremacy; the end of our wars was marked by acts of clemency or by only a necessary degree of severity; the senate was a haven of refuge for kings, tribes, and nations; and the highest ambition of our magistrates and generals was to

---

[15] Cicero, *On Duties*, 35; see also 46.

defend our provinces and allies with justice and honor. And so our government could be called more accurately a protectorate of the world than a dominion.[16]

It is fair for twenty-first-century readers to read this as a hypocritical, ex post facto justification for empire. But Cicero himself seems to have agreed: he used this narrative of Rome's past glories as an indictment of Roman hypocrisy in his day. He believed the Romans in his day were no longer living up to this high calling, and he lamented that they had lost their benevolent protectorate and become an oppressive imperium because they had lost their republican virtue. His critique of Rome was only possible because of the high idealism with which the Romans described their imperial pretentions: hypocrisy is the tribute vice pays to virtue. In that light, the idealism of Cicero's "protectorate of the world" is not the problem; it is the standard that allows self-critique.

Interestingly, Cicero does not blame the loss of Roman integrity on Julius Caesar; he believed the fall came much earlier, during the civil war and the dictatorship of Sulla (81 BC). It was the Romans' complicity in Sulla's extra-constitutional moves, including his seizure and redistribution of Roman citizens' property, which undermined the rule of law and established a destructive populist precedent. If Roman citizens were not safe from the mob, why should Rome's allies expect to be so? Mob rule led to dictatorship, and it became easy for Caesar, the Senate, and later Augustus to subordinate their allies and turn the benevolent protectorate into an exploitative empire. Cicero seems to suggest that the state's virtue in upholding ideals of ordered liberty at home has direct implications for the justice or injustice of its foreign policy. I make this argument explicit in Chapters 6 and 7.

Cicero's early internationalism might even be stretched to suggest endorsement for humanitarian intervention – though Cicero nowhere explicitly addresses the issue. Instead, he addresses sins of omission. One form of injustice, he says, is to fail to help others in need when we are able to help: "He who does not prevent or oppose wrong, if he can, is just as guilty of wrong as if he deserted his parents or his friends or his country." By way of example he complains of philosophers who, so taken with their musings, fail to do their civic duty. Cicero has harsh words for those who "either from zeal in attending to their own business or through some sort of aversion to their fellow-men, claim that they are occupied

---

[16] Cicero, *On Duties*, 26. Aristotle makes a similar argument. "Training for war should not be pursued with a view to enslaving men who do not deserve such a fate. Its objects should be these – first, to prevent men from ever becoming enslaved themselves; secondly, to put men in a position to exercise leadership – but a leadership directed to the interests of the led, and not to the establishment of a general system of slavery." Aristotle, *Politics*, VII. xiv.§21, 319.

solely with their own affairs." Such men "are traitors to social life for they contribute to it none of their interest, none of their effort, none of their means."[17] Cicero's comments here are directed at individuals, rather than states, limiting how much we can read into them an endorsement of humanitarian intervention, though Cicero elsewhere comfortably moves between individual and political ethics. Cicero gives one tantalizing example that is quoted by later authors: "It is more in accord with Nature to emulate the great Hercules and undergo the greatest toil and trouble for the sake of aiding or saving the world, if possible, than to live in seclusion."[18] Among Hercules' exploits were his overthrow of evil kings, including Busiris and Augeias, for their cruelty and faithlessness to him. He also restored the rightful king of Sparta after a coup.

After Cicero neither the Roman Empire nor early Christian thinkers had need for a just war doctrine, representing as they did the two poles – realism and pacifism – between which just war sits. The Roman emperors needed little justification to wage war for their glory and territorial aggrandizement, while most of the Christians whom they persecuted argued that no wars could be justified. The situation changed, naturally, when a Roman emperor took power who professed Christianity. Within a generation of Constantine's ascension, some Christian leaders, such as Ambrose of Milan (340–97), began to argue that the duty of Christian statesmanship might include justly waged wars. Ambrose's student, Augustine of Hippo, worked to synthesize the pagan and Christian worlds, including their just war doctrines.

Augustine of Hippo (354–430)

Like Cicero, Augustine of Hippo was both close to and at a critical distance from power. As an African and a native of Numidia, Augustine was probably ethnically Berber and would have been viewed as a provincial by the imperial elite. But Augustine came from an upper-class family, received a Latin education in the metropolis of Carthage, spent time in Rome and Milan, debated with famed philosophers and theologians, and fully mastered Latin literature and rhetoric. He would be, then, both an insider and an outsider when it came time to critique Rome's use of power, not born to power but one who gained proximity to it through talent and opportunity. Augustine's thinking on the state and war took place against an eventful backdrop: Emperor Theodosius made Christianity the state religion of the Roman Empire around 392, raising important questions about the relationship between sacred and secular

---

[17] Cicero, *On Duties*, 23, 29.   [18] Cicero, *On Duties*, 25.

authority. A series of civil wars wracked the empire between 387 and 394 and again between 406 and 413, giving Augustine ample cause to reflect on the just use of force. Finally, the Visigoths famously sacked Rome in 410, provoking Augustine into writing his magnum opus on the distinction between the cities of God and man.

Augustine is often called the founder of the just war tradition. This is only partly true, and requires at least four caveats.[19] First, the just war tradition that followed Augustine's line of thinking – a paradigm that treats war as an act of loving punishment – essentially ended in the seventeenth century, replaced by the Westphalian paradigm. Augustine can rightly be called the founder of one tradition, which recognized him retroactively as its founding influence (a tradition that was reinterpreted in the twentieth century by thinkers such as Paul Ramsey, Elshtain, Johnson, and Nigel Biggar). Second, the just war conversation he entered was one he did not start: he was, in this respect as in so many others, giving a Christian expression and further development to a preceding tradition of thought. Augustine added a biblical undergirding and patristic exposition to Cicero, Seneca, and Plato, among others (in some cases following the example of Ambrose).

Third, Augustine did not write a treatise or essay on war or even on civil government; his comments on the state and its lethal violence are scattered throughout his sermons, letters, and other works, written over the course of decades. It can be difficult to say with certainty that the Augustine who wrote the *City of God* still agreed with the Augustine from twenty years previously.[20] Augustine seems to have followed a similar course in his life to that which western Christendom would travel over the course of a millennium: from an optimistic belief in the righteous possibilities of Christian imperial power to a chastened vision of "conflicting purposes, of uncertainties of direction, of divergent loyalties and irresolvable tensions" in which "political power has become a means of securing some minimal barriers against the forces of disintegration."[21]

---

[19] Wynn, *Augustine on War and Military Service*, helpfully reminds us that Augustine was not looked to as an authority on war for centuries after his death. That does not change the fact that, eventually, he was seen as an authority, I think because of the power of his integrated political theology. By invoking an "Augustinian tradition" I am not claiming an unbroken line of continuous intellectual endeavor, I am recognizing that Augustine's thought, or a version of it, was taken as central by the tradition that eventually took shape. In a sense, the tradition that bears his name started in the eleventh century, only retroactively recognizing his influence as the cornerstone. Wynn overstates his argument when he says Augustine "did not author a doctrine of just war" (330). As with all matters, Augustine borrowed, reinterpreted, and Christianized, and the resulting political theology was distinctively Augustinian.

[20] Markus, "Saint Augustine's Views on the 'Just War'."

[21] Markus, "Saint Augustine's Views on the 'Just War'," 10. See also Syse, "Augustine and Just War," whose interpretation I broadly echo here.

Fourth, Augustine's lasting influence throughout the Middle Ages was less through his work than through its selective transmission by canon lawyers, especially the twelfth-century jurist Gratian (though by the time of Gentili, scholars had broken free of Gratian and begun to look at Augustine directly). This section thus looks both at Augustine and at Gratian as his primary medieval interpreter. Nonetheless, some things are indisputable. Augustine hated war yet gave qualified approval for it. "Augustine felt compelled to defend such statements [of approval]; ironically, those very statements ultimately motivated by his aversion to war later helped make him into its justifier."[22]

Augustine on Natural Law, Justice, and Sovereignty

Augustine had a conflicted attitude towards the Roman Empire. He clearly admired Rome's glory and breadth. "God willed that there should arise in the West an empire which, though later in time, should be more illustrious still [than the eastern empires] in the breadth and greatness of its sway."[23] This greatness was praiseworthy. Speaking of the Romans, he says that "They were honored among almost all the nations; they imposed the laws of their empire upon many races; and they are glorious among almost all peoples to this day, in literature and history."[24] He asks, speaking of Rome's fame and virtue, "How could these deeds, and the others of the same kind found in the annals of the Romans, have become known, and been proclaimed with so great a fame, had not the Roman empire spread far and wide as its magnificent successes made it greater?"[25]

Augustine also admired what he believed was Rome's fairness and liberality, which Rome's greatness made more possible. "For the Romans themselves did not live exempt from the laws which they imposed upon others," he claims, writing of "the most gracious and humane" policy of admitting "all who belonged to the empire to the

---

[22] Wynn, *Augustine on War and Military Service*, 214.

[23] Augustine, *City of God*, V.13, 210. Some scholars are wary of looking to the *City of God* for the just war tradition because they claim it was not influential during the Middle Ages. First, I note that Gratian used quotations from *City of God* in the *Decretum*, demonstrating that the work was known and that at least portions of it were treated as authoritative through Gratian's transmission. Second, I am concerned not only to trace Augustine's influence but also to understand his thought. *City of God* does provide the broader political and theological framework in which Augustine's understanding of war is best illuminated, making it useful for our purposes. Wynn, for example, exhaustively chronicles Augustine's fragmented comments on war but pays comparatively less attention to the broader political theology of sovereignty and law in which Augustine's just war doctrine needs to be seen.

[24] Augustine, *City of God*, V.15, 213.   [25] Augustine, *City of God*, V.18, 220–221.

fellowship of the city, so that they became Roman citizens."[26] That policy (instituted by the Edict of Caracalla in 212) was an integral part of Rome's breadth and greatness; it made citizenship homogenous and extended its reach to be coextensive with Roman rule, a novel idea for the time. Augustine is praising the idea of using the breadth of imperial rule as a tool for extending the reach of justice and fairness. That is perhaps why Augustine says at another point, "It is beneficial, then, that good men should rule far and wide and long .... Nor is this so much beneficial to them as to those over whom they rule."[27] The largeness of Rome made possible the *Pax Romana*, a blessing to those who lived under it.

However, despite Augustine's clear admiration for Roman glory and greatness, he ultimately seemed to prefer small polities or believe that the smaller the state, the closer it could approach to true justice and peace. He lamented the discord and violence brought by Rome's greatness, even while acknowledging the blessings of a universal rule and the justice of some of Rome's past wars. "Why must an empire be unquiet in order to be great?" he asks. He paints an alternate picture of a small body of "moderate stature" with fewer ills:[28]

The wealthy man, however, is troubled by fears: he burns with greed. He is never secure; he is always unquiet and panting from endless confrontations with his enemies .... By contrast, the man of moderate means is self-sufficient on his small and circumscribed estate. He is beloved of his own family, and rejoices in the most sweet peace with kindred, neighbors, and friends.[29]

Augustine was deeply concerned with the effect of imperial greatness on the character of the people; he believed that the burdens and cares of imperial rule weighed them down and, worse, imperial power and glory were corrupting temptations: "Is it wise or prudent to wish to glory in the breadth and magnitude of an empire when you cannot show that the men whose empire it is are happy?" Such problems are not present in the small city. "If men were always peaceful and just, human affairs would be happier and all kingdoms would be small, rejoicing in concord with their neighbors. There would be as many kingdoms among the nations of the world as there are now houses of a city."[30]

To criticize Rome, Augustine needed a language that could transcend Roman values and Roman norms, yet he also resisted the temptation to frame his argument solely in sectarian or theological terms. Augustine did not write exclusively for the Christian emperor; he framed his argument in

[26] Augustine, *City of God*, V.17, 215.   [27] Augustine, *City of God*, IV.3, 145.
[28] Augustine, *City of God*, III.10, 101.   [29] Augustine, *City of God*, IV.3, 144.
[30] Augustine, *City of God*, IV.15, 159.

universal terms. He did so by founding it not on appeals to God's special commands to the church or to Israel but on the natural law that applies to all. "Since Augustine insists that human fellowship and social life are natural to man, it is not surprising that he follows St. Paul and the Church Fathers" – and their pagan predecessors – "in recognizing the existence of a law of nature, a basic moral law written in the hearts of all men, and that is distinct from human laws or divinely revealed laws," according to Herbert Deane.[31] For Augustine, the content of natural law was summed up by the Golden Rule and given more specific exposition by the Ten Commandments. Natural law is directly tied to, and derived from, God and his eternal law. "The law of nature is God's eternal law because the source of these rules that rational men discover in their consciences is God's Truth," in Deane's summation, though sin has severely damaged our ability to see or understand, much less obey, natural law perfectly.[32] Augustine specifically distinguishes this natural law from the law of self-preservation, the instincts that animate living beings, and the laws of how the physical world operates (distinguishing his understanding of natural law from later, Enlightenment appropriation). Later thinkers continue to develop the idea of natural law and it is crucial to their ability to argue for a universal standard of justice across time and culture.

Nature impels us to pursue justice corporately as well as individually. The purpose of the state is to do justice, without which the state's coercion and violence is mere criminality. As Augustine famously put it, "Justice removed, then, what are kingdoms but great bands of robbers?"[33] The only thing that distinguishes the state from organized crime is its claim to wield force for justice and the common good, not for private gain. Of course, Augustine believed it impossible for an earthly city to attain perfect justice. By that standard, there are no true cities, the Romans are not a true "people," and all sovereign authority is illegitimate (a comment reflecting Augustine's pessimism later in life). Consequently, Augustine offers another definition of a people, less aspirational and more descriptive. "Let us say that a 'people' is an assembled multitude of rational creatures bound together by a common agreement as to the objects of their love."[34] Such a people are capable of disordered loves that orient their cities to evil ends. Thus, the City of Man – the polity of all those who do not rightly worship God – is destined to destruction.

But Augustine does not equate earthly government with the City of Man. The latter is an eschatological concept; the former is a daily reality.

---

[31] Deane, *Political and Social Ideas of St. Augustine*, 85.
[32] Deane, *Political and Social Ideas of St. Augustine*, 87.
[33] Augustine, *City of God*, IV.4, 145.   [34] Augustine, *City of God*, XIX.23, 957.

Earthly government, ruling over both the saved and the damned, has a specific commission from God to pursue earthly peace and justice for all during our earthly sojourn. The damned value peace as an end in itself, while the saved have need of peace to do the work of the Great Commission, to spread the Word of God to the ends of the earth. Regardless, the common ground between the saved and damned is our mutual need for earthly peace. Peace is key to Augustine's thought on war and the state. It is the term he uses for the "Final Good" of human life, the ultimate goal at which all action aims. Peace is the right ordering of things. Peace between people is "ordered agreement of mind with mind." While perfect peace will only be present in the City of God, government is the rightful authority for upholding the best approximation of peace achievable in this life, which Augustine clearly believes will always be flawed, partial, and fleeting but valuable nonetheless. In the city, peace is "ordered concord, with respect to command and obedience, of the citizens." In sum, "The peace of all things lies in the *tranquility of order*; and order is the disposition of equal and unequal things in such a way as to give to each its proper place."[35]

Augustine defines peace, justice, and order in terms of each other, and even seems to equate them or suggest they come in tandem. Order is the arrangement of each thing in its place; justice is rendering to each his due, and peace is the ordered concord of the whole, which is only possible when each thing has its place and is given its due. Because true peace requires the right ordering of things, those who reject the right order cannot be said to be at peace: "In comparison with the peace of the just, the peace of the unjust is not worthy to be called peace at all."[36] For Augustine, the only peace worthy of the name is a just and lasting one. Augustine's arrangement of peace, justice, and order as mutually constitutive is a cornerstone of his thought and a distinctive feature of the Augustinian tradition.

Augustine on War

What, for Augustine, is a just cause for war? The most generic justification he gives, echoing Cicero, is that war should avenge wrongs or respond to an injury. Typically for the ancient and medieval era, Augustine is nonspecific and even inconsistent about what kind of injury, against whom, in whose jurisdiction, and at what frequency or intensity justifies war. As Wynn argues, on this point, "Augustine is

---

[35] Augustine, *City of God*, XIX.13, 936 (emphasis added).
[36] Augustine, *City of God*, XIX.12, 934.

relatively unenlightening."[37] Augustine suggests at various points that injuries as diverse as heresy or the denial of free travel could be just cause for war, comments that show Augustine's changing attitude towards the state throughout his life. Augustine clearly understood some just wars to be those instigated by God, such as the wars of the Old Testament and (at least some of) those fought in defense of the true faith. (This aspect of Augustine's thought led to the later development of holy war doctrine – the very idea that the just war tradition in its mature shape explicitly rejected. In this sense, Augustine is the founder of both the just war tradition and its opposite.)

Setting aside Augustine's holy war line of thought, can we discern any more specific criteria for nonsectarian just war? Augustine's doctrine of peace is crucial here. As we saw above, the purpose of war is to create a better peace. Theologically, Augustine often described war as an ordinance of God's providence, a decree of punishment against the wicked and, simultaneously, a refining chastisement for the righteous. In either case, human combatants use war as an instrument to achieve what they believe will be a better earthly peace:

> For every man seeks peace, even in making war; but no one seeks war by making peace. Indeed, even those who wish to disrupt an existing state of peace do so not because they hate peace, but because they desire the present peace to be exchanged for one of their own choosing. Their desire, therefore, is not that there should be no peace, but that it should be the kind of peace that they wish for.[38]

Augustine is here echoing both Cicero and Aristotle, who both argued that war existed for the sake of peace, but he is also doing something more.[39] The pagans were stating a rather intuitive truth – that even when fought for unjust purposes, war has an endpoint in its own termination and the resumption of public order on the victor's terms, no matter the cause at stake. Augustine is saying something deeper than this: war exists to restore peace, understood not merely as the absence of violence but as the *right ordering of things* – because peace without justice is hardly worthy to be called peace at all. The injury which justifies war, broadly, is the sin of disrupting the tranquility of order with violent injustice.

Augustine's argument is implicit in how he understands the nature and purpose of the state. The state exists to uphold the tranquility of order; it is defined as the institution authorized to uphold and defend that order; it is authorized to act against those who violently disrupt such order. The state's response to disrupted order is a judicial act, executing judgment on the disrupter. Soldiers are part of the same system of justice as judges,

[37] Wynn, *Augustine on War and Military Service*, 249.
[38] Augustine, *City of God*, XIX.12, 932.   [39] Aristotle, *Politics*, VII.xiv.§13, 317.

jailers, and executioners. Keeping in mind the close connection between justice and peace for Augustine, restoring peace means much more than the cessation of political violence. He has in mind the creation, sustenance, and defense of conditions for a just peace, to the extent possible in this sinful and fallen world.[40]

War is a response to a failure or breakdown of right order, of just and lasting peace; it is the means required for the state to restore the "tranquility of order" when such order has been violently disrupted. As Johnson argues of Augustine, "The just cause of defense here was not 'self-defense' as this term is used today but defense of the peace and order both of the immediate community and of the fundamental structure of order on which all communities depended."[41] Frederick Russell similarly describes Augustine as arguing that a just war "avenged the moral order injured by the sins of the guilty party regardless of injuries done to the just party acting as defender of that order."[42] As such, war is a form of punishment against the wicked. "It is the iniquity of the opposing side that imposes upon the wise man the duty of waging wars," Augustine says.[43]

Augustine describes war as a kind of "necessity." "Peace ought to be what you want, war only what necessity demands .... It ought to be

---

[40] Wynn seems to miss this point in his comments about Augustine's understanding of earthly peace. He argues that Augustine was primarily concerned to point out that "the peace that results from the arrogant and militaristic lust to dominate others, *libido dominandi*, can only result in an earthly peace that is unjust and disordered" (Wynn, *Augustine on War and Military Service*, 294). But Wynn fails to notice the converse: that, for Augustine, a peace that results from a rightly intended just war to restore the tranquility of order could be a just peace worth defending, even if still fallible and temporal. That war was an instrument for defending and restoring a just peace suggests Wynn is wrong to characterize Augustine's views here as a "criticism" and "devaluation" of the Roman just war idea (Wynn, *Augustine on War and Military Service*, 249, 252), except insofar as Augustine's Christianization of Roman just war thinking was a criticism of its paganism. Rather than devaluing, Augustine appropriates and improves the Roman tradition by positioning it within a biblical framework which allows princes to see that war, while terrible, might be necessary for justice, which helps the prince resist the temptation so many Romans fell into of reveling in war's glory. Wynn similarly over-interprets Augustine's praise of Theodosius and interpretation of the battle of Frigidus in *City of God*, V.26. He claims that Augustine sees Theodosius as the agent of a divinely instigated war, as evidenced by Augustine's characterization of Theodosius' pious character, Theodosius's visit with John the Hermit, the miraculous wind during the battle, and Theodosius' magnanimity and piety after the battle. But Augustine never says Theodosius was waging a holy war on God's instigation. Augustine's actual argument is plain and straightforward: he characterizes Theodosius' wars as just because his opponents, Maximus and Eugenius, were tyrants and usurpers. Theodosius' other traits and actions were praiseworthy Christian virtues, but Augustine never says they made his wars just or proved their divine origin. See Wynn, *Augustine on War and Military Service*, 256ff and compare Augustine, *City of God*, 231ff.

[41] Johnson, *Ethics and the Use of Force*, 18.   [42] Russell, *Just War in the Middle Ages*, 19.
[43] Augustine, *City of God*, XIX.7, 927.

necessity, and not your will, that destroys an enemy who is fighting you."[44] When the wrongs committed by our enemy have disrupted the right ordering of things, and when there are no other options available for restoring the right order, war becomes the necessary duty of the statesman charged with upholding peace and justice. For Augustine, we ought to fight war only when pressed to it – but when we are pressed, war is necessary not optional. By arguing that war must be only waged when necessary, Augustine rules out what we might call wars of choice, including wars for glory, conquest, profit, or aggrandizement, as he makes clear in his commentary on Rome's wars.

Just cause and right intention are closely linked. It is easy to see how right intention derives from just cause. To have right intention, a sovereign must truly intend to achieve the just cause that has ostensibly triggered the war. Just cause is, therefore, logically prior to right intention and right intention is ancillary to just cause: one cannot have right intention without a just cause, whereas once one has just cause, right intention is relatively straightforward. Augustine argues that just war should be motivated by love for our neighbors and our enemies, as manifested in a desire to do justice and foster peace for both. That he understood love to underlie war is demonstrated by his use of parental punishment as a metaphor for the state's corrective responsibilities: fathers punish their sons because they love them, not because they want to destroy them. The right intention is love – which can include the stern love of retributive justice and forcibly preventing enemies from committing further harm.[45] That is why Augustine often insisted that only good men could wage a just war, because only good men could be trusted to maintain right intention against the temptation of bloodlust. Augustine's "principal argument is that it is our duty to punish evildoers for their sake and for the good of others; we punish them so that we may instill fear into them and into others like them and so keep them from doing further wrong. In acting this way, we are doing them a service," according to Deane. "The punishment of criminal men or nations is justified not only because it protects the innocent but also because it prevents the offender from continuing to misuse his liberty and from adding further crimes to his previous offenses."[46] When someone does evil, he is harming his own soul; if we

[44] Augustine, *Political Writings*, 217.

[45] See Biggar, *In Defence of War*, chapter 2, for a contemporary restatement of this idea.

[46] Deane, *Political and Social Ideas of St. Augustine*, 164. Wynn argues that Augustine only linked love to the domestic use of force, e.g., capital punishment against criminals, not to foreign war. But Augustine viewed war as part of the same judicial function the state played to execute justice on wrongdoers and did not make a strong distinction between foreign and domestic uses of force. It is reasonable to read Augustine as saying that the

stop someone from doing evil, we are helping protect his soul from himself. In Augustine's words:

When, however, men are prevented, by being harmed, from doing wrong, it may be said that a real service is done to themselves . . . . For in the correction of a son, even with some sternness, there is assuredly no diminution of a father's love . . . . The person from whom is taken away the freedom which he abuses in doing wrong is vanquished with benefit to himself.[47]

This approach has implications for how we fight war and how we handle the aftermath. If we love our neighbors and our enemies, we will desire and work for peace in our conduct of war and its outcome: "Be a peacemaker, therefore, even in war, so that by conquering them you bring the benefit of peace even to those you defeat," Augustine writes, "And just as you use force against the rebel or opponent, so you ought now to use mercy towards the defeated or the captive."[48] Augustine is following Ambrose, whose emphasis in his discussion of war was the need for Christian princes and soldiers to treat enemies with magnanimity and charity as befitting their faith. For Augustine and Ambrose, war should result in justice: that means war is about more than achieving military victory. It is about establishing conditions for a better, lasting, just peace. Since the late 1990s, scholars have emphasized the idea of justice after war, or *jus post bellum*, which seems a natural development from the Augustinian (and Ciceronian) seeds we see here. I expand on this at length in my appropriation of the Augustinian tradition in Chapters 6 and 7.

Augustine is concerned to elevate love, peace, and justice as the governing principles of a just war because without them there is no distinction between just war and unjust murder. Interestingly, it is precisely because of the danger of unjust war that he recognizes the necessity of waging just war in response: "The real evils in war are love of violence, revengeful cruelty, fierce and implacable enmity, wild resistance, and the lust of power, and such like; and it is generally to punish these things, when force is required to inflict the punishment, that, in obedience to God or some lawful authority, good men undertake wars."[49] Note that Augustine starts by identifying the evils in war before prescribing war itself as the permissible, and sometimes obligatory, response to war. Augustine is realistic; he understands that war happens and is often (perhaps always)

---

love that should motivate the judicial act against wrongdoers should also motivate just war making.
[47] Quoted in Deane, *Political and Social Ideas of St. Augustine*, 164–165.
[48] Augustine, *Political Writings*, 217.
[49] Augustine, "Against Faustus," book XXII, chapter 74, quoted in Holmes, *War and Christian Ethics*, 64.

marred by evil in the hearts of those who wage it; but it is precisely because there is no other response capable of stopping unjust war that just war must be waged in response.

Because Augustine speaks of war as a loving chastisement of the wicked, he might be accused of romanticizing war, even encouraging it. In fact, Augustine had a stark appreciation for the horrors of war. Long before General William Tecumseh Sherman declared that "war is hell," Augustine argued that this is literally true, in a theological sense. Just as the final state of the just is peace, the final state of the wicked – that is, hell – is a kind of never-ending experience of the horrors of war. For Augustine, the true horror of war was not merely bodily harm and suffering but the inner torment of conflict, which he understood to be the state of souls in hell. Just as the rightly ordered city is an icon of the City of God and the heavenly paradise that awaits the just, the state of war is an icon of hell, the just punishment of the damned.[50]

Gratian on Augustine

That Augustine was broadly understood this way is illustrated by Gratian's use of him in his eleventh-century compendium of canon law. Gratian, while he did not emphasize love as a motive for war, nonetheless echoed and even expanded the conclusions of Augustine's approach. After quoting the theologian Isidore (560–636), Gratian writes in his own words, "That war is just which is waged by an edict in order to regain what has been stolen or to repel the attack of enemies," or, now quoting Augustine, waged for the "avenging of injuries," which includes wars fought (still quoting Augustine) "to constrain a nation or a city which has ... neglected to punish an evil action committed by its citizens."[51] Elsewhere, Gratian again quotes Augustine: "That vengeance which aims at correction is not prohibited; it even belongs to mercy," so long as the one fighting does not fight from hatred.[52] Gratian, in his own words, explains Augustine's analogy of a father lovingly punishing his wayward son for correction (suggesting love is not wholly absent from Gratian's understanding of war): "Vengeance is to be inflicted not out of passion for vengeance itself, but out of zeal of justice."[53] Gratian, again quoting Augustine, reinforces the standard prohibition against killing, "except perhaps by a soldier or by someone held thereto owing to a public function, so that he does not do it for himself but for others, or for the city."[54]

[50] Augustine, *City of God*, XIX.28, 962.   [51] Reichberg et al., *Ethics of War*, 113.
[52] Reichberg et al., *Ethics of War*, 115.   [53] Reichberg et al., *Ethics of War*, 116.
[54] Reichberg et al., *Ethics of War*, 116.

Killing is thus permitted when done for a legitimate public purpose, for the common good. Still later he seems to expand on this, saying (in his own words) that war is just "to defend the oppressed and to fight the enemies of God," because (now quoting Pope Leo IV) "we shall never suffer our men to be oppressed by anyone."[55] Officials of the state may use force because (quoting Augustine) they are acting as "a prosecutor of crime in order to be a liberator of men."[56]

In these passages Gratian interprets Augustine's concept of just cause to include self-defense, the recovery of what has been taken, the response to injury, the defense of the oppressed, liberation, the prosecution of crime, punishment for wrongdoing, and compelling other nations to punish wrongdoing. This broad understanding of just cause, as transmitted by Gratian to the High Middle Ages, is one of the defining features of the Augustinian tradition.

Augustine and his interpreters are thus much more concerned with the defense of the common good and of the innocent than with national self-defense or territorial defense, however defined. "The concept of just cause in Augustine is not centered around a purely defensive stance. It is the pursuit of justice and the punishment of wrongdoing that lie at the heart of his case," according to Henrik Syse.[57] In that respect, Augustine and Gratian anticipated arguments that their successors, from Gentili to Grotius, would elaborate to justify what we would call humanitarian intervention – although it is important to note that the question of intervention was not explicitly raised in the earlier writers.[58] Augustine does not prioritize territorial sovereignty or the protection of international borders, which were ill-defined in his time anyway. Gratian, again, gives support to this reading. Gratian sees war as analogous to a judicial activity: both were processes for pronouncing judgment against injustice.[59] As such, he explicitly argues that "He who fails to ward off an injury from an associate if he can do so, is quite as blamable as he who inflicts it."[60] One scholar has interpreted Gratian as endorsing intervention:

This justified the use of interventional force against injustice on behalf of others; no limitation was imposed by concepts of the inviolability of sovereignty or territory that are the hallmarks of post-Westphalian international law .... Since injustice could be found at both home and abroad, one's obligation to combat injustice did not stop at one's geographic borders, which were often in flux during the Middle Ages .... With Gratian's emphasis on violations of justice rather than violations of

---

[55] Reichberg et al., *Ethics of War*, 123–124.   [56] Reichberg et al., *Ethics of War*, 118.
[57] Syse, "Augustine and Just War," 47.   [58] Russell, *Just War in the Middle Ages*, 305.
[59] Russell, *Just War in the Middle Ages*, 62–63.   [60] Reichberg et al., *Ethics of War*, 114.

territorial integrity, the Decretum offers an approach to the use of just war and intervention that is clearly identifiable in contemporary just war discourse.[61]

Before Gratian, there is no systematic "tradition" of just war thinking. Augustine's writings had been treated as authoritative at various points in the centuries after his death, but no body of thought gathered around his work in a systematic way. With Gratian we see the beginning of scholastic theology and the crystallization of a tradition that retroactively reached back to Augustine and looked to him as its founding authority.

Thomas Aquinas (1225–74)

The scholastic era found its greatest expression, of course, in Aquinas, the prolific thirteenth-century Italian Dominican who gave definition to the High Middle Ages and integrated thinking on just war into his systematic theology. Aquinas' systematization of philosophy and theology was of a piece with the church's effort to systematize canon law and consolidate its authority. The preceding centuries had seen the rise and subsequent fragmentation of Charlemagne's empire, the rise of independently wealthy monasteries and abbeys, the definitive split between the Catholic and the Orthodox Churches, crusades against Muslims in Palestine and heretics in France, and the investiture controversy over the boundary lines between sacred and secular authority. Against this backdrop, the church and its thinkers sought to reformulate and shore up the grounds of its authority.

Aquinas on Natural Law, Justice, and Sovereignty

Building on the Augustinian inheritance, Aquinas' two most important contributions to just war thinking were marrying his doctrine of just war to his doctrine of natural law and his systematic summary of the just war criteria. Aquinas' just war doctrine cannot be understood separately from his doctrine of natural law because the latter shaped his understanding of justice and of the state's jurisdiction or scope of rightful authority.

---

[61] Cox, "Gratian," in Brunstetter and O'Driscoll, *Just War Thinkers*, chapter 3. Russell differs. He acknowledges there is some ambiguity in Gratian's allowance for war on behalf of "associates," but, in his reading, Gratian "did not grant police power or the right of intervention to a third party lacking authority over the 'associates.'" However, what Russell says of later Decretists seems to apply to Gratian as well: "For those who might so wish, there was … a suggestion of the right of intervention of a third party. In effect the author made no distinction between wars, rebellion, armed intervention and the administration of justice over those within one's proper sphere of jurisdiction." See Russell, *Just War in the Middle Ages*, 66, 91.

Aquinas defined natural law as the "participation of the eternal law in the natural creature" and as the "the rational creature's participation of the eternal law."[62] By linking natural law to the eternal law Aquinas suggests the former is partly unchanging and objective; by tying it to the action of a rational creature who exists in time, he also suggests it needs to be interpreted and applied as that creature encounters changing circumstances. Natural law has a dual nature: it is the adaptive application of timeless principles to changing circumstances as practical reason dictates.[63] Aquinas' natural law is teleological: "The first principle in the practical reason is one founded on the notion of good, viz., that good is that which all things seek after. Hence, this is the first precept of law, that good is to be done and pursued, and evil is to be avoided." Like Aristotle, Aquinas believed that we are naturally inclined to strive for the good, and that this fact about our nature is normative: we *should* live in accordance with our nature and strive for the good and for our flourishing. But Aquinas' understanding of human nature and natural law is not solely spiritual. He argues that we strive for good at three different levels. First, like all animals, we strive for self-preservation, and thus "whatever is a means of preserving human life and of warding off its obstacles belongs to the natural law."[64]

Second, Aquinas understands that survival is not enough; we strive after flourishing: "those things are said to belong to the natural law 'which nature has taught to all animals,' such as sexual intercourse, education of offspring, and so forth." In these first two aspects of natural law, Aquinas anticipates Hobbes and other Enlightenment thinkers – but he does not stop there. Unlike Hobbes, he understands there is more to our being: "There is in man an inclination to good according to the nature of his reason, which nature is proper to him; thus man has a natural inclination to know the truth about God and to live in society, and in this respect, whatever pertains to this inclination belongs to the natural law."[65] Natural law teaches us to survive and flourish, and also to seek fellowship with God and our fellow man.

In this last respect, Aquinas' natural law – which broadly serves as the natural law doctrine of Christendom and of the Augustinian tradition of just war until the Wars of Religion – is different from the natural law of the Enlightenment. Natural law cannot be derived from observing people in

---

[62] ST I-II, Q91, article 2, in Aquinas, *On Law, Morality, and Politics*, 20.
[63] Aquinas goes into more detail on this in Q94, article 3, stating that general principles are unchanging, but their applications are not.
[64] ST I-II, Q94, article 2, in Aquinas, *On Law, Morality, and Politics*, 47.
[65] ST I-II, Q94, article 2, in Aquinas, *On Law, Morality, and Politics*, 48. For more on the evolution of natural law, see Rommen, *Natural Law*.

a hypothetical state of nature and describing what is necessary for survival and civilization. Natural law must also account for that towards which humanity's moral nature impels us. Aquinas' natural law stipulates that humanity act in a way that fulfills the purpose or goals of human nature, as defined by the natural moral and spiritual impulses found therein.

The teleological nature of natural law shapes Aquinas' understanding of justice because justice is part of natural law; natural law commands that we do justice. Broadly, justice is the virtue that "directs man in his relations with other men," and, when other men are considered corporately, his relations with society as a whole. It is the "general virtue" insofar as other virtues, when directed to the common good, support and "pertain to" justice. Justice is the virtue of living well with others; it is the fulfillment of natural law's requirement towards others and towards society. Because justice fulfills natural law's command to "know the truth about God and to live in society," it is more than procedural. In fact, Aquinas' justice is quite broad and includes charity and mercy: "Mercy, liberality, and the like, are connected with [justice] .... To succor the needy, which belongs to mercy or pity, and to be liberally beneficent, which pertains to liberality, are by a kind of reduction ascribed to justice as to their principal virtue."[66] Remarkably, Aquinas seems to be arguing that justice entails and requires generosity and charity.

Aquinas expands on this in a later article. He acknowledges some key differences between liberality and justice – for example, justice is the giving to each his legal due, whereas liberality is giving beyond what is legally required – but he stresses that both are other-directed virtues of providing to others what they deserve. In the case of liberality, the virtue "considers a certain moral due ... based on a certain fittingness and not on an obligation."[67] When Aquinas suggests that giving succor to the needy is part of justice based on their moral due, he likely means that human beings possess intrinsic dignity and worth because they are made in the image of God; that no one deserves the indignity of poverty or suffering; and that to give the needy succor is to recognize their worth and treat them with the dignity they deserve – not the desert of their legal rights, but the desert of their inherent moral worth. As Johnson argues, in medieval Christian understanding, "justice, being informed by charity, expresses itself through mercy and not only through vindication."[68] This starting point – humanity's obligation to help those in need, understood as part of justice, derived from a teleological understanding of natural law,

---

[66] ST II-II, Q58, article 12, in Aquinas, *On Law, Morality, and Politics*, 162.
[67] ST II-II, Q117, article 5, www.newadvent.org/summa/3117.htm#article5.
[68] Johnson, *Ideology, Reason, and the Limitation of War*, 30.

founded on the natural moral impulses of our nature – has profound consequences for Aquinas' understanding of politics and war.

We can begin to see the impact of Aquinas' view of natural law and justice on war in his discussion of right authority, a major concern in the High Middle Ages as princes worked to consolidate their authority and eliminate the banditry and competing centers of power that had marked the earlier Middle Ages.[69] Aquinas starts, as do all thinkers, with the obligatory statement that only the sovereign has just cause to wage war. But, as we shall see, Aquinas undermines this and argues that right authority belongs to whoever possesses just cause or whoever is fighting in defense of public order. Initially, he argues that a just war requires "the authority of the ruler, by whose command the war is to be waged; it is not the business of a private individual to declare war, because he can seek for redress of his rights from the tribunal of his superior."[70] Feuds, clan or tribal conflict, dueling, and civil war are examples of the sin of strife. "Strife is a kind of private war, because it takes place between private persons, being declared not by public authority, but rather by an inordinate will …. Strife is always sinful."[71] However, Aquinas essentially strips this of meaning because he allows for personal self-defense; strife is only, and by definition, *unjust* private violence.

It is a mortal sin in the man who attacks another *unjustly* … but in him who defends himself, it may be without sin … and this depends on his intention and on his manner of defending himself. For if his sole intention be to withstand the injury done to him, and he defend himself with due moderation, it is no sin, and one cannot say properly that there is strife on his part. But if, on the other hand, his self-defense be inspired by vengeance and hatred, it is always sin.[72]

Aquinas does the same thing, with greater consequence, in his discussion of sedition. Sedition is always sinful; indeed, it is "a special kind of sin" because it is "opposed to a special kind of good, namely the unity and peace of a people."[73] But sedition is defined as opposition to a just government, opposition to which is unjust by definition.

The unity to which sedition is opposed is the unity of law and common good; whence it follows manifestly that sedition is opposed to justice and the common good. Therefore *by reason of its genus* it is a mortal sin, and its gravity will be all the greater according to the common good which it assails surpasses the private good which is assailed by strife.

---

[69] See Johnson, *Sovereignty*, chapter 2, for a similar interpretation.
[70] ST II-II, Q40, article 1, in Aquinas, *On Law, Morality, and Politics*, 221.
[71] ST II-II, Q41, article 1, www.newadvent.org/summa/3041.htm.
[72] ST II-II, Q41, article 1, www.newadvent.org/summa/3041.htm (emphasis added).
[73] ST II-II, Q42, article 1, www.newadvent.org/summa/3042.htm#article1.

He goes on:

Discord from what is not evidently good, may be without sin …. A tyrannical government is not just, because it is directed, not to the common good, but to the private good of the ruler …. Consequently there is no sedition in disturbing a government of this kind, unless indeed the tyrant's rule be disturbed so inordinately, that his subjects suffer greater harm from the consequent disturbance than from the tyrant's government. Indeed it is the tyrant rather that is guilty of sedition, since he encourages discord and sedition among his subjects, that he may lord over them more securely; for this is tyranny, being conducive to the private good of the ruler, and to the injury of the multitude.[74]

Aquinas' reasoning is tautological: strife and sedition are opposition to just government, therefore strife and sedition are unjust; but if the government is not just, opposition to it is not seditious and therefore not unjust. In both examples – sedition and strife – Aquinas locates right authority with the party who has just cause, whether it is private individuals defending themselves from personal attack, a group of citizens resisting a tyrannical government, or a sovereign state fighting against an aggressor. Justice is found with those fighting in defense of public order, which can come under attack from an external aggressor, a private criminal, or from the government itself when it acts contrary to justice. Aquinas cautions against rebellion against tyranny that is not "excessive" because the evils of rebellion are hard to outweigh, but, in a move that will become conventional by the early modern era, he opens the door to legitimate revolt: "If, however, a tyranny were so extreme as to be intolerable, it has seemed to some that it would be an act consistent with virtue if the mightier men were to slay the tyrant, exposing themselves even to the peril of death in order to liberate the community."[75] Though he seems to equivocate on whether or not he agrees with this view, counseling Christians to suffer injustice peacefully and advising against private persons assuming the responsibility to slay tyrants, he also suggests other magistrates might justifiably lead people in a revolt against a tyrant. For "the tyrant who has failed to govern the community faithfully, as the office of king requires, has deserved to be treated in this way," that is, forcibly deposed.[76] Aquinas is creating grounds on which to criticize the arbitrary tyranny and warlordism prevalent in feudal Europe. As Gregory Reichberg argues, Aquinas "quietly displaced the focus [of justice] from loyalty to the person of the prince to respect for the underlying subject of this competence – the political community."[77]

[74] ST II-II, Q42, article 2, www.newadvent.org/summa/3042.htm#article2 (emphasis added).
[75] Aquinas, *Political Writings*, 18–19.   [76] Aquinas, *Political Writings*, 20.
[77] Reichberg, "Thomas Aquinas," in Brunstetter and O'Driscoll, *Just War Thinkers*, chapter 4.

In this decidedly un-Hobbesian view, justice is separable from and enjoys lexical priority over the institution of government and territorial boundaries. The presence of justice makes right authority; right authority does not make justice. Put another way, justice constitutes government, not vice versa. This is a deeper way of saying *lex rex*, that law is king and even the government must obey the rule of law. Indeed, Aquinas is saying, more or less, *ius rex*, that justice is sovereign and a government that does not do justice is not a government. As Johnson argues:

> the just war idea, as it came together in the late twelfth and thirteenth centuries, centered on a conception of sovereignty as responsibility for the common good of society that is to be exercised to vindicate justice after some injustice has occurred and gone unrectified or unpunished. This responsibility is fundamentally to and for the moral order itself, understood as an order in accord with the natural law.[78]

Elshtain makes much the same argument in her discussion of the evolution of sovereignty. In Aquinas (and for much of Christendom), "The king or emperor is not free to do anything he wills . . .. The ruler who fails to fulfill his respective office with its distinctive and particular responsibilities, is a tyrant, not king," Elshtain argues. "Magistracy was bound by an objective legal order that transcended the positive law of particular entities of rule. This order is part of God's creation, a manifestation of God's fullness of goodness, reason, and love."[79] Aquinas may have equivocated mildly in other writings, and his view was of course contested by others in the Middle Ages, but his view here is representative of the Augustinian tradition.

Aquinas on War

Aquinas' discussion of right authority brings us around to the question of just cause. Aquinas argues that "A just cause is required [for war], namely that those who are attacked, should be attacked because they deserve it on account of some fault." Like Augustine, Aquinas declines to define further what "some fault" might be, nor what criteria of desert should be used to determine who "deserves" to be attacked. He simply quotes Augustine: "Wherefore Augustine says, 'A just war is wont to be described as one that avenges wrongs, when a nation or state has to be punished, for refusing to make amends for the wrongs inflicted by its

[78] Johnson, *Sovereignty*, 19. Johnson says elsewhere: "this classic just war idea serves as a reminder – a very useful one, I think – that the leaders of sovereign states have important responsibilities for order, justice, and peace both in their own communities and in others," Johnson, *Ethics and the Use of Force*, 9.
[79] Elshtain, *Sovereignty*, 15, 16.

subjects, or to restore what it has seized unjustly.'"[80] (Aquinas cites or quotes Augustine nine times in his first article on war.)

Aquinas seems to give two examples of just cause in this passage, but his examples are clearly meant to be illustrative rather than exhaustive since they do not cover the paradigmatic case of repelling a foreign invasion.[81] By remaining nonspecific with his own words but quoting Augustine at length, and leaning on Augustine's authority throughout his work, Aquinas implicitly adopts in to the Augustinian understanding of just cause. As we saw earlier, Augustine himself was vague about just cause, but his understanding of natural law and justice suggests that the defense and preservation of the "tranquility of order" was the primary justification for the state and the source of its authority to wield lethal force. Aquinas gets close to this when he links the authority to wage war to the state's responsibility for the "common weal." He writes:

Since the care of the common weal is committed to those who are in authority, it is their business to watch over the common weal of the city, kingdom, or province subject to them. And just as it is lawful for them to have recourse to the sword in defending that common weal against internal disturbances ... so too is it their business to have recourse to the sword of war in defending the common weal against external enemies.

War is an instrument of the state for protecting and restoring the common good. That Aquinas understood this to include the virtues of liberality and charity is evident in his next sentence: "Hence it is said to those who are in authority: 'Rescue the poor and deliver the needy out of the hand of the sinner.'"[82] Aquinas clearly links war to our obligation to "rescue the poor and deliver the needy," and later describes the vocation of soldiering in the same way.[83] Joseph Boyle interprets these passages this way: "What grounds the sovereign's authority, in both these relationships, is the fact that the care of the community is entrusted to the prince, who has the responsibility to look after its welfare. This responsibility includes authority to use force not only internally against domestic criminals but also against outsiders who harm the polity."[84] Aquinas' emphasis on the responsibilities of the sovereign was likely a response to the failure of the sovereigns in his day to do so.

That Aquinas had something like this in mind is likely when we recall his discussion of natural law, justice, and liberality. Natural law requires

---

[80] ST II-II, Q40, article 1, in Aquinas, *On Law, Morality, and Politics*, 221.
[81] On Aquinas and self-defense, see Johnson, *Ethics and the Use of Force*, chapter 9.
[82] ST II-II, Q40, article 1, in Aquinas, *On Law, Morality, and Politics*, 221.
[83] ST II-II, Q188, article 3, in Aquinas, *On Law, Morality, and Politics*. I am indebted to Russell, *Just War in the Middle Ages*, 261, for this latter point.
[84] Boyle, "Traditional Just War Theory and Humanitarian Intervention," 36.

that we cultivate the virtues necessary for living well in society, which might be thought of in Augustinian terms as a commandment to do one's part to live in harmony with the "tranquility of order." There is a relationship of mutual reciprocity between the *tranquilitas ordinis* and the virtues of justice and liberality: upholding the tranquility of order and living well in society includes liberality towards those in need, while liberality includes doing one's part to preserve and cultivate the tranquility of order because such an order is a blessing to those in need, as to all people. The state acts justly when it upholds and defends the tranquility of order, by law when possible and by force when necessary. In Aquinas' own words, he defends war as an action "necessary . . . for the common good," including "the good of those with whom he is fighting."[85]

This is a crucial point for my overall argument, so it bears repeating and unpacking. If justice includes liberality, mercy, and charity – if justice means giving succor to the needy based on their moral due – then a *just war* must include such virtues as well. Such a war should exhibit love for both our neighbors and our enemies in how it is fought and how it is ended; additionally, war on behalf of the innocent or to punish the wicked becomes conceivable. Such a view of justice rests on a teleological understanding of natural law: nature teaches us that we must obey the goal or purpose of our natures, including the goals of seeking truth, knowing God, and living in society. Because natural law is teleological, not descriptive, it includes all acts of virtue among its precepts, including the virtues of liberality and charity, which are essential to living in society. War itself, to be just, must include such virtues: war must be liberal, magnanimous, and loving. That is why Aquinas, and other scholars in the Augustinian tradition, discusses just war under the heading of charity, not justice. War, placed alongside discord, contention, schism, strife, and sedition in Aquinas' discussion, was understood as a breach of the right ordering of things and a sin against charity, but, unlike the other sins, war itself was also the right response to the sin of war. War was understood to be an act of love, fulfilling the command to love our enemies and our neighbors by working for justice and peace in society from which they might benefit.

Francisco de Vitoria (1492–1546)

Aquinas consolidated the template that his successors would build upon until the Reformation and the Wars of Religion. Those events, along with

---

[85] ST II-II, Q40, article 1, in Aquinas, *On Law, Morality, and Politics*.

the Age of Exploration, proved the catalyst for the next major developments in just war thinking. Theologians faced new questions about the ethics of using force against schismatic Christians and unbelieving Native Americans; relatedly, they faced new questions about the relationship between church and state, specifically about the different legitimating authorizations behind each institution. Francisco de Vitoria, a Spanish Dominican of the sixteenth century, continued and deepened the Thomist tradition. He worked to respond to Renaissance humanism and the Reformation by updating Thomism and reviving the ideas of natural law and natural rights. Vitoria was animated, above all, by the question of whether or how Spain's conquest of the New World could be justified. The question presented novel challenges because, since Europe lacked prior contact with Native Americans, there was no customary law and no formal agreements to regulate intercourse between them. Vitoria appealed to natural law as the only possible standard of conduct that could apply across culture and time to govern the rights and privileges of diverse peoples – and he concluded, courageously for his day, that Spain lacked natural title to conquer the Indians. His major works on war, *On the Indians* and *On the Law of War*, appeared in 1532.

Vitoria on Natural Law, Justice, and Sovereignty

Vitoria, like Aquinas, roots natural law in divine law. "Law is of two kinds, divine and human; and the first of these is of two kinds, natural and positive."[86] He affirms that our judgments about natural law are binding and obligatory precisely because "it [natural law] derives from eternal law."[87] Vitoria's natural law shares Aquinas' teleology: he argues that the goal of law, including natural law, is to "make men good,"[88] and that "What a man is naturally inclined towards is good, and what he naturally abhors is evil," because God is the author of our natural inclinations.[89] Natural law commands us to obey our natural inclinations to pursue the good; this is only intelligible if we understand our natural inclinations to include the sort of moral aspiration towards truth and goodness that Aquinas had in mind.

Nature also impels us to seek fellowship with other people. "We are all, as Aristotle says, impelled by nature to seek society," Vitoria argues, which, when coupled with our moral aspirations, means we naturally incline to help one another. "Human partnerships arose for the purpose of helping to bear each other's burdens." The city and its government are

---

[86] Vitoria, *Political Writings*, 159.   [87] Vitoria, *Political Writings*, 163.
[88] Vitoria, *Political Writings*, 165.   [89] Vitoria, *Political Writings*, 171.

the institutions by which we exercise our communal care for one another in public matters. The city is "the most natural community, the one which is most conformable to nature," a view that leads Vitoria specifically to deny that cities are a "human invention or contrivance," which seems to be a preemptive rebuttal of social contract theory.[90]

If there is a shift in Vitoria from the reasoning of earlier ages, it is in his treatment of sovereignty. In contrast to Aquinas, who locates sovereignty in the person of the prince under commission from God, Vitoria locates sovereignty in the body politic, the commonwealth, the *respublica* or public thing that embodies the people as a whole. He argues that the commonwealth is the material cause of civil power, that is, the stuff out of which government is made. Government has no intelligibility apart from the body politic, the corporate entity it exists to govern, and the good of that entity in turn provides government with its purpose. "The common-wealth takes upon itself the task of governing and administering itself and directing all its powers to the common good," Vitoria says. Vitoria spe-cifically vests sovereignty in the body politic as a whole: "There is no convincing reason why one man should have power more than another," and so it follows that "this power be vested in the community, which must be able to provide for itself." Vitoria goes on to argue that monarchy is the best form of government, but he does so not on the basis of the divine right of kings but because of their superior effectiveness when compared with republics.[91]

Importantly, as with Aquinas, the ultimate standard of justice is not the state but that which the state serves and from which it derives its legitim-acy. Government exists "to guard public property and look after the common good," he says; "public power is founded upon natural law" and "natural law acknowledges God as its only author."[92] Natural law and the defense of the common good are the purposes of the state; states that do not serve the common good or govern in accord with natural law lack legitimacy: "Tyrants have no legitimate power whatever."[93] However, Vitoria does acknowledge that tyrants still retain the authority to enforce law and that non-Christian princes are legitimate. On the whole, for Vitoria, "The law of God directs the state, not immediately from above, but from below through natural law," according to Johnson.[94]

---

[90] Vitoria, *Political Writings*, 8–9.   [91] Vitoria, *Political Writings*, 11, 20.
[92] Vitoria, *Political Writings*, 9–10.   [93] Vitoria, *Political Writings*, 42.
[94] Johnson, *Just War Tradition*, 100. Johnson exaggerates Vitoria's departure from Aquinas when he writes that it was a novelty in Vitoria that "just war theory is grounded exclusively in appeals to nature" (94).

Vitoria on War

Vitoria, quoting the key Augustinian texts, echoes the by-then conventional view that "difference of religion," "enlargement of empire," and "personal glory" are not just causes for war: "The sole and only just cause for waging war is when harm has been inflicted."[95] He echoes Augustinian language about the need for right intention: "The prince should press his campaign not for the destruction of his opponents, but for the pursuit of the justice for which he fights and the defense of his homeland, so that by fighting he may eventually establish peace and security."[96] Similarly, Vitoria denies that unbelief, heresy, or madness deprives people of the right to their property or land or makes them justly subject to a war waged against them.[97] He specifically denies that the Spanish emperor, the pope, or any emperor has universal jurisdiction or legitimate title to be emperor of the world. This is an important limitation: Vitoria denies that anyone could claim global authority on the basis of natural or divine law. He denies that Spain could conquer the Indians because they refused to convert; refusing to accept Christ is not legitimate grounds for regime change: "If the barbarians have done no wrong, there is no just cause for war."[98] (Somewhat contradictorily, he does allow war in response to blasphemy.) In his work to defend the Indians' rights against Spain, Vitoria definitively breaks from the "holy war" strand of thought that also had roots in some of Augustine's writing.

But Vitoria does allow a very expansive set of just causes for war. Vitoria allows for "offensive war," by which he means punishment or vengeance in response to an attack: "It is lawful to avenge the injury done by the enemy, and to teach the enemy a lesson by punishing them for the damage they have done."[99] More broadly, for Vitoria, the "harm" to which war is a response might include the denial of free travel, free trade, immigration, the freedom to proselytize, the Indians' freedom to convert, protection of Indian Christians, and the naturalization of children born of Spanish fathers and Indian mothers. And the Spaniards could also wage war on behalf on an ally that has been attacked. "If war is necessary to obtain their rights, they may lawfully go to war."[100] Vitoria is careful to say that such wars should be subject to the criteria of last resort and proportionality, suggesting that he wants to avoid justifying wars of conquest or total wars for a perceived slight over a small matter of immigration or trade. Broadly, we can see that Vitoria's understanding of the Augustinian and Thomist inheritance leads to an expansive writ to defend public order.

---

[95] Vitoria, *Political Writings*, 297, 312.   [96] Vitoria, *Political Writings*, 327.
[97] Vitoria, *Political Writings*, 243.   [98] Vitoria, *Political Writings*, 270.
[99] Vitoria, *Political Writings*, 303, 305.   [100] Vitoria, *Political Writings*, 282.

We see this most clearly, and most interestingly, when Vitoria addresses the thorny question of humanitarian intervention, apparently the first (or at least most prominent) to do so explicitly and at length in the western tradition. Vitoria at first denies that the barbarians' violation of the laws of nature through cannibalism, incest, or sodomy gives Spain the right to wage war because the pope and the emperor do not have jurisdiction over barbarians' crimes.[101] But he turns around and justifies war on humanitarian grounds anyway – not on the grounds of the Indians' sins against nature but because of how such sins oppress the innocent. The Spaniards may, on the grounds of the general moral obligation to defend the innocent and love one's neighbor, wage war on the Indians. I quote at length here to demonstrate how Vitoria further elaborates the Thomist logic of including liberality as a component obligation of justice. Just war, he argues, could be waged in response to

the personal tyranny of the barbarians' masters towards their subjects, or because of their tyrannical and oppressive laws against the innocent, such as human sacrifice practiced on innocent men or the killing of condemned criminals for cannibalism. I assert that in lawful defense of the innocent from unjust death, even without the pope's authority, the Spaniards may prohibit the barbarians from practicing any nefarious custom or rite ... *The barbarians are all our neighbors*, and therefore anyone, and especially princes, may defend them from such tyranny and oppression. A further proof is the saying: "deliver them that are drawn unto death, and forebear not to deliver those that are ready to be slain," (Prov. 24:11). This applies not only to the actual moment when they are being dragged to death; they may also force the barbarians to give up such rites altogether. If they refuse to do so, war may be declared upon them, and the laws of war enforced upon them; and if there is no other means of putting an end to these sacrilegious rites, their masters may be changed and new princes set up. In this case, there is truth in the opinion held by Innocent IV and Antonino of Florence, that sinners against nature may be punished. It makes no difference that all the barbarians consent to these kinds of rites and sacrifices, or that they refuse to accept the Spaniards as their liberators in the matter.[102]

Vitoria recognizes the implications of this argument for other aspects of his just war doctrine and, commendably for his intellectual consistency, he carries the argument right through to its conclusion. For example, in his discussion of right authority, he begins with the conventional view that right authority rests with sovereign governments – but, he argues, that does not limit their authority to crimes only within their territory. Governments have authority to "punish those of its own members who are intent on harming it." And "if the commonwealth has these powers

---

[101] Vitoria, *Political Writings*, 274.
[102] Vitoria, *Political Writings*, 288 (emphasis added).

against its own members, there can be no doubt that the whole world has the same powers against any harmful and evil men. And these powers can only exist if exercised through the princes of commonwealths."[103] If just cause includes the defense of the innocent, right authority must give governments extraterritorial jurisdiction over those who commit crimes against nature. This is an example of how just war doctrine is best understood as an integrated whole, not a separable checklist. The conceptual center of gravity for the Augustinian tradition – that governments have an obligation to pursue justice, defined as the tranquility of order, motivated by love for our neighbors and enemies alike – has implications for the whole fabric, not only for just cause.

Vitoria even approaches the idea of intervening to save a failed state from itself:

> These barbarians, though not totally mad, as explained before, are nevertheless so close to being mad, that they are unsuited to setting up or administering a commonwealth both legitimate and ordered in human and civil terms. Hence they have neither appropriate laws nor magistrates fitted to the task. Indeed they are unsuited even to governing their own households; hence their lack of letters, of arts and crafts (not merely liberal, but even mechanical), of systematic agriculture, of manufacture, and of many other things useful, or rather indispensable, for human use. It might therefore be argued that for their own benefit the princes of Spain might take over their administration, and set up urban officers and governors on their behalf, or even give them new masters, so long as this could be proved to be in their interest .... Such an argument could be supported by the requirements of charity, since the barbarians are our neighbors and we are obliged to take care of their goods.[104]

Vitoria's argument foreshadows contemporary debates over the ethics of intervening in failed states, such as Somalia, Haiti, or the Democratic Republic of the Congo, to provide governance where it seems to be absent. Vitoria isn't naive; he realizes this argument could be used as a pretext for exploitative imperialism, and that the idea of disinterested, charitable intervention is extraordinarily unlikely. It only holds "if everything is done for the benefit and good of the barbarians, and not merely for the profit of the Spaniards. But it is in this latter restriction that the whole pitfall to souls and salvation is found to lie." That is why Vitoria adds extra caveats to the argument, claiming to have explicated it for the sake of argument, "though certainly not asserted with confidence ... I myself do not dare either to affirm or condemn [this argument] out of hand."[105] Similarly, Vitoria argues that regime change is only justified in the most extreme cases: "Although the harm done by the enemy may be

---

[103] Vitoria, *Political Writings*, 305–306.   [104] Vitoria, *Political Writings*, 290–291.
[105] Vitoria, *Political Writings*, 290–291.

a sufficient cause of war, it will not always be sufficient to justify the extermination of the enemy's kingdom and deposition of its legitimate native princes; this would be altogether too savage and inhumane." Such an extreme step is only justified in rare cases: "this may be because of the number or atrocity of the injuries and harm done by the enemy, and especially when security and peace cannot otherwise be ensured, when failure to do so would cause a dangerous threat to the commonwealth."[106]

Vitoria was pushed to think through these extreme scenarios because of the novel case of the Spanish encounter with the New World. He criticized Spain for its conduct towards the Indians and denied most of the grounds on which Spain claimed its right to conquer and rule the Americas. But, in passing, Vitoria also explicated other grounds for war that Spain had not invoked for its New World conquests that could, in principle, be used to justify humanitarian intervention. Some have accused Vitoria of defending imperialism with these arguments. But given his critique of the actual practice of Spanish imperialism, it seems more consistent to interpret Vitoria as doing the same thing Cicero and Augustine did when the former praised the Roman "protectorate of the world" and the latter expressed admiration for Roman greatness. Both held up the empire's self-image as a standard against which to judge the hypocrisy of the imperial practice of their day. Vitoria, similarly, is describing the high standard against which any imperial pretension should be judged, and he uses that standard to show how radically Spain's actual conduct fell short.

Conclusion

With Vitoria the Augustinian tradition reached an inflection point. His thorough and systematic treatment of war, compared to the scattered reflections in Augustine and the brief treatment by Aquinas, showed the promise of Augustinian thinking in full flower. But just war thinking

---

[106] Vitoria, *Political Writings*, 326. Vitoria's argument here casts doubt on Tuck's argument that the scholastic tradition differed significantly from the so-called "humanist" tradition in its evaluation of wars for humanitarian intervention. Tuck argued that the humanists, among whom he wrongly places Gentili, were more open to such warfare because they "saw a dramatic moral difference between Christian, European civilization and barbarism." He goes so far as to speak of "the critical struggle between humanist and scholastic over the right to inflict violence on barbaric peoples." Tuck may be right that the scholastics and humanists had different views about whether the Indians retained rights or whether their civilization was on an equal moral footing with Europe, but he is wrong that the scholastics therefore drew a different conclusion about humanitarian intervention. Vitoria and Suárez clearly favored it. See Tuck, *Rights of War and Peace*, 78, 89.

would undergo profound changes within a century because of the Reformation, just in the process of breaking out when Vitoria published his treatises (the Diet of Worms confronted Martin Luther just eleven years prior). The great schism in the western church, and the emergence of Protestant thinkers willing to challenge the Roman church's teachings on natural law and its interpretation of scripture, forced all thinkers, Protestant and Catholic alike, to argue anew from the ground up. Even as they continued to share much in common and operate with the broader Augustinian worldview, they introduced subtle changes in the structure of just war thinking, as we see in the next chapter.

3   The Transition

The Protestant Reformation ushered in a prolonged period of warfare across Europe. Some thinkers used the wars as occasion to argue in favor of religious or holy war: war commissioned by God for the gain of his people and the advance of the true faith. The holy war challenge forced thinkers in the just war tradition to refine their arguments and explain why just war must exclude war for religion. In doing so, just war thinkers were forced to reexamine the premises on which the Augustinian tradition stood, including their understanding of natural law, justice, and sovereignty. This reexamination brought the late Augustinian just war tradition to its classic expression – but the social and political fracture of those wars also brought Christendom to an end. The Augustinian tradition, then, reached its zenith just as the cultural context it presumed and depended on fractured and vanished.

This chapter examines three thinkers crucial to the transition between the Augustinian tradition and its successor: Gentili, Suárez, and Grotius. I classify them as part of the Augustinian tradition, but they clearly show signs of subtle departure from their predecessors. Grotius, especially, is a hybrid between the Augustinian past and the Westphalian future. Their inclusion with the Augustinians is justified, I think, because they understood themselves to be engaged in a project of continuity: they wanted to salvage and reinterpret the intellectual inheritance of Christendom and reapply it to the changing and fracturing landscape of their day. That project, and Christendom itself, essentially came to an end with the Peace of Westphalia, which arrived just two short decades after the first edition of Grotius' masterwork in 1625.

Alberico Gentili (1552–1608)

Gentili represents the beginning of a shift in just war thinking. Born and educated in Italy but Protestant by conviction, Gentili (and his father) fled the Inquisition when he was in his twenties. After temporary stays in

Germany and Slovenia (and after his formal excommunication from the Catholic Church) he settled in England, already a famed jurist and law teacher. He took up a post teaching law at Oxford University, which he held until his death two decades later, while also practicing law in London. As an Italian Protestant refugee who won fame and influence in England, he once again had the mix of an outsider's perspective and an insider's access that marked so many just war thinkers. His distinctions are many: he was the first important Protestant thinker on war; he was a lawyer, not a theologian; and he wrote, essentially, Europe's first book on international law. His *Three Books on the Law of War* appeared in 1598. His Protestantism and his legal approach to the subject introduced subtle shifts of emphasis in the tradition.[1] (For example, Gentili dismisses the category of right intention as outside his concern: "Some raise the question whether or not it is necessary for the justice of a war that the leader have a good motive, which is a problem for theologians.")[2]

Gentili on Natural Law, Justice, and Sovereignty

Gentili begins with a brief reflection on what he alternately calls natural law and the law of nations. The latter (Latin: *ius gentium*) had not been an important concept for the theologians discussed in the previous chapter. Gentili's appeal to it is one among many indications of his departure from them. But Gentili's use of the law of nations, and its relationship to natural law, is ambiguous. In fact, it is unclear if the two are distinct for Gentili and, if so, what the nature of their relationship is. In defining the law of nations Gentili offers what could be one of the better definitions of natural law, one that accurately reflects the tradition in which he stood and to which his predecessors would surely assent: "Such laws are not written, but inborn; we have not learned, received, and read them; but we have wrested, drawn, and forced them out of nature herself. We have not received them through instruction, but have acquired them at birth; we have gained them, not by training, but by instinct."[3] However, Gentili quickly shows his divergence from Thomism: "It does not appear to be the function either of the moral or of the political philosopher to give an

---

[1] His divergence from other just war thinkers is why Tuck chooses him as representative of what he calls the "Humanistic" just war tradition, loosely analogous to what I have called the Westphalian tradition. Tuck is right to distinguish between differing traditions of just war thought, but his chapter on Gentili is mostly about pagan and Renaissance thinkers, not about Gentili himself. Ultimately Tuck overemphasizes the Renaissance influence, and underemphasizes the religious influence, in Gentili's thought. As a Protestant who paid a steep cost for his Protestantism, Gentili is an Augustinian before he is a neo-Roman.
[2] Gentili, *Three Books on the Law of War*, 35.
[3] Gentili, *Three Books on the Law of War*, 10.

account of the laws which we have in common with our enemies and with foreigners."[4] Philosophers, he claims, confine themselves to affairs of one city, whereas the law of nations and the law of war consider relations between cities. Gentili, claiming to see an unmet need that philosophers and theologians have ignored, aspires to elaborate this law – but he claims his qualifications to do so are as a jurist rather than a philosopher or theologian.

Gentili treats theologians' arguments with a very Protestant skepticism: "Although international law is a portion of the divine law, which God left with us after our sin, yet we behold that light amid great darkness; and hence through error, bad habits, obstinacy, and other affections due to darkness we often cannot recognize it."[5] Gentili is echoing Calvin and other Protestant thinkers (and, dimly, Augustine and even Plato) in their insistence that sin and passion had corrupted man's intellect as much as his soul and that therefore we should be skeptical of our ability to read truth clearly and straightforwardly off the book of nature. Church fathers and past theologians and their opinions about nature are insufficient; some other foundation is needed. Fortunately, for Gentili, such a foundation is provided by the world's lawyers and jurists:

Abundant light is afforded us by the definitions which the authors and founders of our laws are unanimous in giving to this law of nations which we are investigating. For they say that the law of nations is that which is in use among all the nations of men, which native reason has established among all human beings, and which is equally observed by all mankind. Such a law is natural law.[6]

Interestingly, Gentili identifies both universal practice and common reason as the source of this law, which he names both natural law and the law of nations. The emphasis of his work, in fact, focuses more on the law of nations than natural law. And elsewhere he does distinguish the two: the law of nations is not the same as natural law, but, as a body of international common law, it was understood to "express" the natural law.[7] The difference reflects a longstanding ambiguity about the law of nations: past thinkers sometimes described it as a component of natural law, sometimes as a body of international customary or common law. Gentili leans towards the latter, perhaps reflecting an English influence. (I trace the evolution of the "law of nations" at the end of Chapter 4.)

His belief that common practice is a source of the law of nations is why Gentili approaches his subject as a Renaissance scholar who appeals to comparative history and pagan philosophy alongside church authorities.

---

[4] Gentili, *Three Books on the Law of War*, 3.
[5] Gentili, *Three Books on the Law of War*, 8.
[6] Gentili, *Three Books on the Law of War*, 8.   [7] Johnson, *Just War Tradition*, 93.

His method throughout his work is to pile historical examples and quotations from the pagans on top of another to show by weight of evidence what the common practice of nations has been, punctuated by obligatory references to Christian thinkers (including, of course, Augustine). He works inductively, reasoning from historical data and jurists' views of particular cases to generalizable principles. Gentili did not invent this mode of scholarly inquiry, which had risen to prominence throughout the Renaissance and marked the work of other scholars, such as Desiderius Erasmus; but among just war thinkers, Gentili's work stands in contrast to Vitoria and Suárez, who appealed to church fathers and the magisterium. Their method had largely been deductive, applying principles captured in doctrine to particular problems of war and peace. By linking natural law to the law of nations (or customary law) rather than directly to divine law, Gentili shifts the emphasis of his subsequent thought. He plays down the teleological aspect of natural law, the idea of natural law as leading to the fulfillment of man's purpose or God's design. Natural law in Gentili, tied so closely to the customary law of nations, begins to look more like the descriptive natural law of the Enlightenment thinkers, the law of the "state of nature."

Gentili thus represents the beginning – though only the beginning – of a transition in the just war tradition away from church doctrine and towards secular law. His work is still very much steeped in the broader Christian and Augustinian tradition and a Christian understanding of justice and charity. The full implications of Gentili's approach were not apparent for half a century after his death, until after Grotius and, later, Pufendorf had taken Gentili's premises to their logical conclusions. It was for later thinkers to complete the transition from the Augustinian to the Westphalian tradition. That is why, despite his departures from a Thomist understanding of natural law, the bulk of Gentili's just war doctrine lies squarely within the Augustinian tradition of just war thinking. Gentili continues to see war as an act of loving punishment and he stridently agrees with Vitoria's and Suárez's views on humanitarian intervention, the right of revolt, and state building.

His views on sovereignty are also similar to his predecessors'. He recites the pro forma view that "the sovereign has no earthly judge."[8] But he also clearly understands natural law and the law of nations to be binding on sovereigns. That in itself does not differentiate him from the Westphalian thinkers, but it does when he continues by recognizing some divine connection to natural law: God, even if more removed, is still at the back of sovereignty and his natural law still operates as an external

---

[8] Gentili, *Three Books on the Law of War*, 15.

standard to which sovereigns are accountable. Gentili asks, "are not the following principles from the books of Justinian" – he had previously argued that the Justinian code expressed natural law and the law of nations – "applicable to sovereigns: to live honorably, not to wrong another; to give every man his due; to protect one's children; to defend oneself against injury; to recognize kinship with all men; to maintain commercial relations, [etc.]?"[9] His view that sovereignty involves a responsibility to "recognize kinship with all men" and to "give every man his due" shows similarities with the Augustinian and Thomist view of sovereignty as responsibility for the common good.

Gentili on War

Gentili regularly invokes Augustine,[10] alongside scores of other authorities, to position himself firmly in the mainstream of the received just war discourse. Doing so allows Gentili more flexibility to stretch the boundaries of the tradition. Gentili argues that war is justified for self-defense and for securing anything that "is refused us which Nature herself has bestowed upon mankind," the latter including, presumably, free travel, access to waterways, and so on.[11] Gentili's view of self-defense is conventional to us, and his successors have no problem reiterating it, but it is different in emphasis from his predecessors. Augustine, Aquinas, and Vitoria had emphasized war in response to an injury received and war to defend the common good, protect the innocent, and punish the wicked. Gentili speaks more plainly of war to defend ourselves, our territory, and our property from attack. He even gives broad writ for preemptive self-defense when attack is imminent or when a rival power threatens to amass so much power as to be beyond check.[12] "We should oppose powerful and ambitious chiefs. For they are content with no bounds, and end by attacking the fortunes of all," he says, giving as examples both the Ottoman and Habsburg empires, the Islamic and Catholic threats to Protestant survival. In this, Gentili anticipates the arguments that Wolff and Emerich de Vattel will develop about war to maintain the balance of power.[13]

---

[9] Gentili, *Three Books on the Law of War*, 18. Tuck is wrong when he claims that "Gentili's state was already in effect the autonomous agent of the great seventeenth-century writers, governed by an extremely thin set of moral requirements" (Tuck, *Rights of War and Peace*, 228). Bellamy, similarly, exaggerates when he says Gentili "discarded ... the Just War tradition's theological foundations" (Bellamy, *Just Wars*, 61).

[10] Gentili cites Augustine on at least fourteen occasions in volume 1 alone: *Three Books on the Law of War*, 10, 15, 20, 28, 32, 36, 59, 67, 79, 83, 86, 87, 96, 122.

[11] Gentili, *Three Books on the Law of War*, 58.

[12] Gentili, *Three Books on the Law of War*, 61ff.

[13] Gentili, *Three Books on the Law of War*, 64.

But if Gentili seems to narrow just cause by focusing on self-defense, he dramatically enlarges it again by expanding the "self" whom we are obligated to defend. Gentili, reflecting both Christian and Renaissance universalism, endorses the view that "The whole world is one body, that all men are members of that body, that the world is their home, and that it forms a state." Gentili here anticipates Wolff's argument that the states of Europe form a universal commonwealth or republic, but he is more expansive in applying his universalism to the whole world. Since we belong to the universal republic of humanity, defending others is akin to defending ourselves: "the defense of one's own people and of strangers is equally necessary." This is a simple obligation of love: "Men will aid one another, since society cannot be maintained except by the love and protection of those who compose it." We have an obligation to protect each other's interests and safety: "This is due to any man from any other, for the very reason that they are alike men; and also because human nature, the common mother of them all, commends one to the other."[14] Gentili clearly echoes Aquinas' view that doing justice means recognizing the equal moral worth of every person.

Gentili applies this argument to humanitarian intervention and comes to some strident conclusions. Indeed, Vitoria and Suárez's views are qualified and modest by comparison. Perhaps because Gentili looks more to history than to theology for guidance, he sees ample proof of humanity's capacity for atrocity. At the same time, he does not sacralize international borders the way the Westphalians do, and thus sees fewer obstacles to their abrogation. "So far as I am concerned, the subjects of others do not seem to me to be outside of that kinship of nature and the society formed by the whole world," he writes, the denial of which would "destroy the union of the human race." Gentili is writing in this passage about foreign intervention in civil wars to help subjects in rebellion against oppression. "When a dispute arises regarding the commonwealth, there are no competent judges in the state, nor can there be any," in consequence of which, Gentili argues, only external powers can serve as judges. "For if a war is just when its purpose is to ward off injury ... it would seem that the same thing may be established for the same reason with regard to the defense of others, even though they be subjects [of another]."[15] Rebellion against an unjust tyrant and foreign intervention in a civil war to uphold justice are both, for Gentili, just cause: "A vassal

---

[14] Gentili, *Three Books on the Law of War*, 67–69. Again, this demonstrates that Tuck is wrong to see Gentili's state as akin to the autonomous state of the seventeenth century. Compared to Hobbes and Pufendorf, Gentili treats international borders as radically contingent and gives essentially no support at all to the principle of noninterference.

[15] Gentili, *Three Books on the Law of War*, 75.

may defend himself by war against the injustice of his lord ... a prince may defend subjects who are not his own."[16]

As a Protestant who fled persecution, Gentili was keenly aware that Protestantism would likely not have survived the sixteenth century without Protestant foreign powers intervening to support their coreligionists, as, for example, England supported the Netherlands in its war for independence against Catholic Spain. England extended military aid and diplomatic recognition to the Dutch rebels in 1585, thirteen years before Gentili published his work and likely when he was solidifying his convictions on international law, intervention, and the right of rebellion. Interestingly, however, Gentili does not frame his argument in terms of a holy war or war for religion, as many Protestant thinkers did in the sixteenth century. Instead, Gentili finds a universal language – that of natural law and the law of nations – to describe the justice of one sovereign intervening to support the people of another sovereign. In doing so, he elevated what would have been another unremarkable sectarian argument for holy war into a just war argument about oppression and tyranny generally, without regard to the particular sect, religion, or ideology of the oppressor or oppressed.

Gentili goes further along this line of thinking, permitting even an offensive war against tyrants and oppressors: "We are right in protecting even unjust sons against the cruelty of a father, and slaves against the inhumanity of their masters .... Aid may be given to the subjects of another even when they are unjust, but only with the purpose of saving them from immoderate cruelty."[17] Gentili devotes a whole chapter to discussing "an honorable reason for waging war," that is, "a war which is undertaken for not private reason of our own, but for the common interest and in behalf of others. Look you, if men clearly sin against the laws of nature and mankind, I believe that any one whatsoever may check such men by force of arms .... To make war upon such men was, and is, lawful."[18]

At this crucial juncture in his argument, Gentili invokes Augustine as his authority for supporting a doctrine of humanitarian intervention: "'If some earthly city should decide to commit certain great crimes, it would have to be overthrown by decree of the human race,' says Augustine."[19] Gentili is either misquoting or mistranslating Augustine, who in the passage in question is actually refuting the idea that the mere alignment of stars could decree that "crimes are to be committed of such a kind that,

---

[16] Gentili, *Three Books on the Law of War*, 126–127.
[17] Gentili, *Three Books on the Law of War*, 76.
[18] Gentili, *Three Books on the Law of War*, 122–123.
[19] Gentili, *Three Books on the Law of War*, 122.

if any earthly city had decreed them, the whole human race would deem it worthy of destruction!"[20] Augustine's purpose in the passage is plainly not to endorse intervention but to refute astrology. However, Gentili believed he was drawing on an Augustinian authority for his doctrine of intervention – demonstrating, in passing, the endurance of Augustinian authority into the sixteenth and seventeenth centuries – and, with more justification, he also believed it meshed well with the rest of the inheritance of Christendom in which he was working.

In his passage about intervention, Gentili has in mind human sacrifice and piracy: "If a war against pirates justly calls all men to arms because of love for our neighbor and the desire to live in peace, so also do the general violation of the common law of humanity and a wrong done to mankind." Gentili even says that private individuals may act against such criminals: "No rights will be due to these men who have broken all human and divine laws and who, though joined with us by similarity of nature, have disgraced this union with abominable stains."[21]

From the same framework Gentili, like Vitoria and Suárez, comes close to addressing the question of failed states and the justice of state building: "Subjects deprived of the aid of their prince, as the Romans were by the removal of the emperor to Constantinople, and harassed by the arms of foes, as the Romans then were by the Lombards, may take refuge with another sovereign and adopt him as their own." The Romans in question were living in conditions of state failure because the western empire fell in 476 and the eastern emperor was unable or unwilling to reassert sovereignty there (the emperors had split the empire into eastern and western halves in 285 and moved the capitol to Constantinople in 330). The Roman government, then, had ceased to function; it was no longer able to provide basic governance or public order. The Roman people were justified in seeking another sovereign. Gentili appeals to a version of social contract theory to justify the Roman people's right to do this: "By making oneself subject to a superior, one imposes an equal obligation on the superior .... The vassal and the lord exchange oaths as to that fidelity, and it is just not to keep faith with a lord who does not himself keep faith," which may not be how the Romans actually thought of their relationship to their emperor but does reflect how the English thought of their sovereign after the Magna Carta and how Gentili thought of sovereignty in his day.[22]

Behind these views is an understanding of sovereignty and justice. Earlier I suggested that Aquinas implicitly held the view that not only is

[20] Augustine, *City of God*, 186.   [21] Gentili, *Three Books on the Law of War*, 124.
[22] Gentili, *Three Books on the Law of War*, 115.

lex rex but *ius rex* – that whoever could claim the mantle of justice thereby could claim rightful authority. Gentili adapts this emphatically un-Hobbesian view and makes it more explicit. He clearly believes there are limits to sovereignty: "Unless we wish to make sovereigns exempt from the law and bound by no statutes and no precedents, there must also of necessity be someone to remind them of their duty and hold them in restraint."[23] Pithily, he argues, "Kingdoms were not made for kings, but kings for their kingdoms," and, later, "It is not lawful, I repeat, to do to subjects whatever one wishes."[24] Sovereignty imposes positive obligations on the king, dereliction in which justifies a response by the subjects and by outside powers who might come to their aid: "He who does not aid his people slays them, and thus the justice of his subjects' action gains strength."[25] Gentili could hardly be more clear that sovereignty is a commission of responsibility towards one's commonwealth, not a plenary grant of authority to do whatever one pleases. Once again, Gentili's Protestantism probably gave him great sympathy with Protestant suffering under Catholic monarchs on the continent, such as during the St. Bartholomew's Day Massacre of 1572 in which leaders of the French Huguenots were judicially executed and thousands more were murdered in several days of mob violence with the tacit approval of the French monarchy.

In passing, it is worth noting that Gentili, though he earlier disparaged the idea of right intention, essentially reintroduces it at the end of his work in his of discussion of the end and aftermath of war. "One should ask the question, not what the victor is able to do and what victory may demand, but what befits the character of the victor, as well as that of the vanquished," he writes, gesturing towards the *jus post bellum* that scholars would expand on four centuries later; "in the case of the victor in particular, it should be considered what becomes him and also the nature of the war which is being carried on. But everything must be directed towards the true purpose of victory, which is the blessing of peace."[26] To that end Gentili devoted an entire volume to post-conflict problems, including tribute, prisoners, the sacking of cities, "ensuring peace for the future," alliances, treaties, and more. Such was the natural outworking of the Augustinian framework in which Gentili operated.

---

[23] Gentili, *Three Books on the Law of War*, 74.
[24] Gentili, *Three Books on the Law of War*, 76, 78.
[25] Gentili, *Three Books on the Law of War*, 116. Again, the contrast with Tuck's characterization of Gentili is stark.
[26] Gentili, *Three Books on the Law of War*, 293.

Francisco Suárez (1548–1617)

At the same time that Gentili was introducing a new angle to just war thinking through his Protestant sensibilities and legal training, Suárez was working to reinforce its traditional shape. Suárez was the son of a wealthy lawyer who became a Jesuit and a student of the law. Famed for his intellect, he started teaching philosophy at age twenty-two and was ordained at twenty-four. Like Aquinas, he lived a relatively quiet life of contemplation and writing, teaching theology in Spain, Portugal, and briefly Rome until his death at sixty-nine. He found fame and controversy by critiquing the Spanish empire's treatment of the indigenous peoples of the New World and denying many of the justifications the Spanish crown offered for its conquests. Like Vitoria, Suárez stands solidly in the Augustinian and Thomist tradition.[27] However, Suárez was writing a century later than Vitoria (most of his work dates from between 1612 and 1621) and almost contemporaneously with Gentili, when the Protestant Reformation was mounting its challenge to the claims of universality of the Roman Catholic Church and its theologians.

Suárez on Natural Law, Justice, and Sovereignty

In response to these challenges, Suárez subtly adapted and developed the foundations of the just war tradition. Unlike past thinkers, he acknowledges and comments upon the different uses of the term "natural law." He cites Plato and Aquinas but then denies that natural law could properly be said to apply to "insensate" things of the natural or animal worlds, apparently from a concern to root natural law even more squarely in divine law and the character of God and to avoid the pitfall of letting natural law become nothing more than the law of the jungle. He concludes that natural law "is that form of law which dwells within the human mind, in order that the righteous may be distinguished from the evil," and describes it as "a kind of characteristic of nature, and because God Himself has annexed that law to nature. Moreover, in this respect the natural law is also divine, being decreed, as it were, directly by God Himself."[28] Later he discusses the ways in which natural law could be understood in relation to rational nature itself, at one point defining it as

[27] In his disputation on war Suárez cites Augustine on (at a minimum) pages 911, 913, 914, 939, 949, 956, and 969, and Aquinas on 911, 917, 923, 924, 925, 927, 960, 967, 969, 973, 976, and 977; see Suárez, *Selections from Three Works*. Augustine's influence is even clearer in Suárez's *Treatise on Laws* (also in *Selections from Three Works*), in which there are some ninety references to Augustine's works.
[28] Suárez, *Selections from Three Works*, 42ff.

"the natural light of the intellect."[29] He also argues that natural law "embraces all precepts or moral principles which are plainly characterized by the goodness necessary to rectitude of conduct," which echoes the idea of justice as the sum of all virtue.[30] Suárez might here be responding, consciously or not, to the Protestant challenge. If Gentili had seemed to conflate natural law with the law of nations, which was derived inductively from the data of history and different human societies, Suárez is emphasizing the more traditional view that natural law can be reached deductively, by the light of reason, deriving natural law from the mind of God.

Suárez introduces an interesting distinction. Because humanity lives in a world of both nature and grace, and human nature can be understood from both standpoints, so too natural law can be seen as both "absolutely natural" and as "supernatural," that is, "in relation to grace." He appears to be trying to give us two perspectives on natural law: a strictly natural view from the ground up, so to speak, and a view from the top down, or from the perspective of revealed religion. This might be a small concession to the various ways diverse writers of the past understood natural law that Suárez had noted earlier, but he again stresses that "even in its purely natural form," natural law is "divine, its source being God," though we experience it "from God through the medium of nature." One gets the sense that Suárez is trying to unify various types of natural law and incorporate them under the traditional umbrella of divine law.

Suárez is especially interesting because he took up systematically the question of the *ius gentium,* or law of nations, and its relation to the natural law. Vitoria made use of the concept of the law of nations and Gentili invoked it frequently but often treated it as a synonym for natural law.[31] Suárez spends considerable time interrogating the relationship between the two. He insists they are distinct, though related, and even that they overlap. The law of nations "has a close affinity with the natural law, so that many persons confuse it therewith, or hold that the *ius gentium* is a part of the natural law," which is mistaken, even though Suárez concedes that "the kinship is very close and the *ius gentium* constitutes an intermediate form (so to speak) between natural and human law."[32] The difference is that natural law is derived from divine law and human reason while the law of nations is derived from "the common usage of mankind."[33] The two are similar in that they both have universal applicability to all humanity. And in principle, they can and should overlap

[29] Suárez, *Selections from Three Works,* 205.
[30] Suárez, *Selections from Three Works,* 234.
[31] Kingsbury and Strauman, *Roman Foundations of the Law of Nations,* chapter 14.
[32] Suárez, *Selections from Three Works,* 374.
[33] Suárez, *Selections from Three Works,* 375.

insofar as the common law of humanity is rightly formed – but even when they overlap, the law of nations is more specific, and thus changeable, than natural law. The law of nations does not command or proscribe anything as intrinsically mandatory or wicked; it only makes contingent judgments based on the cases at hand – which is why it is close to being a kind of positive law – "accordingly, it is from this standpoint that the *ius gentium* is outside the realm of natural law."[34]

In the course of his discussion of the law of nations, Suárez paints a striking picture of the human community unified by the common law of humanity. Despite the differences he had with Gentili, they are agreed on this point:

> The human race, into howsoever many different peoples and kingdoms it may be divided, always preserves a certain unity, not only as a species, but also a moral and political unity (as it were) enjoined by the natural precept of mutual love and mercy; a precept which applies to all, even to strangers of every nation. Therefore, although a given sovereign state, commonwealth, or kingdom may constitute a perfect community in itself, consisting of its own members, nevertheless, each one of these states is also, in a certain sense, and viewed in relation to the human race, a member of that universal society; for these states when standing alone are never so self-sufficient that they do not require some mutual assistance, association, and intercourse . . . . Consequently, such communities have need of some system of law whereby they may be directed and properly ordered with regard to this kind of intercourse and association.[35]

Passages like this are why Suárez is counted among the fathers of international law. He envisioned humanity as constituting one community and thus bound by one law – albeit a different kind of law than bound together a domestic society under an acknowledged rulership. His comments echo both Augustine's hope for a *tranquilitas ordinis* and Gentili's vision of a unified human family, and prefigure Vattel's and Wolff's argument that the nations of Europe constitute a republic of humanity bound together by laws of ordered liberty. It is remarkable that this idea recurs throughout history in different guises and with different rationales, as if the idea itself may be part of the received customary usage of nations. (I will later use a similar argument to argue for the justice not of international law but of a system of ordered liberty among nations that we today call the liberal international order.)

Suárez's insistence on the unity of humanity probably reflects his generation's wish for peace in a tumultuous era. The Anglo-Spanish War – the war in which the Spanish Armada famously foundered off the

---

[34] Suárez, *Selections from Three Works*, 384.
[35] Suárez, *Selections from Three Works*, 402–403.

coast of the British Isles in 1588 – had ended in 1604. The Netherlands were in the midst of their eighty-year revolt against Spanish rule. Bubonic plague had killed several hundred thousand Spaniards around the turn of the century. Reeling from the financial setback of continuous warfare and expansion, Philip III signed peace agreements and withdrew from Europe's wars for two decades at the beginning of the seventeenth century – precisely when Suárez wrote and published most of his work. On the other hand, Suárez's vision of the commonwealth of humanity may also echo the Habsburg pretension towards universal monarchy. As one of the two major Habsburg monarchs, after the Holy Roman Empire, the Spanish Crown played a leading role in the Wars of Religion, trying to reimpose Catholic Christendom on a divided and pluralistic Europe, though its hope for universal monarchy had largely died with Charles V in the preceding century.

In keeping with his desire to emphasize the naturalness of order and good government, Suárez turns his attention to justice and gives it the same careful treatment he had given to natural law. He notes a variety of possible derivations and meanings of justice (specifically, the Latin word *ius*) and highlights two: justice as the sum of all virtue and justice as rendering to each his due. Suárez appears to prefer the latter, more specific definition: *ius* is "a certain moral power which every man has, either over his own property or with respect to that which is due to him." *Ius* is the moral claim a person has to that which is due him. But he also concedes ground to another, broader meaning, saying that *ius* can almost be equated with law itself, or at least with the ordering principles and effects of rightly ordered law, and also with the act of judgment by a judge. In keeping with convention, Suárez rests justice on nature, speaking of "what is naturally just, this being equivalent to what is right according to natural reason."[36]

As with his predecessors, Suárez understands government to be natural, under the authority of natural law, and dedicated to the common good. "A civil magistracy accompanied by temporal power for human government is just and in complete harmony with human nature," he writes. He comments on the grant of power given by God to Israel and other governments in the Bible and notes that "power of that kind is in harmony with nature itself, in so far as it is necessary to the proper government of a human community," clearly reflecting his belief that government is legitimate because it is essential to human life.[37] As proof, he cites and endorses the view held by Aristotle and Aquinas that

[36] Suárez, *Selections from Three Works*, 26ff.
[37] Suárez, *Selections from Three Works*, 418–419.

"man is a social animal, and cherishes a natural and right desire to live in a community."[38] Government exists to protect the common good of this community: "No body can be preserved unless there exists some principle whose function it is to provide for and seek after the common good thereof, such a principle as clearly exists in the natural body, and likewise (so experience teaches) in the political."[39] Following Vitoria, Suárez argues that sovereignty "resides not in any individual man but rather in the whole body of mankind." He continues by appealing to a state-of-nature argument: "in the nature of things all men are born free; so that, consequently, no person has political jurisdiction over another person, even as no person has dominion over another," such that sovereignty must belong to all humanity, not to any individual person.[40] Princes, therefore, are accountable to the commonwealth to govern for its good, as defined by the dictates of nature; their power is not "immutable" but it derives from the commonwealth "by its own consent or through some other just means."[41]

Suárez on War

It is within this context that we must understand Suárez's views on war. He sustained the Augustinian and Thomist understanding of natural law but strove to respond to the emerging challenges from Europeans' encounters with the native peoples of the New World and from the Protestant Reformation at home. As such, his discussion of natural law, justice, and the law of nations shows greater nuance and attentiveness to areas of divergence and disagreement. Like Aquinas, and following Augustine's lead, Suárez's treatise on war is subsumed under the theological category of charity. Neither of the earlier writers drew much explicit attention to the connection between love and war, but Suárez writes, "War is not opposed to the love of one's enemies; for whoever wages war honorably hates, not individuals, but the actions which he justly punishes."[42] He similarly argues that war is not opposed to peace per se but to injustice: we "may deny that war is opposed to an honorable peace; rather, it is opposed to an unjust peace, for it is more truly a means of attaining peace that is real and secure," suggesting, like Augustine, a mutually constitutive relationship between justice and peace.[43]

---

[38] Suárez, *Selections from Three Works*, 419.
[39] Suárez, *Selections from Three Works*, 422.
[40] Suárez, *Selections from Three Works*, 430.
[41] Suárez, *Selections from Three Works*, 439.
[42] Suárez, *Selections from Three Works*, 913.
[43] Suárez, *Selections from Three Works*, 913.

Suárez reiterates Aquinas' criteria for just war, including his rather vague description of just cause: a "just and sufficient reason for war is the infliction of a grave injustice which cannot be avenged or repaired in any other way."[44] But where Augustine and Aquinas had been relatively silent on what offenses constituted a just cause for war, Suárez follows Vitoria in elaborating several examples, including the seizure of property, the denial of free travel and trade, and "any grave injury to one's reputation or honor."[45] He later amends his formulation, adding a crucial extension: "a Christian prince may not declare war save either by reason of some injury inflicted *or for the defense of the innocent.*"[46] He also echoes, and makes more explicit, Aquinas' prioritization of just cause over right authority: "the power of defending oneself against an unjust aggressor is conceded to all."[47]

Suárez continues and elaborates Aquinas' and Vitoria's line of reasoning regarding the relationship between justice, right authority, and just cause in cases of humanitarian intervention, civil war, and revolution. Regarding the complex issues surrounding civil war, revolt, and sedition Suárez holds that domestic conflict is always unjust on the part of the aggressor, but, he argues, "a war of the state against the prince, even if it be aggressive, is not intrinsically evil." Revolt is justified "only when the prince is a tyrant," and a specific kind of tyrant at that. Suárez distinguishes between the tyranny of jurisdiction, tyrants who claim universal dominion – whom we might call totalitarians – and tyrants "merely in regard to his acts of government," that is, tyrants whose policies are oppressive. "When the first kind of tyranny occurs, the whole state, or any portion thereof, has the right [to revolt] against the prince ... [because] the tyrant in question is an aggressor, and is waging war unjustly against the state and its separate parts."[48] Suárez seems to be saying that a totalitarian ruler who asserts universal dominion is no longer a servant of the common good but its enemy; his assertion of unlimited power and unlimited jurisdiction is a kind of aggressive warfare against which defensive rebellion is justified. With regard to the second kind of tyrant, Suárez equivocates: the right of revolt is granted not to individuals or portions of the state but only to "the state as a whole," because only the state as a whole is "superior to the king" and can sit in judgment on his tyranny. "The state, when it granted him his power, is held to have granted it upon these conditions: that he should govern in accord with

[44] Suárez, *Selections from Three Works*, 929.
[45] Suárez, *Selections from Three Works*, 943.
[46] Suárez, *Selections from Three Works*, 942 (emphasis added).
[47] Suárez, *Selections from Three Works*, 917.
[48] Suárez, *Selections from Three Works*, 976.

the public weal, and not tyrannically; and that, if he did not govern thus, he might be deposed from that position of power."[49] It is unclear just what "the state as a whole" is or would look like in a historical example and how we would distinguish it from a portion of the state.

In one compact passage, Suárez endorses war on behalf of an ally who has suffered injury and intends to exact punishment but simultaneously denies that any state has universal jurisdiction to seek out and punish any wrong done to any person.

> Furthermore, the cause [for war] is sufficient if the wrong be inflicted upon any one who has placed himself under the protection of a prince, or even if it be inflicted upon allies or friends .... But it must be understood that such a circumstance justifies war only on condition that the friend himself would be justified in waging the war, and consents thereto, either expressly or by implication. The reason for this limitation is that a wrong done to another does not give me the right to avenge him, unless he would be justified in avenging himself and actually proposes to do so. Assuming, however, that these conditions exist, my aid to him is an act of cooperation in a good and just deed; but if [the injured party] does not entertain such a wish, no one else may intervene, since he who committed the wrong has made himself subject not to every one indiscriminately, but only to the person who has been wronged. Wherefore, the assertion made by some writers, that sovereign kings have the power of avenging injuries done in any part of the world, is entirely false, and throws into confusion all the orderly distinctions of jurisdiction; for such power was not [expressly] granted by God and its existence is not to be inferred by any process of reasoning.[50]

Suárez seems to want to endorse a qualified right of intervention, akin to Vitoria's, while guarding against the more sweeping language of Gentili (though he nowhere explicitly cites or quotes Gentili). He is likely responding to Protestant and Catholic partisans who claimed that their monarchs had a right to overthrow rulers of the opposing sect. Suárez seeks to circumscribe such claims by arguing that any state that embarks on punitive war must be responding to a wrong done either directly to itself or to any ally. Relatedly, Suárez rejects "sins against nature" as just cause for war, though, unlike other writers, he uses the phrase to mean idolatry, blasphemy, and other crimes against God – which belligerents in the Wars of Religion claimed were just causes for war – not crimes such as cannibalism and piracy.[51] In his argument opposing war in response to crimes against nature, he explicitly allows war for "the defense of the innocent,"[52] without specifying that the protecting state must be related

---

[49] Suárez, *Selections from Three Works*, 977.
[50] Suárez *Selections from Three Works*, 931.
[51] Suárez, *Selections from Three Works*, 938.
[52] Suárez, *Selections from Three Works*, 873, 939, 942, 943.

to the innocent victims. And he gives extremely cautious, limited endorsement to the idea of waging war on "barbarians" because they "are incapable of governing themselves properly." "The order of nature demands that men of this condition should be governed by those who are more prudent"; commenting on this idea, Suárez says:

> In order that the ground in question may be valid, it is not enough to judge that a given people are of inferior natural talents; for they must also be so wretched as to live in general more like wild beasts than like men, as those persons are said to live who have no human polity, and who go about entirely naked, eat human flesh, &c. If there are any such, they may be brought into subjection by war, not with the purpose of destroying them, but rather that they may be organized in human fashion, and justly governed. However, this ground for war should rarely or never be approved, except in circumstances in which the slaughter of innocent people and similar wrongs take place; and therefore, the ground in question is more properly included under defensive than under offensive wars.[53]

Like Vitoria, Suárez seems to endorse state-building interventions in failed states, but only when the conditions of state failure demonstrably harm the innocent or permit war crimes.

Suárez emphasizes several features that will become familiar in later formulations of just war thinking. For example, he expands on Aquinas' just war criteria slightly, adding that "the method of [war's] conduct must be proper, and due proportion must be observed at its beginning, during its prosecution, and after victory."[54] Suárez's concern for justice "after victory," like Gentili's, shows that concern for *jus post bellum* is not a novelty and that it flows naturally out of the Augustinian tradition. We also see the appearance of the "reasonable chance of success" criterion. Suárez argues that "for a war to be just, the sovereign ought to be so sure of the degree of his power, that he is morally certain of victory . . . . otherwise the prince would incur the evident peril of inflicting upon his state losses greater than the advantages involved."[55] These are developments in just war thinking that take on much greater significance in the twentieth century.

Hugo Grotius (1583–1645)

Grotius is a pivotal figure in this story. Like Gentili, he was a Protestant and was not a theologian. He was more a man of the world than even Gentili: born to a wealthy family, he had relatives who fought for Dutch

---

[53] Suárez, *Selections from Three Works*, 941.
[54] Suárez, *Selections from Three Works*, 916.
[55] Suárez, *Selections from Three Works*, 937.

independence from Spain and others who were shareholders in the Dutch East India Company. "The generation before Grotius's birth, his relatives had fought in the great struggle that established the freedom of the northern provinces of the Netherlands from the rule of the Spanish Crown, and many of Grotius's writings display the intense patriotism engendered by that struggle," according to Tuck.[56] Grotius subsequently served as an advisor and secretary to the Dutch prime minister, supported a failed coup, was imprisoned and escaped, served as the Swiss ambassador to France, took part in the negotiations to end the Thirty Years War, and was killed in a shipwreck before he could conclude his work. Once again, as with so many just war thinkers, Grotius was both close to and at a critical distance from power: close as a ministerial advisor and ambassador, distant as a dissident, prisoner, and exile. He is widely hailed as a – or sometimes as *the* – father of international law because of *The Rights of War and Peace* (sometimes translated as *The Law of War and Peace*), the first edition of which appeared in 1625 and the fourth edition in 1632.

With a major transitional figure like Grotius, we should expect to find elements of continuity and discontinuity from his predecessors. In some respects, especially in his conception of just cause and his doctrine of humanitarian intervention, he is the last representative of the Augustinian tradition described in this chapter. At the same time, Grotius furthered the transition initiated by Gentili away from the Augustinian tradition and laid the groundwork for the emerging Westphalian tradition, which is unsurprising from a diplomat who helped create the Westphalian treaties. In particular, Grotius' understanding of natural law and the law of nations had more in common with Gentili and their early Enlightenment contemporaries and successors, such as Hobbes, than with his Augustinian predecessors, though it is not a complete departure. "It was to a kind of natural theology that Grotius appealed rather than to the modern rationalist's denial of the relevance of God to political theory," as one scholar has rightly noted.[57] Grotius' thought was part of the broader movement away from theological and teleological ways of reasoning and towards secular and scientific modes of thought. The part he plays in this story,

---

[56] Tuck, "Introduction," in Grotius [Morrice/Tuck], *Rights of War and Peace*. I have consulted several versions of Grotius' work. The 1925 translation of the fifth edition by Francis Kelsey as edited and abridged by Stephen Neff is the most accessible and I have used it where possible, noted as [Kelsey/Neff]. It is, unfortunately, severely abridged. The next most accessible is the 1901 translation by A. C. Campbell, noted as [Campbell]. But the 1901 translation appears to be from one of the earlier editions of Grotius' text, missing several key chapters added in later editions. For those passages, I have used the 1738 John Morrice translation of the Barbeyrac edition edited by Richard Tuck available through Liberty Fund, noted as [Morrice/Tuck].

[57] Sigmund, *Natural Law in Political Thought*, 65.

then, is of one who, despite shifting the foundations – pulling the philosophical rug from under the Augustinians' feet, so to speak – nonetheless continued to support many of the conclusions and applications of their just war doctrine. That includes Gentili's conclusions about the ends and aftermath of war: Grotius, unlike most of his contemporaries, included a full discussion of what to do about spoils, prisoners, conquered territory, treaties, and other post-conflict issues; and he spent a considerable part of his final volume describing the necessity of moderation, magnanimity, and good faith. The full implications of the Westphalian philosophical revolution would not be apparent until a generation after Grotius.

Grotius on Natural Law, Justice, and Sovereignty

Grotius mixes Enlightenment and Christian language in his definition of natural law: "The law of nature is a dictate of right reason ... in consequence, such an act is either forbidden or enjoined by the author of nature, God."[58] The precise role that God played in Grotius' understanding of natural law seems to have shifted over time and between revisions of his work, partly to respond to the sensibilities of different audiences, though it is clear Grotius is within the mainstream of natural law thinking.[59] Throughout his work Grotius emphasizes human sociability as something natural: "Among the things which are unique to man is the desire for society, that is for community ... though not a community of any kind, but one at peace, and with a rational order."[60] This emphasis increases in later revisions of his work. Aristotle and Aquinas would not find much to disagree with here.

Like Gentili and Suárez, Grotius distinguishes between the natural law and the law of nations, though not always consistently: there are "some laws agreed on by common consent, which respect the advantage not of one body in particular, but of all in general. And this is what is called the law of nations, when used in distinction to the law of nature."[61] Grotius appeals to history, experience, and precedent to illuminate the content of the law of nations: "The proof for the law of nations is similar to that for unwritten municipal law; it is found in unbroken custom and the testimony of those who are skilled in it."[62] Like Gentili, he appeals to historical precedent throughout his work to justify or illustrate his

---

[58] Grotius [Kelsey/Neff], *Law of War and Peace*, 28–29.
[59] See Tuck, *Rights of War and Peace*, 99ff.
[60] Quoted in Tuck, *Rights of War and Peace*, 97.
[61] Grotius [Morrice/Tuck], *Rights of War and Peace*, 94.
[62] Grotius [Kelsey/Neff], *Law of War and Peace*, 32.

conclusions.[63] He elsewhere echoes Suárez in describing natural law as derived from the "principles of nature," and the law of nations from "universal consent."[64] Grotius "learned to separate a historical *ius gentium* from natural law," according to one scholar, and study the former through empirical investigation into how nations actually conducted themselves.[65]

We see a similar trend in Grotius' divergent understanding of sovereignty, another aspect of his thought more in line with the Westphalian than the Augustinian tradition. Grotius anticipates Hobbes in deriving government from tacit agreement by people in the state of nature:

> Again, since the fulfilling of covenants belongs to the Law of Nature ... from this very foundation civil laws were derived. For those who had incorporated themselves into any society ... must be understood to have tacitly promised, that they would submit to whatever either the greater part of the Society, or those on whom the Sovereign Power had been conferred, had ordained.[66]

Government is a construction of contracting parties interested in securing their rights: "The state is a complete body of free persons, associated together to enjoy peaceably their rights, and for their common benefit."[67] That does not mean that the people are the source of the state's legitimacy. Grotius specifically denies that "supreme power" is vested in the body of the people "that they may restrain or punish their kings, as often as they abuse their power."[68] He will later make allowances for the punishment of tyrants, but here he is at pains to emphasize the unconditional nature of the state's authority. We see here a different vision of government than is found in the work of Grotius' predecessors, for whom government was a natural institution commissioned by God to pursue the common good. The locus of sovereignty begins to shift from *ultimate responsibility* to *ultimate power*: "That is called supreme, whose acts are not subject to another's power, so that they cannot be made void by any other human will."[69] Continuing a shift that began with Vitoria, Grotius

---

[63] I disagree with Coates' characterization that Grotius "understood natural law itself in abstract rational terms, as the product of individual reasoning rather than the fruit of social and historical experience" (Coates, "Humanitarian Intervention," 67). Grotius quite clearly made ample use of historical experience in illustrating the content of natural law. Coates locates Grotius' difference in how he understands the state. I will split a hair and say, rather, that Grotius' difference is in how he understands justice, with implications for the state and war alike.

[64] Grotius [Morrice/Tuck], *Rights of War and Peace*, 112.

[65] Koskenniemi, "Methodology and Theory," in Fassbender et al., *Oxford Handbook*, 948.

[66] Grotius [Morrice/Tuck], *Rights of War and Peace*, 93.

[67] Grotius [Morrice/Tuck], *Rights of War and Peace*, 162.

[68] Grotius [Morrice/Tuck], *Rights of War and Peace*, 261–262.

[69] Grotius [Morrice/Tuck], *Rights of War and Peace*, 260.

now begins to describe sovereignty as a collective right of self-rule and self-defense, rather than a responsibility for order and justice. But, demonstrating that he is truly a transitional figure, Grotius hedges; he speaks of the "observation of the natural and divine law, or even of the law of nations, to which all kings stand obliged," which suggests rulers are, to some degree, accountable to standards external to themselves. Then, pages later, he defines sovereignty as having supreme power "accountable to none,"[70] reflecting his view that the corporate polity is the repository of sovereignty, not individual rulers. Grotius at least has a conflicted and ambiguous vision of sovereignty, mixing some elements of both the Augustinian heritage and the Westphalian future.[71]

Grotius' historical methodology coupled with his Christian sensibilities leads to a two-tier ethic of statesmanship: one for relations between Christian statesmen and a second for relations between a Christian and a non-Christian prince and among non-Christians generally. "The virtues which are required of Christians," he writes, "are either recommended or enjoined to the Hebrews [i.e., non-Christians], but not enjoined in the same degree and extent as to Christians."[72] Natural law is the ethic for non-Christians, a common moral basis to regulate behavior among those with no shared conception of the divine. But the effect of Grotius' move is to separate natural law from Christianity. In Augustine and Thomas, the two were closely aligned: natural law was defined as the manifestation of the divine law in the rational creature, or the participation of the rational creature in God's law. As a result, natural law was more easily understood as teleological, commanding the same thing as the divine law because God required the same behavior of Christian and heathen alike. But because of Grotius' separation of natural law and Christianity, natural law and the divine law might not always agree (reflecting the lack of agreement between Protestants and Catholics on the content of the divine law). The moral aspiration present in older natural law begins to fade; it begins to be less prescriptive and more descriptive. The high moral code of Christianity becomes supererogatory: admirable, and perhaps obligatory for Christians privileged to operate within Christendom, but impractical and thus optional in other circumstances. "Many things which are permitted by the law of nature, and the civil law, should be forbidden by

---

[70] Grotius [Morrice/Tuck], *Rights of War and Peace*, 300, 305–306.
[71] Johnson sees only the Westphalian future in Grotius. He writes that, for Grotius, "the idea of sovereignty defined in terms of the moral responsibility of the ruler to ensure the common good effectively disappeared, as sovereignty became a possession of the territorially defined state" (Johnson, *Sovereignty*, 25). I think the picture is more mixed than that.
[72] Grotius [Morrice/Tuck], *Rights of War and Peace*, 308.

the divine law, that being the most perfect of all laws, and proposing a reward above human nature," Grotius argues, "and to obtain such a reward, it is no wonder if virtues that exceed the bare dictates of nature are required."[73]

For example, a large part of Grotius' argument in Book 1 is to show that Christianity does not require pacifism or withdrawal from the affairs of state, despite Jesus' admonition to turn the other cheek and his disavowal of earthly political power. Grotius argues that the Christian ethic, whatever higher standard it may encourage us towards, does not prohibit warfare and statecraft, an argument he does not have to make regarding non-Christian peoples. "All these counsels [of the Gospel] are good, recommending excellent attainments, highly acceptable to God, yet they are not required of us, by any absolute law."[74] Or again: "The right of war is not taken away by the law of the gospel ... that Christian piety in kings is acceptable to God, [and] their profession of Christianity does not abridge their rights of sovereignty."[75] There is no comparable discussion about the claim of pacifism on the pagans because Grotius does not treat Jesus' commands as binding on them and because the law of nations, based on the common practice of humanity, was not pacifist.

In a second example, Grotius goes to great lengths to show that deception in war is permitted, even to Christian princes. He has a comparatively easier time showing that pagans accepted and practiced deception, whose historical record is replete with such example. He is at pains to list historical examples of non-Christian rulers, including Nero and Agrippa, whose behavior illuminates the natural law. He eventually concludes that Christian princes may follow suit, despite the apparent contradiction with the Christian prohibition against lying, but only after an extended discussion showing that deception in war is not incompatible with the gospel.[76] He lets pagans off the hook because of the lower standard to which he holds them.

In a third example, Grotius argues that while fellow Christians have a "preferable claim to our support," we nonetheless have equal legal obligations to all people, Christian and non-Christian alike: "The gospel has made no change in this respect, but rather favors treaties, by which assistance in a just cause may be afforded even to those, who are strangers to religion.... For in imitation of God, who makes his sun to rise upon the righteous and the wicked, and refreshes them both with his gracious rain, we are commanded to exclude no race of men from their due share of our

---

[73] Grotius [Morrice/Tuck], *Rights of War and Peace*, 415.
[74] Grotius [Morrice/Tuck], *Rights of War and Peace*, 48.
[75] Grotius [Campbell], *Rights of War and Peace*, 41–42.
[76] Grotius [Kelsey/Neff], *Law of War and Peace*, 329ff.

services."[77] And he argues that selflessness in war is a virtue for all but should be especially easy for Christians because of Jesus' example of selflessness: "how honorable it is to be regardless of our own lives, where we can preserve the lives, and promote the lasting welfare of others. A duty that should operate with greater force upon Christians, who have before their eyes continually the example of him, who died to save us."[78] To that end he argues that natural law allows a lax standard for civilian casualties and Christian charity a higher standard.[79] Similarly, Grotius recommends arbitration and congresses for settling disputes between Christian princes but not as a general, global norm.

In one case, Grotius overrules the precedent of the pagan world in favor of the Christian ethic. He acknowledges the widespread practice of executing hostages in the ancient and non-Christian world but argues in this case that universal practice (otherwise the grounds of natural law) has been overtaken by the ethic of Christianity, which requires war to be "tempered with moderation and humanity."[80] It is not clear what standard Grotius used to decide when to appeal to Christian doctrine and when to pagan practice, but he seems largely to favor the latter as the grounds of the law of nations and reserve the former exclusively for Christian princes.

Grotius on War

Despite his subtly different understanding of natural law and his increased reliance on the law of nations, Grotius otherwise follows the Augustinian tradition in his understanding of just cause, right authority, and the other components of just war thinking. Grotius quotes Augustine and others to the effect that just cause is an injury received.[81] Like Gratian, he views war as a judicial activity to redress grievance: "The grounds of war are as numerous as those of judicial actions. For where the power of law ceases, there war begins."[82] He simplifies by grouping just causes into three categories: defense, recovery of property, and punishment. He forswears conquest, glory, religion, and the preservation of the balance of power as just causes, staying well within the conventions of the Augustinian tradition.[83]

---

[77] Grotius [Campbell], *Rights of War and Peace*, 172.
[78] Grotius [Campbell], *Rights of War and Peace*, 280.
[79] Grotius [Campbell], *Rights of War and Peace*, 77.
[80] Grotius [Campbell], *Rights of War and Peace*, 359.
[81] Grotius [Campbell], *Rights of War and Peace*, 74–75.
[82] Grotius [Campbell], *Rights of War and Peace*, 75.
[83] This rather conventional view suggests Tuck is unfair to suggest Grotius was "an enthusiast for war around the globe" (Tuck, *Rights of War and Peace*, 95). Coates similarly

The inclusion of punishment (different from revenge) is distinctive to the Augustinian tradition, and Grotius clearly embraces it: "But among the dictates laid down by nature, as lawful and just ... the following maxim may be placed, that it is right for everyone to suffer evil proportioned to that which he has done."[84] In addition to deterrence, punishment serves another purpose that, again, places Grotius in the Augustinian tradition: the reformation of the offender. Just as Augustine argued war was an act of love against the wrongdoer, helping the wicked cease from the evil they intend, so Grotius envisions force as an act to help the aggressor stop his crime.[85] Despite the similarity between Grotius and Augustine, it is clear that the foundations of the just war tradition were shifting: while Augustine could simply assert punishment was a just cause for war, Grotius felt compelled to devote a substantial portion of his treatise – over 24,000 words in the English translation – to justifying, explaining, and circumscribing the use of punishment in war.

Grotius' different understanding of natural law, and his two-tier ethic, accounts for his strained and ambiguous treatment of civil war, rebellion, and the right of revolt. As a Protestant and a Dutchman who supported his ancestors' rebellion against Spain, Grotius might be expected to have sympathies for the right of revolt; as an ambassador trying to bring an end to the Thirty Years War and as counselor to a prime minister, he might be expected to show the opposite sympathies. The resulting tension in his work is unsurprising. Gentili and Suárez had allowed for a relatively straightforward right of revolt against unjust kings. Grotius equivocates. He initially, and at length, denies any such right, explaining from both sacred and secular precedent how it endangers the principle of (Westphalian) sovereignty. In an illuminating comment, Grotius argues that "if that promiscuous right of resistance should be allowed, there would be *no longer a state,* but a multitude without union."[86] Statehood, for him, effectively disappears if the people are given jurisdiction over their government's behavior or responsibility for holding it accountable for abuses through force of arms. "[T]here is nothing more considerable than the order of government I have spoken of, which is incompatible with the right of resistance left to private persons," he argues, quoting Cassius Dio that, "I think it neither decent for a prince to submit to his

over-interprets Grotius' endorsement of intervention; see Coates, "Humanitarian Intervention," 67.

[84] Grotius [Campbell], *Rights of War and Peace,* 221.
[85] Grotius [Campbell], *Rights of War and Peace,* 226–227.
[86] Grotius [Morrice/Tuck], *Rights of War and Peace,* 338–339 (emphasis in original).

subjects, nor can one ever be in safety, if those who ought to obey pretend to command."[87]

His denial that "private persons" have a right to stand in judgment over the state reflects the Thomist concern for right authority and is by itself unremarkable. But even Aquinas had qualified his emphasis on right authority by arguing that such authority is constituted by its responsibility to uphold justice, and thus a state could lose its rightful authority if it acted unjustly. Grotius, when contemplating this scenario, first enjoins civil disobedience rather than rebellion in response to unjust government: "if the civil powers command anything contrary to the law of nature, or the commands of God, they are not to be obeyed ... but if for this, or any other cause, any injury be done us by the will of our sovereign, we ought rather to bear it patiently, than to resist by force."[88] Grotius, and the subsequent Westphalian thinkers, had seen the chaos of the culminating battles of the Wars of Religion and wanted to shore up state authority and the principle of noninterference to prevent their recurrence.[89]

But then Grotius follows the Augustinian tradition by introducing a backdoor through which the right of revolt might nonetheless be recognized. "A more difficult question is, whether the law of non-resistance obliges us in the most extreme and inevitable danger," he writes. "I dare not condemn indifferently all private persons, or a small part of the people, who finding themselves reduced to the last extremity, have made use of the only remedy left them, in such a manner as they have not neglected in the mean time to take care, as far as they were able, of the public good."[90] Grotius here introduces something akin to what Walzer later calls the "Supreme Emergency," which suspends the normal rules of war. If an innocent people are suffering especially grievously, Grotius concedes, no one should condemn them for resisting by force of arms.

After introducing this loophole, Grotius goes on to delineate its exact dimensions. Even during justified rebellion, rebels must respect the person of the king. Rebellion is easier to justify for a free people to whom the sovereign is explicitly beholden by an agreement to govern for their good. Rebellion is justified against a king who has abdicated, abandoned his kingdom, surrendered its independence to another, or violated any separation of powers that limited the scope of his authority. Finally, Grotius invokes language that echoes what Suárez and Gentili had argued: "If

---

[87] Grotius [Morrice/Tuck], *Rights of War and Peace*, 347–348.
[88] Grotius, [Morrice/Tuck], *Rights of War and Peace*, 102.
[89] Johnson, *Ethics and the Use of Force*, chapter 9.
[90] Grotius [Morrice/Tuck], *Rights of War and Peace*, 111, 112.

a king shall, like an enemy, design the utter destruction of the whole body of his people, he loses [the right to] his kingdom."[91]

It is only after his admission of a right of revolt that Grotius takes up the issue of humanitarian intervention. Specifically, he follows Vitoria's and Suárez's conclusions on the matter. "The fact must also be recognized that kings, and those who possess rights equal to those kings, have the right of demanding punishments not only on account of injuries committed against themselves or their subjects," he writes, "but also on account of injuries which do not directly affect them but excessively violate the law of nature or of nations in regard to any persons whatsoever." Grotius seems even to suggest such wars enjoy a superior moral status than wars of mere self-defense: "Truly, it is more honorable to avenge the wrongs of others rather than one's own," he argues, specifying vengeance against pirates, cannibals, and those who act with "impiety towards their parents." Such wars are just because they vindicate the law of nature: "Regarding such barbarians, wild beasts rather than men, one may rightly say . . . that war against them was sanctioned by nature." Grotius directly rebuts his critics who say the state lacks jurisdiction to punish such crimes on the grounds that they misunderstand the locus of sovereignty: "For they claim that the power of punishing is the proper effect of civil jurisdiction, while we hold that it also is derived from the law of nature."[92] This is why Grotius is ultimately more an Augustinian than a Westphalian.[93]

Grotius' argument about punishing crimes against nature lays the groundwork for his views on why sovereigns may wage war on behalf of allies, friends, and indeed the whole human race: "The final and most wide-reaching cause for undertaking wars on behalf of others is the mutual tie of kinship among men, which of itself affords sufficient ground for rendering assistance."[94] We are obligated to punish gross wickedness and help the oppressed because of our common humanity. Grotius, like Suárez, places a limit on this obligation: we are not obligated to risk our national survival for others. And Grotius adds a word of caution similar to Suárez's: "those wars which are undertaken for the exacting of punishment, are suspected to be unjust, unless the crimes be very heinous and manifest."[95] But with that exceptional limitation,

---

[91] Grotius [Morrice/Tuck], *Rights of War and Peace*, 120.

[92] Grotius, [Kelsey/Neff], *Law of War and Peace*, 285–286.

[93] Johnson has overlooked this aspect of Grotius in his argument that, for Grotius, "the particular sort of injury that may be vindicated or punished has here been reduced to the violation of territory" (Johnson, *Sovereignty*, 85).

[94] Grotius [Kelsey/Neff], *Law of War and Peace*, 317.

[95] Grotius [Morrice/Tuck], *Rights of War and Peace*, 440. Tuck is therefore wrong to say that Grotius "specifically aligned himself . . . against Vitoria on this crucial issue" (Tuck,

intervention is justified to stop abnormal tyranny and wickedness: "Where a Busiris, a Phalaris or a Thracian Diomede provoke their people to despair and resistance by unheard of cruelties, having themselves abandoned all the laws of nature, they lose the rights of independent sovereigns, and can no longer claim the privilege of the law of nations."[96] Busiris was the mythological Egyptian king whose overthrow by Hercules was praised by Cicero because, instead of offering hospitality to visitors, Busiris offered them as human sacrifices to the gods. Phalaris, the tyrant of Akragas in the sixth century BC, was renowned for excessive cruelty and alleged cannibalism, including of human infants. The mythological King Diomedes of Thrace was said to have fed captives and visitors to his horses. Their crime was reasonless, sadistic murder, killing with no discernible purpose except for a perverse enjoyment of human suffering. Sovereignty was never designed to shield such murderous tyranny, even in the hands of Hugo Grotius.

Conclusion

No tradition is static. The Augustinian tradition evolved and developed over centuries, especially as contact with the New World, the Reformation, and the Wars of Religion compelled thinkers to examine the source and nature of natural law. The commonality I emphasize here is these thinkers' agreement that there is such a thing as natural law; that it enjoins humanity to strive to live up to its moral aspirations; that these aspirations include charity; and that loving others politically means doing justice. These thinkers further agreed that doing justice means safeguarding the common good, or what Augustine called the *tranquilitas ordinis*, the conditions for order, peace, and flourishing; and that doing so in the face of violent opposition required the use of force. This, the use of force as an act of love to defend public order and human flourishing, is the Augustinian doctrine of the state and just war.

The age of modernity inaugurated by the treaties of Westphalia inherited the rhetoric of the Augustinian just war tradition but transformed it in subtle but important ways, most prominently by secularizing its discourse and changing its understanding of natural law. To split a very fine hair, Johnson is almost right when he says "the ideological value base for just war ideas had shifted from the religious – the church's notion of

---

Rights of War and Peace, 103). As we saw above, Vitoria does allow humanitarian intervention, not on the grounds of the Indians' barbarism, but on the grounds of the Spaniards obligation to love the Indians who were suffering under barbarous rule.

[96] Grotius [Campbell], *Rights of War and Peace*, 288.

'divine law' – to a secular concept of 'natural law,' as conceived by Grotius, Locke, and Vattel."[97] In fact, just war had always rested on natural law; the shift was not from divine to natural law, but from one understanding of natural law to another. Regardless, these changes prefigured, and were part of, the broader changes in Western public philosophy during the Age of Reason and the Enlightenment, inaugurating the Westphalian just war tradition.

[97] Johnson, *Just War Tradition*, ix.

4   The Westphalian Tradition

The Protestant Reformation and the ensuing Wars of Religion fractured the religious consensus in Western Christendom and made urgent the search for new grounds on which to base claims of political legitimacy and the use of force. The Peace of Westphalia marked a sea change in the political order of Europe, codifying religious pluralism and a multipolar order and rejecting the aspiration of a religiously homogenous universal empire. The Treaty of Osnabrück, one of a trio of treaties codifying the Westphalian settlement, specified that, "adherents of the Augsburg Confession [i.e., Lutherans] who are subjects of the Catholics, and the Catholic subjects of the estates of the Augsburg Confession ... shall be patiently tolerated and have liberty of conscience." It specified religious minorities' rights to public-worship services, religious education for their children (even education abroad), and their freedom from employment discrimination on the basis of their faith: "In these and all other similar things, they shall be treated in the same manner as brethren and sisters with equal justice and protection." The treaty specifically barred resumption of warfare on grounds of religion: in cases of religious dispute, "the dispute is to be decided by amicable agreement alone."[1] These and other provisions effectively declared that differences of religion were to be tolerated within and between nations, abandoning the ideal of a religiously unified Christian Europe that had animated much of European political aspirations since Constantine.

The Renaissance had prepared the ground by recovering pre-Christian influences on Western thought, influences which thinkers turned to as a resource for rebuilding the social order in the absence of religious uniformity. At the same time, the European encounter with the New World made the task doubly important: what were the rules for interacting with a non-Christian people? What laws or moral standards regulated

---

[1] "Treaties of Westphalia," German History in Documents and Images, http://ghdi.ghi-dc.org/docpage.cfm?docpage/id=4548.

their conduct? The answers to these challenges included, eventually, the Enlightenment, the creation of the secular state, the emergence of classical liberalism, and the birth of modernity – historians' shorthand for the wide and deep changes that overtook almost every aspect of European life between roughly 1500 and 1700. Thinking about war was no exception: as change overtook everything else, so too did it mark intellectuals' arguments about sovereignty, natural law, justice, and war.

Natural law, in particular, came to mean something very different from what it had meant in the Augustinian tradition. In the words of a historian of natural law, "A bewildering variety of doctrines have been associated with the term 'natural law.'"[2] Thinkers have "equated the natural with the rational; the divine; the distinctively human … the primitive; the elements not subject to human artifice or control; the self-evident; and the non-historical."[3] In the early modern era, natural law "frees itself from its close association with theology and the medieval church; it breaks with the hierarchical and group-oriented aspects of medieval theory; and it becomes a revolutionary ideology or justification for the transformation of political, economic, and social relationships."[4] Elshtain, in her sweeping history of the concept of sovereignty, notes, "The use of the word *nature* or *natural* doesn't mean a thinker is using these terms in the same way as classical natural-law philosophers and theologians."[5] Coates, in his discussion of the relationship between Vitoria and Grotius, for example, comments, "Though both are classifiable as natural law thinkers, their conceptions of natural law are of radically different pedigree and import."[6]

One consequence was, in Johnson's evaluation, that

In the hands of the secularizers the *jus ad bellum* of the classic doctrine became increasingly formalized, and the doctrine as a whole increasingly reduced to a set of limits on the pursuit of wars between sovereign states … they did so by eliminating the concept of just cause …. The *jus ad bellum* conceived as *competence de guerre* was one result; by this doctrine each sovereign had the right and authority to decide when just cause for war existed.[7]

The concept of sovereignty also underwent change. What Johnson calls "the Grotian–Westphalian" approach "sacrificed the idea of sovereignty

---

[2] Sigmund, *Natural Law in Political Thought*, vii.
[3] Sigmund, *Natural Law in Political Thought*, ix.
[4] Sigmund, *Natural Law in Political Thought*, 55. See also Rommen, *The Natural Law*, esp. 75ff.
[5] Elshtain, *Sovereignty*, 39. Johnson makes a similar point in tracing the medieval use of the Latin word *ius* (Johnson, *Sovereignty*, 17–18).
[6] Coates, "Humanitarian Intervention," 65.
[7] Johnson, *Ethics and the Use of Force*, 16.

as service of the common good, focusing on the right of states to protect
their territories and defining political authority in terms of the obligation
to protect such territory."[8] Rengger similarly argues that, "States were
presumed from roughly the eighteenth century onwards to have a right of
war in defense of their interests, which therefore made the traditional
questions of the *jus ad bellum* largely irrelevant."[9]

In this chapter I demonstrate how these changes, especially to
thinkers' understanding of natural law, sovereignty, justice, and just
cause, were so fundamental as to mark the end of the Augustinian
tradition and the inauguration of a distinct Westphalian tradition of
just war. The Westphalian tradition rooted itself in a different understanding of natural law than the Augustinians'. Instead of understanding natural law as part of divine law and reflecting humanity's moral
aspirations, the Westphalians' natural law was rooted in the "state of
nature" and reflected what reason and custom told us about humanity's
actual conduct.

Justice, in this view, did not include liberality or charity; it involved the
protection of rights – not human rights, but the rights of sovereigns.
Above all, in this era, international justice became equated with the rights
of sovereign autonomy and the reciprocal noninterference associated with
the treaties of Westphalia. The just war thinkers of this era are consequently more hesitant to endorse a right of rebellion, intervention to
support rebels, humanitarian intervention, war as punishment, war to
defend the innocent, or war against those who commit crimes against
nature.[10] There are similarities: like the Augustinians, the Westphalian
thinkers argue that states have presumptive authority within their borders
and allow qualified exceptions for extreme circumstances. The difference
is one of emphasis: the Augustinian stressed the sovereigns' responsibilities; the Westphalians focused on the sovereigns' rights and privileges.
Intervention and rebellion are easier to justify in the Augustinian framework. For the Westphalians, war becomes, above all, an instrument to
defend international borders not to enforce an abstract ideal of justice.
This leads to the signature contribution from the Westphalian tradition:
the preservation of the balance of power is a just cause because it preserves
the independence and territorial integrity of every state.[11]

---

[8] Johnson, *Sovereignty*, 26.   [9] Rengger, "On the Just War Tradition," 359.
[10] Bellamy, *Just Wars*, 203ff.
[11] I focus on the seventeenth and eighteenth-century thinkers because, as others have noted,
just war thinking in the "long nineteenth century" from the Napoleonic era through
World War I focused almost exclusively on *jus in bello* and thus lies outside the scope of my
focus on *jus ad bellum* considerations. See O'Driscoll, *Renegotiation of the Just War
Tradition*, chapter 1.

Samuel von Pufendorf (1632–94)

Pufendorf approached the study of war as a jurist and philosopher who had deliberately rejected the study of theology in the immediate aftermath of the Peace of Westphalia. Born in Saxony, the son of a Lutheran pastor, he was sent to study for the ministry at the University of Leipzig but abandoned his religious studies for law at the University of Jena, where he studied the works of contemporary and early Enlightenment thinkers, including Grotius and Hobbes. In his choice of studies and his choice of interlocutors Pufendorf perfectly represents the transition from theology to international law in just war thinking. He is the first major just war thinker not to appeal to, cite, or quote Augustine or Aquinas as authorities. He discusses Cicero and Grotius at length and consults several pagan authorities, including Roman law, Pliny, and Lucretius, but the clear and overwhelming influence is Hobbes, to whom he devotes several chapters in his book. If a tradition is constituted, in part, by what is treated as a source of authority and legitimacy, and by what is replicated and quoted across generations, we see the end of the tradition that looked to Augustine and other theologians and treated them as authoritative and worthy of citation and commentary.[12]

Unlike Grotius, Pufendorf was not politically active: his most significant exposure to the world of politics was, first, losing his academic chair for publishing ideas unfavorable to the Holy Roman Empire and, subsequently, working as a tutor to a diplomatic official of the Swedish court, because of whom he spent several months as a political prisoner during a dispute between Sweden and Denmark. His work on war, *Of the Law of Nature and Nations*, appeared in 1672, a generation after the Peace of Westphalia and just over two decades after Hobbes' *Leviathan*. His work captures the emerging contours of the early Westphalian and Enlightenment age.

Pufendorf on Natural Law, Justice, and Sovereignty

Pufendorf follows Hobbes' method to discern the content of natural law: he imagines a state of nature devoid of the artifices of civilization or the protections of government. "The essential distinguishing mark" of early modern natural law "was the importance of the doctrine of the state of nature," according to Heinrich Rommen.[13] "Law" in this understanding

---

[12] Pufendorf's work happily is accompanied by an index of authors cited, making it easy to verify his inattention to Augustine and Aquinas in favor of Hobbes and Grotius. See Pufendorf, *Of the Law of Nature and Nations*, "An Index of the Authors Explain'd or Cited in the Text or Notes of This Edition," on unnumbered pages directly following page 878.
[13] Rommen, *Natural Law*, 80.

is less an imperative maxim prescribing how humans ought to act than a descriptive generalization illustrating how humanity does in fact behave in the imagined state of nature. In this respect, the Enlightenment version of natural law attempts to be akin to scientific laws (generalizations that describe observed phenomena) rather than ethical laws (teleological principles for humanity to fulfill its purpose), although it is typically coupled with an implicit (and groundless) leap over the is–ought divide: whatever can be derived about natural law from the state of nature is taken as normative.

Pufendorf is at pains to distance natural law from divine law and from the character of God. The law that governs God's conduct towards humanity – if indeed "law" can be used to describe that relation at all – is inscrutable and thus cannot be the foundation for the law that governs humanity's conduct towards itself. The effect of this move is that "we ought not to admit any law common to both God and man." Natural law is consequently wholly derived from and confined to mortal matters.[14] Pufendorf is echoing Grotius' creation of a two-level ethic: a lower ethic for relations among all humanity and a higher one for relations exclusively among Christian princes. Whether sealing off a zone for Christian princes (in Grotius) or for God's character (for Pufendorf), the effect is the same: to remove natural law from theology and to derive ethics from secular reason. "The law of nature is to be drawn from man's reason, flowing from the true current of that faculty," Pufendorf writes.[15] He attempts to thread a very fine needle, at one point acknowledging that "reason, properly speaking, is not the law of nature itself" but only a means to its discovery;[16] but in another place he says natural law is "the dictate of right reason," and "that the understanding of man is endued with such a power, as to be able from the contemplation of human condition, to discover a necessity of living agreeably to this law."[17] It is difficult to see the difference between natural law as reason and natural law as the dictate of reason.

Regardless, we are very far from Aquinas' understanding of natural law as "the rational creature's participation of the eternal law." What is novel in Pufendorf is not that unaided human reason can access and understand natural law but that reason itself is the source, foundation, and justifying principle of natural law. Natural law binds and obligates humanity not because it is rooted in God's character or the eternal law but because it is "the dictate of right reason." Near the end of his discussion about the

---

[14] Pufendorf, *Of the Law of Nature and Nations*, 123.
[15] Pufendorf, *Of the Law of Nature and Nations*, 132–133.
[16] Pufendorf, *Of the Law of Nature and Nations*, 145.
[17] Pufendorf, *Of the Law of Nature and Nations*, 132–133.

origins of natural law Pufendorf is at pains to deny that this is the implication of his argument. He acknowledges that natural law would have no power to bind or obligate if rooted only in human consent, will, mind, or command and that therefore "the obligation of natural law proceeds from God himself."[18] Yet it is hard to escape the sense that, for Pufendorf, this is an obligatory concession rather than an integral part of how he thought of natural law. Pufendorf shoehorns God into his argument without much groundwork: "It must be supposed that God has laid an obligation on man to obey this law," he concedes.[19] But the weight of his argument about natural law and his method of deriving it from reason and through reason leaves little purpose for God. Pufendorf's appeal to God is purely instrumental rather than foundational; "it must be supposed," he says, because it has not been argued or demonstrated. "It must be supposed" because the course of Pufendorf's argument leaves him in need of the supposition. God shows up only as a kind of ultimate enforcer or backstop in case readers are skeptical of the project of refounding natural law on purely secular, rational grounds.

Pufendorf does, however, acknowledge people's social nature, which Hobbes does not. He is more optimistic than Hobbes and does not see the state of nature as necessarily leading to a state of war. Humanity can, in fact, live in peace – peace "which the Law of Nature was given to men principally to establish and preserve." Peace is natural to humanity, whereas war is common to both people and beasts, showing that war is natural to people's animal, not spiritual, nature. Nonetheless, Pufendorf deems the peace of the state of nature untrustworthy because of "the great wickedness of men, their unbridled lust for power, and their desire of encroaching on the rights and possessions of others."[20] Pufendorf places less emphasis on the individual than Hobbes, arguing that humanity's need for society is part of what leads it out of the state of nature. Natural law, in fact, demands it: because each individual needs others to ensure his or her own survival, it is a "fundamental law of nature" that "every man ought, as far as in him lies, to promote and preserve peaceful sociableness with others, agreeable to the main ends and dispositions of the human race in general."[21] These, for Pufendorf, are the determinative grounds in favor of entering into civil society and creating government (in this respect anticipating Locke more than echoing Hobbes).

Starting from the state of nature and appealing only to human reason, Pufendorf argues that the law of nature begins with humankind's survival

---

[18] Pufendorf, *Of the Law of Nature and Nations*, 144.
[19] Pufendorf, *Of the Law of Nature and Nations*, 144.
[20] Pufendorf, *Of the Law of Nature and Nations*, 116.
[21] Pufendorf, *Of the Law of Nature and Nations*, 137.

instinct and natural liberty, consonant with an equal liberty for others. Here he again echoes Hobbes, for whom "self-preservation through rational conduct is the single 'natural law.'"[22] Immediately following his analysis of the origin of natural law, he moves directly to an examination of "the duties and performances of man towards himself,"[23] as the first dictate of the law of nature, followed by discussions on self-defense, mutual nonaggression, the importance of keeping faith in contracts, the importance of "promises and pacts," the nature of "consent required in making promises and pacts" and several more chapters dealing with the details of promises and contracts.[24] This is what a discussion of justice looks like for Pufendorf: a careful detailing of the rights rational individuals have against one another and how to go about guarding and enforcing them. Elshtain's interpretation of Hobbes seems apt for Pufendorf too: in his natural law doctrine he "set forth as primary a drive toward self-preservation that is essentially individualistic."[25]

The law of nature includes "all possible ways of preserving their body and their life, and of overcoming all such things, as seem to drive at their destruction," and allows that people "may use and enjoy the common goods and blessings, and may act and pursue whatever makes for their own preservation, while they do not hence injure the right of the rest,"[26] which is how Pufendorf begins to derive the rights of war from the law of nature. The law of nature dictates that "no man should offer unjust violence or injury to another" and that "all men should show kindness and humanity to one another." Aquinas similarly recognized humanity's survival instinct as part of natural law but had not stopped there. Pufendorf's natural law does not account, as Aquinas' had, for humanity's moral aspirations or spiritual nature.

Pufendorf derives government along Hobbesian lines, as the product of a covenant in the state of nature. Here we see one of the most important changes in Westphalian thought, one that marks it out as a distinct tradition. Sovereignty is conceived as supreme authority, territorial integrity, and political independence, not primarily as responsibility for the common good. Pufendorf defines "the freedom of a community or body of men" as their ability "independent of the will of any superior, to resolve and decree such matters, as appear conducive to the general benefit and safety." Any interference in their ability to conduct their own affairs is an abridgment of their freedom and, thus, their sovereignty. Pufendorf is at pains to describe this as starkly and unconditionally as possible: "Such

[22] Sigmund, *Natural Law in Political Thought*, 79.
[23] Pufendorf, *Of the Law of Nature and Nations*, 153.
[24] Pufendorf, *Of the Law of Nature and Nations*, 183ff.   [25] Elshtain, *Sovereignty*, 38.
[26] Pufendorf, *Of the Law of Nature and Nations*, 105–106.

a power being supreme, or not acknowledging any superior upon earth, the acts, which proceed from it, cannot be disannulled at the pleasure of any other mortal." In short, "For the same reason must the sovereign be acknowledged unaccountable," that is, not answerable to any other authority.[27] He even denies that sovereigns are accountable to human laws and denies that sovereignty derives from the people, differing not only from Vitoria and the late Augustinian line of thinking but also from Locke and the future course of liberalism; rather, Pufendorf argues that princes must be considered above or exempt from human law to be truly sovereign, describing the sovereign as "sacred" and counseling citizens to bear patiently with rulers who make mistakes or rule unjustly in light of their indispensable service in helping us escape the state of nature.[28] Subjects suffering under unjust cruelty or tyranny should flee, hide, or suffer; "if all means of escaping are cut off, we ought rather to be killed than to kill" (more on Pufendorf's extremely limited right of revolt below). He counsels that we accept martyrdom "out of regard for the commonwealth, which on such an occasion, cannot but be embroiled in the most unhappy troubles."[29] Pufendorf could not be clearer that state sovereignty trumps individual rights and is not accountable to any external standard of justice. He later acknowledges that the sovereign is responsible for the safety of his people – "Let the safety of the people be the supreme law" – but the grounds on which dereliction in this responsibility could be used to abrogate sovereignty are extremely limited.[30] Pufendorf's emphasis is on the sovereign's responsibility to enforce the terms of the covenant by which his government was created from the state of nature: the enforcement of public order and the protection of individuals' right to physical safety. Compared to the Augustinian notion that sovereigns are responsible for promoting the tranquility of order, Pufendorf's vision of sovereignty is thinner, more legalistic, and more focused on the state's prerogatives than its responsibilities. He acknowledges that sovereigns are under the authority of God but denies that anyone can act to enforce God's judgments – rendering God superfluous to the picture: "As for the laws of God and Nature, to bring them into the question, would be no less absurd than impious."[31]

That is one reason why Pufendorf sees no essential difference between the law of nature and the law of nations, as evidenced by the title of his work. He approvingly cites Hobbes to the effect that the law of nations is

[27] Pufendorf, *Of the Law of Nature and Nations*, 687.
[28] Pufendorf, *Of the Law of Nature and Nations*, 716, 718.
[29] Pufendorf, *Of the Law of Nature and Nations*, 719–720.
[30] Pufendorf, *Of the Law of Nature and Nations*, 737.
[31] Pufendorf, *Of the Law of Nature and Nations*, 688.

the law of nature (the law of self-preservation, self-defense, liberty, and mutual nonaggression) as applied to nations. He acknowledges the body of custom that had grown up surrounding the conduct of war and diplomacy but insists that violating such customs would not be a breach of law but only a sort of amateurism, a lack of skill or finesse in the profession of statecraft. Nations should not feel morally bound to restrict themselves by the customs of other nations but only by the dictates of natural law, a much more reliable safeguard of the nation's security and liberty.[32] Pufendorf's treatment of the law of nations is a natural extension of how he understood natural law. Since natural law was not derived from God's character or law, it becomes little more than the law of the state of nature – which is to say, it was a description of customs that developed to regulate the state of nature, exactly what previous thinkers had said was the defining characteristic of the law of *nations*, not the law of nature. The two laws collapsed into each other. Pufendorf denies that natural law depends on consent or custom, but that is the effect of his argument.

He does acknowledge a natural-law obligation to show benevolence to all humankind, which is the doctrine the Augustinians used to argue in favor of humanitarian intervention. Pufendorf has in mind a different and more limited kind of obligation. He argues that our first obligation of benevolence is to be engaged in some form of useful employment for the good of society; he especially praises great inventors and innovators whose discoveries benefit all humanity. Second, he argues we have a more specific obligation to help other individuals in need – but this duty "we may often perform not only without our own loss and prejudice, but likewise without giving ourselves any labor or trouble." He is more explicit later: "Whatever we can part with to another, without any danger to ourselves, this it is our duty to give, though to a stranger."[33] We are obligated to help others only so far as such help is costless and riskless to ourselves; this clearly sets up Pufendorf's later rejection of, or at least hesitance to endorse, humanitarian intervention.

Pufendorf on War

Given Pufendorf's departure from the Augustinian tradition's understanding of natural law, we should be unsurprised to find that he also diverges from them on the question of justice and war. And, in fact, Pufendorf is remarkable for having explicitly raised the question of offensive war to punish the wicked or defend the innocent, only to explicitly, if

[32] Pufendorf, *Of the Law of Nature and Nations,* 149ff.
[33] Pufendorf, *Of the Law of Nature and Nations,* 235–236.

inconsistently, reject it. He frames his argument about just cause in terms that are clearly indebted to a social contractarian or transactional understanding of human society:

> The Law of Nature obliges men to a mutual exercise of the office and duties of peace; and the person that first violates them to my prejudice, releases me, as far as lies in his power, from paying any of those offices to himself. And in consequence, as long as he professes himself my enemy, he gives me a liberty to use violence against him *in infinitum,* or as far as I am able.[34]

Pufendorf roots just cause in violated rights, not the obligations of love or the tranquility of order. In this respect, Pufendorf perfectly captures the transition of just war thinking to the new Westphalian tradition. (And the rights he has in mind are the rights of sovereign states, not individuals, distinguishing him from the later Liberal tradition.)

Pufendorf describes three causes of a just war, all of which are versions of self-defense: defense from immediate attack; defense of the sovereign's rights; and recompense for damages. Pufendorf does not include punishment of the wicked, defense of the innocent, or defense of the common good among his just causes. Indeed, Pufendorf notes that though God might use war to punish humankind for its sins, sovereigns may not do so: "When princes make war without any other design than [punishment], it is the greatest impiety."[35] He summarily dismisses the possibility of a just rebellion against one's prince, though he later seems to endorse rebellion against a foreign occupier.[36] Strikingly, Pufendorf endorses revenge as a just cause of war because, he argues, it would be an effective deterrent to future aggression. All told, Pufendorf "reject[ed] many of the extensive rights of war that [previous] writers had embraced and instead offered a remarkably statist interpretation of the principles of just war that prioritized and defended the rights and liberties of the territorial sovereign state," according to one scholar.[37] Along the way, Pufendorf completes the transformation of the meaning of sovereignty started by earlier thinkers. In Johnson's assessment, sovereignty for Pufendorf meant "the moral obligation for self-preservation of each of its members, and the fundamental moral obligation of the state is thus its own self-preservation, that is, its defense against attacks and threats." Johnson argues, "The vindication of justice is thus reduced to defense against attack."[38]

---

[34] Pufendorf, *Of the Law of Nature and Nations,* 837.
[35] Pufendorf, *Of the Law of Nature and Nations,* 836.
[36] Pufendorf, *Of the Law of Nature and Nations,* 840; compare with page 848.
[37] Glanville, "Samuel Pufendorf," in Brunstetter and O'Driscoll, *Just War Thinkers,* 145.
[38] Johnson, *Sovereignty,* 96.

Pufendorf's departure from the Augustinian tradition's understanding is significant, but I do not want to exaggerate the difference. All three of Pufendorf's causes are necessarily ways of defending the common good, and recompense from damages might be considered a means of punishing the wicked, both of which are Augustinian grounds for war. Pufendorf's argument is not diametrically opposed to the Augustinian scheme; it is a divergence from it. They overlap in significant ways, but Pufendorf introduces a different emphasis, relies on a different rhetoric of justification, and invokes subtly different concepts. He thereby re-centers the justification for war away from the Augustinian concepts of love, justice, and the tranquility of order.

We have already seen that Pufendorf's understanding of sovereignty strongly frowns on any kind of right of revolt or rebellion. He expressly denies that tyrants can be deposed. He argues that the business of government is too complicated and obscure for private citizens to judge its conduct; good princes might be unfairly maligned if a precedent of citizens judging princes was established; and the standard of tyranny is vague. Even if individual citizens might be justified in resisting a specific and discrete act of injustice against themselves that would lead to their imminent death, such a course of action would not give other citizens a right to revolt in kind; one person's suffering of injustice does not confer a general right of rebellion onto the whole people. Pufendorf seems to allow only the very narrowest possible exception: "a people may defend themselves against the extreme and unjust violence of their prince," an act that is only justified when the prince "by thus changing himself into an enemy, seems to absolve the subjects of their obligation towards him."[39] Pufendorf seems to have in mind cases in which the sovereign murders his own people out of mere entertainment or whimsy. This is such a narrow exception that Pufendorf specifically excludes the case in which a people has sold itself into slavery to a tyrant because to rebel in those conditions would be to violate the contract whereby they enslaved themselves. He also allows subjects to take on the burden of ruling themselves when a king has "utterly deserted and abandoned the kingdom," when he violates a specific written clause in the covenant establishing his rule, or when he "shall go about to alienate the kingdom, or to change the manner of holding the government," a sort of regime change from the top in which the king seeks to alter or transfer the government against the conditions of his reign.[40]

Pufendorf takes up the question of whether crimes against nature justify war, specifically addressing cannibalism. As I showed in the

[39] Pufendorf, *Of the Law of Nature and Nations*, 722ff.
[40] Pufendorf, *Of the Law of Nature and Nations*, 723–724.

previous chapters, the Augustinian tradition endorsed the idea that sovereigns might wage a war of punishment against those who commit such crimes, but Pufendorf dissents. He says he "cannot agree" with those who hold "that sufficient reason for making war upon the [Native] Americans" is that they are "proscribed by the law of nature, inasmuch as they had a barbarous custom of sacrificing men, and feeding upon man's flesh."[41] He argues that it is of no concern to the Europeans if Native Americans eat their own people, or eat criminals or enemies. It is only a problem for European monarchs to address if the Native Americans killed and ate a European visitor who came in peace, and then not because of the cannibalism, but because it is a straightforward obligation of self-defense.

Pufendorf requires that any third party that comes to the aid of one state against another "should be under some particular ties and obligations to him that is principally concerned in the war." He frowns on disinterested, nonobligatory, or supererogatory intervention "because otherwise it would be very unjust to assist one man against another, since as they are men they both equally deserve favor." Pufendorf disregards the justice or injustice of the cause in question or of the two sides involved, focusing only on the procedural question of whether the outside power had bound itself by treaty to one or the other side.[42]

Confusingly, in the next section Pufendorf does seem to endorse a sort of humanitarian intervention, just before reiterating his opposition to it. Like Grotius and others, he acknowledges that we owe a degree of concern to all mankind "by the common affinity and public relations of mankind" and that these concerns "sometimes ... alone may be sufficient motives to us to undertake the defense of a person manifestly injured and abused." In fact, he says, such an intervention is just because "nothing can tend more to promote the public good than to punish those that take pleasure in disquieting and injuring others," despite his earlier disavowal of punishment as a just cause for war. However, two sentences later, Pufendorf equivocates, as if recalling his opposition to such interventions: "But then we are not to imagine that every man ... has a right to correct and punish with war any person that has done another an injury, barely upon pretense that common good requires that such as oppress the innocent ought not to escape punishment, and that which touches one ought to affect all." He argues that such a doctrine would multiply war and misery rather than alleviate it and that no sovereign has rightful authority to stand as judge over others and adjudicate their quarrels:

[41] Pufendorf, *Of the Law of Nature and Nations*, 837.
[42] Pufendorf, *Of the Law of Nature and Nations*, 842.

It is also contrary to the natural equality of mankind for a man to force himself upon the world for a judge, and a decider of controversies. Not to say what dangerous abuses this liberty might be perverted to, and that any man might make war upon any man upon such a pretense. The wrong therefore another man suffers is not reason sufficient to engage me in his quarrel.[43]

Similarly, he denies that any state has jurisdiction over crimes committed by other states or in the course of other wars: "one should not pass judgment on upon the wars another engages in"; "it is safer to leave these things to the conscience of the parties engaged in the war." This seems definitive, especially given its consistency with Pufendorf's condemnation of rebellion and third-party intervention – except that he yet again equivocates, allowing intervention when specifically requested by the injured party. Towards the end of Pufendorf's life, the Holy Roman Empire became embroiled in a major war with the Ottoman Empire (1683–99), in the course of which the Habsburg monarchy allied with rebel Serbian militias against Ottoman rule, aiding fellow Christians against a Muslim despot – a suggestive illustration of Pufendorf's comments on intervention. "We cannot lawfully undertake to defend the subjects of a foreign commonwealth in any other case, than when they themselves may lawfully take arms to repress the insupportable tyranny and cruelties of their own governors,"[44] an odd exception given that Pufendorf earlier disallowed rebellion in any case except against foreign conquest. Even more confusingly, Pufendorf then defers the whole question to Grotius' judgment, and he *had* endorsed humanitarian intervention.

We are forced to conclude that Pufendorf had no consistent doctrine of intervention – he appears to have grown more amenable to the idea later in life as persecution against Protestants in Europe grew[45]– but at the very least he made several arguments against it and he was clearly more hesitant to declare such military operations just than the thinkers of the Augustinian tradition. One scholar has concluded that Pufendorf's view "was a firmly statist rendering of the principles of justice that restricted the rights of war primarily to defensive wars waged in response to injuries to oneself or to others."[46]

Pufendorf shows his departure from the Augustinian tradition (and from most just war thinkers) in another respect, one that is less central to my overall argument but useful for how it illustrates Pufendorf's

---

[43] Pufendorf, *Of the Law of Nature and Nations*, 842–844.
[44] Pufendorf, *Of the Law of Nature and Nations*, 842–844. Tuck seems to have missed the sections in which Pufendorf briefly endorsed intervention and focused only on the sections in which he opposed it.
[45] Tuck, *Rights of War and Peace*, 162–163.
[46] Glanville, "Samuel Pufendorf," in Brunstetter and O'Driscoll, *Just War Thinkers*, 153.

thinking. He seems to reject the idea of limits in war, an idea that is central to just war. In response to attack, he allows reprisals "in *infinitum*, or as far as I am able." If a person is denied that liberty "but [is] necessarily obliged to confine [their] violence within certain bounds, and in no case to proceed to extremities, the proper end of war, whether offensive or defensive, can never be obtained." Pufendorf argues that limitless war is necessary to success in war. This is true even if the enemy does not go to extremities. We are authorized not only to defend ourselves and get reparations, he argues, but to go further and inflict more evil on them than they on us to deter them and others from future evil. Pufendorf does not expand greatly on the idea but his brief comments are against the grain of past (and future) just war thinking, which explicitly and strongly insists on limits in warfare. Similarly, Pufendorf gives little consideration to the end or aftermath of war. Gentili had started a conversation in that direction, suggesting a fruitful avenue for the development of the just war tradition, one that would not be followed by the Westphalians.

Christian von Wolff (1679–1754)

Wolff was, like Pufendorf, a German thinker of the early Enlightenment and the early Westphalian age. Unlike Pufendorf, Wolff was not a jurist (nor a theologian) but an intellectually omnivorous philosopher and polymath. A scholar who lectured on mathematics, physics, law, and philosophy, Wolff was known for his search for, and insistence on, absolute certainty in all subjects – as well as for his championing of academic freedom and religious pluralism. His stance eventually got him into trouble: he was fired from his chair at the University of Halle and exiled from Prussia on charges, essentially, of heresy. Known for his arrogance and rigidity, Wolff's personality may have contributed to his professional setback. Regardless, he found a new home at the University of Marburg until his triumphal return to Halle in 1740. His major work, *The Law of Nations Treated According to a Scientific Method*, appeared in 1749.

Wolff on Natural Law, Justice, and Sovereignty

Wolff's understanding of natural law is similar to Pufendorf's. He asserts without much ceremony the view, conventional by his time, a century after Hobbes, that natural law is derived from humanity's condition in the state of nature. It is "derived from the essence and nature of man as a source whence flows the very immutability of natural law."[47]

---

[47] Wolff, *Law of Nations*, 10.

According to Wolff, "The right of a nation is only the right of private individuals taken collectively . . . .Every right is derived from these rights, even the right of war against rulers."[48] In turn, "the law of nations is originally nothing except the law of nature applied to nations," which echoes both Pufendorf and Hobbes.[49] Natural law gives to nations the right to whatever they need for survival: "Since every nation is bound to preserve itself, since, moreover, the law of nature gives to men the right to those things without which they could not perform their obligation, every nation has the right to those things without which it cannot preserve itself."[50] Wolff's natural law is exhausted with rights; it has no component of liberality, charity, or reciprocal altruism. God has dropped out of the conversation entirely.

Wolff furthers Pufendorf's reinterpretation of sovereignty and his hard view of mutual noninterference among nations. "Nations are regarded as individual free persons living in a state of nature," he argues.[51] As such, they are equal to one another and obliged to regard one another as equals by the law of nature and law of nations. "All acts are illegal by which any ruler of a state indicates that he does not look upon another as equal by nature to himself . . . much more illegal are the acts by which he shows that he judges another unworthy to be considered as ruler of a state."[52] Because they are equal, no nation may govern another or interfere in another's affairs: "No nation ought to do anything which is opposed to the purpose of another state, nor in any way prevent another nation from attaining the purpose of its state."[53] He casts this view of noninterference in terms of sovereignty: "By nature no nation has the right to any act which belongs to the exercise of the sovereignty of another nation. For sovereignty, as it exists in a people or originally in a nation, is absolute."[54] Wolff belabors his point, stressing that sovereignty means noninterference: "To interfere in the government of another, in whatever way indeed that it may be done, is opposed to the natural liberty of nations . . . . A perfect right belongs to every nation not to allow any other nation to interfere in any way in its government."[55] Wolff extends this argument beyond military interference to include even mere acts of exhortation and persuasion. A sovereign "cannot urge that another should establish anything in its state or do anything, or not do anything,"[56] a view that occasionally held sway among European diplomats through the nineteenth century.

---

[48] Wolff, *Law of Nations*, 315.   [49] Wolff, *Law of Nations*, 9.
[50] Wolff, *Law of Nations*, 23.   [51] Wolff, *Law of Nations*, 9.
[52] Wolff, *Law of Nations*, 129.   [53] Wolff, *Law of Nations*, 93.
[54] Wolff, *Law of Nations*, 130.   [55] Wolff, *Law of Nations*, 131, 137.
[56] Wolff, *Law of Nations*, 131.

In describing the nature, origin, and function of government, Wolff leans heavily on the idea of "the purpose of the state": "The perfection of a nation depends upon its fitness for accomplishing the purpose of the state, and that is a perfect form of government in a nation, if nothing is lacking in it which it needs for attaining that purpose."[57] Wolff's precise meaning involves idiosyncratic and technical definitions of "state," "nation," and "government," but for our purposes we can note that Wolff seems to argue that the state exists to fulfill its purpose. States were formed by people "to accomplish the purpose on account of which the state was established."[58] From subsequent discussion Wolff makes clear that the purpose of the state includes, as a matter of first principles, defense and survival. Within that broad understanding, the purpose of the state also includes acquiring the means or resources that would contribute to its safety and perpetuation, including a general grant of authority to pursue power as the *sine qua non* of the state's purpose: "Nations ought to strive as far as they are able to be powerful."[59] But there is at least a suggestion in Wolff that the "purpose of the state" is whatever the ruler deems it to be:

The ruler of a state has the care of perfecting and preserving his nation or people and likewise its form of government, and also of guarding against and avoiding, so far as possible, all imperfection and destruction. For it belongs to the ruler of a state to exercise the civil authority, consequently *to determine those things which are required to advance the public good, and therefore to accomplish the purpose of the state.*[60]

With this foundation we see in Wolff the emergence of the notion of the *raison d'état* as a self-justifying principle (what will later be called "realism"). If the ruler determines the purpose of the state, the ability of the ruler to accomplish his or her will becomes the standard of the state's legitimacy. Put another way, if natural law is only concerned with survival, then the survival of the state and the power of the state become the highest good (perhaps foreshadowing Hegel's understanding of the state as the unfolding of the Absolute in history). "In regard to those things which affect nations, natural reasons are to be derived from the purposes of the state," Wolff argues, "from which is to be measured the right of the whole against individuals." The "purposes of the state" are the measure of right, not measured by it. Individual rights are relatively less important than the ability of the ruler to accomplish his or her will and thus achieve the purpose of the state: "The law of nature, which makes the public welfare the supreme law of the state, restricts natural liberty also in regard

---

[57] Wolff, *Law of Nations*, 20–21.   [58] Wolff, *Law of Nations*, 20-21.
[59] Wolff, *Law of Nations*, 42.   [60] Wolff, *Law of Nations*, 26 (emphasis added).

to those things which are opposed to the purposes of the state."[61] We see here the theoretical justification for the idea that monarchs possessed a *competence de guerre*, a presumptive right of war that needed no additional justification, which helped justify the "sovereigns' wars" of the seventeenth and eighteenth centuries.

Wolff on War

With these considerations in mind, we can consider Wolff's views on war. War is justly fought only for defense, survival, or for securing the means of survival: "A just cause of war between nations arises only when a wrong has been done or is likely to be done."[62] As with Pufendorf, Wolff's examples are all variations of what we would broadly call self-defense: he specifies that just war is war that aims to right a wrong, gain reparations, or deter further wrongdoing. He uses the language of punishment but only as a form of deterrence or reprisal, not for any intrinsic value.[63] His doctrine of punishment is relevant for his later discussion of humanitarian intervention: only the person directly harmed by an injury has a right to impose punishment on the wrongdoer, severely circumscribing the right of punishment.

Wolff is significant for his development of perhaps the main contribution of the Westphalian tradition of just war thinking: the preservation of the balance of power is a just cause.[64] Vattel takes up the issue in greater detail, but we first see Wolff devoting special attention to the justice of wars against aggressor states, "whom war as such delights," as against a common enemy of civilized nations: "A right of war belongs to all nations in general against those who, in their eagerness for wars as such, are carried into wars for reasons neither justifying nor persuasive." Wolff begins here to articulate an important idea and to develop it in new directions: the "self" whose defense is a just cause is larger than any single state (expanding on an idea found in germ in Gentili and elsewhere[65]). "Nature herself has united all nations into a supreme state for no other purpose than that for which individual states have been established," he argues, echoing Gentili, perhaps unconsciously. Wolff uses this idea differently than Gentili: for Gentili, the universal state of mankind was reason to intervene to stop humanitarian atrocity; for Wolff, it is a reason to intervene to defend the balance of power and preserve territorial

---

[61] Wolff, *Law of Nations*, 173.   [62] Wolff, *Law of Nations*, 314.
[63] Wolff, *Law of Nations*, 315–316, 325–326.
[64] Bellamy is therefore wrong to say of Wolff and Pufendorf that "substantively, they offered very little that was new." See Bellamy, *Just Wars*, 78.
[65] See Tuck, *Rights of War and Peace*, 74.

integrity. This "supreme state" is what we today call the *international community*, and it exists for "the security of nations as a whole." Because humanity is united in a supreme state, nations may wage wars in defense of the international system of sovereign states. Aggressors who violate the principle of national sovereignty are common enemies of all independent states. Military force is justified against "monsters of the human kind," whom Wolff compares to brigands and thieves and whom he accuses of being "enemies of the whole human race."[66]

Some of the language here – the talk of "monsters" and being an enemy of the human race – is reminiscent of how Suárez, Vitoria, Gentili, and Grotius describe especially oppressive tyrants, cannibals, pirates, and others whose brutality is so extreme as to violate the law of nature and undermine human dignity. The earlier thinkers used this argument to justify humanitarian intervention. It is important to note that is not what Wolff is arguing. The true monster, for Wolff, is not the oppressive tyrant, war criminal, pirate, or cannibal; the monster is the international aggressor whose boundary-crossing military adventurism threatens to overturn and undo the precarious international system painfully wrought by the Peace of Westphalia. For Wolff, the worst crime is to violate the principles of the newly emerging international system and plunge the world back into the chaos of the Wars of Religion. War to defend the Westphalian system is a just cause for war. Indeed, Wolff might go further. Insofar as the Westphalian system of states is, for Wolff, a precondition for the sovereignty and independence of all the states within it, the defense of the Westphalian system and the Westphalian notion of sovereignty might be, in Wolff's mind, the preeminent just cause for war.

Wolff's concern for the balance of power is an accurate reflection of the politics of his day. The Holy Roman Empire fought a succession of wars for virtually the entirety of Wolff's life to sustain a precarious balance against French and Bourbon power to the west and against Turkish power to the south and east. In the Nine Years War of 1688–97, the empire fought against the French armies of Louis XIV, who had invaded to consolidate his place as the preeminent power of Europe. The wars of Spanish Succession (1701–14) and Polish Succession (1733–5) were fought over essentially the same issue, to check French and Bourbon power. Facing the other direction, the Holy Roman Empire participated in the War of the Holy League against the Ottoman Empire (1683–99), when Wolff was coming of age. The empire threw back an Ottoman invasion and subsequently allied with the Polish-Lithuanian Commonwealth, the Russian Empire, the Republic of Venice, and others

---

[66] Wolff, *Law of Nations*, 319.

to seize large swaths of Ottoman territory. The Ottoman invasion was a blatant land grab, the very sort of disrespect for sovereignty that Wolff detested. The victorious alliance against the Ottomans was a coalition to restore the balance of power; and the crippling of Ottoman power was surety against future imbalance. The Ottomans were dissatisfied with the treaty that ended the war and resumed fighting in the war's sequel, the Austro-Turkish War of 1716–18 (and another, from 1737 to 1739). The period did not lack for wars over the balance of power.

The defense of the balance of power was a novel and important extension of the idea of "self-defense," a version of which I will use later to argue for the justice of defending the liberal international order, so it is worth dwelling on it. Wolff is careful to distinguish between international aggressors and those whom we merely fear may become aggressors in the future. States may not wage preemptive war against rising powers whose power they suspect may overturn the established order, nor against a neighboring power that builds fortifications, engages in an arms buildup, or otherwise prepares for war. They must wait for the rising power to commit an act of aggression or actually inflict injury to respond.

Augustine had suggested that the defense of the common good or the tranquility of order was the primary moral justification for force; Wolff goes in a different direction. Wolff applies intrinsic moral worth and legitimizing authority not to the common good but to the preservation of the balance of power among rival states – what he calls the "equilibrium of nations," a relatively new concept in the Westphalian order in which states accept coexistence with rivals whom they must deter rather than defeat in pursuit of universal empire. Wolff favors the balance of power as a useful mechanism for "the common security of nations," and even argues that states have a right to preserve the balance of power because they "are jointly bound also to look out for the common security." But again, he insists that states wait until actual aggression against the balance has occurred before responding. He does allow a hair-trigger response and a low threshold of injury in extreme cases: "If any nation should manifestly be considering plans for subjecting other nations to itself, these ought to provide for their common security by alliances, and the slightest wrong gives them the right to overthrow the growing power by armed force."[67] Wolff comes near to contradicting his earlier principles that states must wait for actual injury to respond with war, arguing that if states have rational grounds to fear subjugation by a hostile rising power they may wage war "to avert it if threatened." He argues that rulers can and should judge the character of a regime based on its past behavior and

[67] Wolff, *Law of Nations*, 333–334.

likely intentions: "When, indeed, one who manifests the intention of doing wrong to others, does not hesitate to do a very trivial wrong, he is properly assumed to be likely to do a greater one," an argument that has some bearing on the debate over the Iraq War, as I discuss in Chapter 8.[68]

Finally, Wolff also argues that states possess a general commission to defend the international system. States are "bound to protect the common security by their combined powers," and "in the supreme state [or international community] the right to punish a disturber of the common security of nations belongs to nations as a whole . . . [and] this right can be exercised in general by those who have the most interest in diminishing the excessive power of the disturber."[69] With these important boundaries in place, we can recognize Wolff's contribution in extending the "self" of "self-defense."[70]

The upshot of Wolff's understanding of states' responsibilities to uphold the international system is a more permissive mandate to wage war, even preemptive war, than most of Wolff's predecessors would have been comfortable with. For Wolff, the defense of Westphalian sovereignty meant the defense of the Westphalian system and the balance of power that undergirded it, any disruption to which – even any *threat* of disruption – could be met with force. And Wolff's prescription would lead naturally to a world dominated by powerful states, who might intentionally disrupt the balance of power to provoke a war by smaller neighbors that the strong state will inevitably win.[71] Scholars have often accused Grotius of being too quick to license a resort to war, but Wolff appears to be even quicker, given his expansion of the "self" to encompass the Westphalian system and his ease with preventive war against potential aggressors who might threaten the balance.

The self is not, however, the kinship of all humanity or all individuals. He severely circumscribes the right of revolt and humanitarian intervention. Early in his work he distinguishes between barbarous and civilized nations depending on whether they cultivate the intellect. While the latter are superior, they may not coerce the former: "If any nation wishes to promote the perfection of another, it cannot compel it to allow that to be done; if some barbarous and uncultivated nation is unwilling to accept aid offered to it by another in removing its barbarism and rendering its manners more cultivated, it cannot be compelled to accept such aid." This is because "Barbarism and uncultivated manners give you no right against a nation . . . . Therefore a war is unjust which is begun on this

---

[68] Wolff, *Law of Nations*, 335.   [69] Wolff, *Law of Nations*, 336.
[70] Wolff, *Law of Nations*, 328–336.
[71] I am indebted to James Turner Johnson for this insight.

pretext." He explicitly rejects Grotius' argument that nations ought to punish crimes against nature.[72]

For the same reason, while states may band together against an international aggressor who threatens the system of independent states, they may not band together against a tyrant who oppresses his or her own people: "Since a punitive war is not legal except for one who has received irreparable injury from another, a punitive war is not allowed against a nation for the reason that it is very wicked, or violates dreadfully the law of nature, or offends against God."[73] Again, he argues, "If the ruler of a state should burden his subjects too heavily or treat them too harshly, the ruler of another state may not resist that by force."[74]

Wolff specifically criticizes Grotius on this point and claims that the problem is that Grotius fails to demonstrate why or how any nation has gained the right to exact punishment when it was not itself wronged. In this respect Wolff, like Pufendorf, relies exclusively on a theory of violated rights for his understanding of justice. Grotius had argued that nations are under the law of nature and have responsibilities derived directly from it, including to punish crimes against nature, even absent any positive law or treaty obligation. Wolff warns that the doctrine of humanitarian intervention invites abuse: "those who had no just case for war, have drawn a pretext from the law of punishment." Wolff is unfair to Grotius, however, in conflating his argument about humanitarian intervention with an argument about a war to defend religion. Grotius and every other just war thinker would agree with Wolff's contention that nations have no right to punish offenses against God – "God himself is capable of punishing a wrong done to himself, nor for that does he need human aid" – but Wolff implies that rejecting a war for religion is part of the same argument that should lead us to reject wars to defend the innocent and punish the wicked.[75]

Because of his philosophical method that stressed consistency and rigor, Wolff produced probably the most stringent version of the Westphalian tradition of just war thinking. Whereas Pufendorf and Vattel (and Grotius before them) allowed more nuance, tension, and even contradiction into their work, Wolff is more straightforward and consistent. He lacks the loopholes and caveats that allow the others to justify intervention or revolt, even as those justifications are at odds with the rest of their work. The result is that Wolff's position is a minority view yet also represents the ideal type of his tradition when its premises are carried to their logical conclusion.

---

[72] Wolff, *Law of Nations*, 89.   [73] Wolff, *Law of Nations*, 326.
[74] Wolff, *Law of Nations*, 132.   [75] Wolff, *Law of Nations*, 326.

Emerich de Vattel (1714–67)

Vattel was a Francophone Swiss jurist, born in a region ruled by Prussia, the son of an ennobled Protestant clergyman. He studied theology, metaphysics, and philosophy in Basel and Geneva, attending lectures on Pufendorf and closely reading the work of Wolff. He held a minor government post until after the publication in 1758 of his magnum opus, *The Law of Nations*, when he received a job in Dresden advising the government of Saxony. His view of sovereignty "marks a sharp departure from the classical just war tradition – the view that sovereigns had a moral obligation to secure justice in the world at large . . . and was the final step in the secularization of just war thinking," according to one scholar.[76] This sweeping judgment may be unfair, however, as Vattel introduced a measure of nuance and moderation to the Westphalian tradition that eluded Wolff.

Vattel on Natural Law, Justice, and Sovereignty

Vattel outlines his understanding of natural law in a separate essay. He is commendably clear: "*natural laws, in particular, are those that we derive from nature, or whose rationale is found in the essence and nature of man, and of things in general.*"[77] Like other thinkers since Hobbes and Pufendorf, Vattel firmly rooted natural law in human nature and reason alone: "If by the foundation of natural law we understand the source from which can be derived the rules and precepts; the principle in which is found what can provide an explanation for why these rules and precepts are as they are, then we would not wish to look further than in *the essence and nature of man and things in general.*"[78]

Invoking God is superfluous for our understanding of natural law: "God could only give laws suitable to the nature of things, and particularly to the essence and nature of man, whom he instructs to observe them; laws whose rationale is found in this essence and nature."[79] If we argue that God is the source of natural law, we still face the question of what that law is, the answer to which is found not in the character of God but in the nature of man. Thus, even if we consider God the source of natural law, he adds nothing to our understanding of the law. We are still compelled to adopt the same method as those who think of natural law only in secular terms: we must derive it from human nature: "This is sufficient to show that natural law is founded on the essence and nature of

---

[76] Christov, "Emer de Vattel," in Brunstetter and O'Driscoll, *Just War Thinkers*, 157.
[77] Vattel, *Law of Nations*, 747.   [78] Vattel, *Law of Nations*, 748 (emphasis in original).
[79] Vattel, *Law of Nations*, 749.

things and of men in particular."[80] The natural law is such that we ought obey it whether or not God commanded it:

The will of a superior, as we have just seen, is not the first principle or the *foundation of obligation* ... men would be obliged to follow natural laws even by setting aside the will of God, because they are praiseworthy and useful .... In no way does it detract from the authority of God to say that everything he ordains for us in natural laws is so *fine* and *useful* in itself that we would be *obliged* to adopt it, even if God had not ordered it."[81]

Vattel follows the convention, by then, of defining the law of nations as the law of nature as applied to nations, though he insists that, because it is applied to different subjects than individuals, it will have different precepts. This kind of law of nations, which he calls the necessary law of nations, is the unique application of natural law to nations and, as such, is unchanging and absolutely binding. He contrasts necessary law with several other subtypes, including voluntary, customary, and conventional laws of nations (the latter constituted by formal treaties), which together make up a newly emergent positive law of nations. This recalls, once again, Suárez's distinction between natural law, as derived by reason and Scripture, and the law of nations, derived by custom; except, for Vattel, the former has been entirely replaced by the necessary law of nations. With the idea of a positive law of nations created by nations' mutual consent, we see the emergence of what will be called international law.

Vattel also follows the view of post-Hobbesian thinkers on the nature of the state: "Nations or states are bodies politic, societies of men united together for the purpose of promoting their mutual safety and advantage by the joint efforts of their combined strength," created by agreement among people in the state of nature; the community of states are as "free persons living together in the state of nature."[82] As such, all states are equal to one another and autonomous within their own jurisdiction: "Power or weakness does not in this respect produce any difference. A dwarf is as much a man as a giant; a small republic is no less a sovereign state than the most powerful kingdom."[83] It is a fundamental law of nature "that each nation should be left in the peaceable enjoyment of that liberty which she inherits from nature. The natural society of nations cannot subsist, unless the natural rights of each be duly respected." Vattel, like Wolff, belabors the principle of mutual noninterference. "It exclusively belongs to each nation to form her own judgment of what her conscience prescribes to her – of what she can or cannot do – of what it is proper or improper for her to do," he argues, "no other nation can compel her to act in such or such

---

[80] Vattel, *Law of Nations*, 749.   [81] Vattel, *Law of Nations*, 757 (emphasis in original).
[82] Vattel, *Law of Nations*, 67–68.   [83] Vattel, *Law of Nations*, 75.

particular manner: for any attempt at such compulsion would be an infringement on the liberty of nations."[84]

Vattel emphasizes the rights and prerogatives of sovereignty. "Since then a nation is obliged to preserve itself, it has a right to everything necessary for its preservation," he argues, specifying that "a nation has an indisputable right to form, maintain, and perfect its constitution ... and that no person can have a just right to hinder it."[85] Some of his language is reminiscent of Wolff's emphasis on fulfilling the "purpose of the state"; he explains that sovereignty exists "to obtain the end of its institution," or establishment, leaving for later a discussion of what those ends actually are.[86] At one point Vattel seems to come close to arguing that sovereignty is comprised exclusively of actual control or power, that de facto sovereignty is all the sovereignty that counts: "To give a nation a right to make an immediate figure in this grand society, it is sufficient that it be really sovereign and independent, that is, that it govern itself by its own authority and laws."[87] If Vattel left the discussion there, it would seem to leave no room to judge a state's legitimacy by any measure external to the state itself.

Vattel does, however, stress the responsibilities of sovereignty more than Pufendorf or Wolff, and ends up with a nuanced position that moderates some of the harder edges of the former two. He elaborates at length on the sovereign's duty to work for the perfection of the state and the common good of the nation:

The end or object of civil society is to procure for the citizens whatever they stand in need of, for the necessities, the conveniences, the accommodation of life, and, in general, whatever constitutes happiness, – with the peaceful possession of property, a method of obtaining justice with security, and, finally a mutual defense against all external violence. It is now easy to form a just idea of the perfection of a state or nation: – every thing in it must conspire to promote the ends we have pointed out.[88]

The just sovereign bears responsibility for the common good. Vattel uses language that would not be out of place in the Augustinian tradition: "It is evident that men form a political society, and submit to laws, solely for their own advantage and safety. The sovereign authority is then established only for the common good of all the citizens."[89] The sovereign "ought, therefore, as a tender and wise father, and as a faithful administrator, to watch for the nation, and take care to preserve it, and render it more perfect, – to better its state, and to secure it, as far as possible,

---

[84] Vattel, *Law of Nations*, 74.   [85] Vattel, *Law of Nations*, 88, 94.
[86] Vattel, *Law of Nations*, 97.   [87] Vattel, *Law of Nations*, 83.
[88] Vattel, *Law of Nations*, 86.   [89] Vattel, *Law of Nations*, 97.

against everything that threatens its safety or its happiness."[90] And like the Augustinians, Vattel sees here grounds for recognizing when the sovereign has failed in upholding his responsibilities. The sovereign is obliged to protect and defend the lives of his subjects; if he does the opposite, the people are not bound to him: "This high attribute of sovereignty is no reason why the nation should not curb an insupportable tyrant, pronounce sentence on him (still respecting in his person the majesty of his rank), and withdraw itself from his obedience."[91] This opens the door for a relatively more straightforward right of revolt, as we will see below.

Vattel's moderation probably had many sources. He was writing a full century after the Peace of Westphalia. Memories of the Wars of Religion had faded; with them, the felt urgency of finding a new ordering principle for Europe after the fracture of Christendom. A return of some older ideas about the responsibilities of sovereigns was perhaps more acceptable by Vattel's day. He was also writing as the Enlightenment was reaching full flower – his contemporaries included Jean-Jacques Rousseau, Voltaire, and the Baron de Montesquieu – and was likely influenced by broader intellectual currents that emphasized reason, individual liberty, and equality of persons. Finally, Vattel studied theology and philosophy; those studies, in addition to whatever religiosity he may have absorbed from his clergyman father, may have inclined Vattel to recognize, haltingly and inconsistently, a higher authority than the state, vague though it often was in his work. As we will see, Vattel appeared profoundly conflicted on the issues we have been tracing throughout this story.

Vattel on War

Vattel starts simply enough, and entirely in line with Pufendorf and others of the Westphalian tradition: "The right of employing force, or making war, belongs to nations no farther than is necessary for their own defense and for the maintenance of their rights."[92] As had become conventional by then, he specifies what kind of injury against rights is a sufficient cause for war: war is justified for recovering things taken, deterring future aggression through punitive reprisals, and defense from immediate attack.[93]

Vattel does allow for punishment as a just cause for war, though, like Pufendorf, only insofar as punishment is a means to deterrence: "We are authorized to provide for our own safety, and even for that of all other

[90] Vattel, *Law of Nations*, 99.   [91] Vattel, *Law of Nations*, 104.
[92] Vattel, *Law of Nations*, 483.   [93] Vattel, *Law of Nations*, 484.

nations, by inflicting on the offender a punishment capable of correcting him, and serving as an example to others."[94] And Vattel, like Pufendorf, is at pains to distinguish this limited right of punishment from a universal writ to enforce good conduct. "The offended party alone has a right to punish independent persons," he argues, because it is a "dangerous mistake or extravagant pretensions of those who assume a right of punishing an independent nation for faults which do not concern them, – who, madly setting themselves up as defenders of the cause of God, take upon them to punish the moral depravity or irreligion of a people not committed to their superintendency."[95] As we will see, Vattel means this as a direct criticism of Grotius.

Despite this, and unlike Pufendorf and Wolff, Vattel is straightforward and clear in recognizing a right to revolt and the right of other nations to intervene in a civil war. His comments here seek to balance between the pre- and post-Grotian views – or, perhaps, they show Vattel having a debate with himself about where that balance lies – and so are worth quoting at length: "If [the prince] becomes the scourge of the state, he degrades himself; he is no better than a public enemy, against whom the nation may and ought to defend itself."[96] Later, he continues in this vein:

When the injuries are manifest and atrocious – when a prince, without any apparent reason attempts to deprive us of life, or of those things the loss of which would render life irksome, who can dispute our right to resist him? ... The prince who violates all laws, who no longer observes any measures, and who would in his transports of fury take away the life of an innocent person, divests himself of his character, and is no longer to be considered in any other light than that of an unjust and outrageous enemy, against whom his people are allowed to defend themselves.[97]

As an example, Vattel praises the French magistrates who refused to obey King Charles IX's command to murder the Huguenots in the St. Bartholomew's Day Massacre. Vattel explicitly draws the obvious conclusion that if a people has a right to revolt, other states may help their cause: "If the prince, by violating the fundamental laws, gives his subjects a legal right to resist him, – if tyranny, becoming insupportable, obliges the nation to rise in their own defense, – every foreign power has a right to succor an oppressed people who implore their assistance."[98] This is despite Vattel's earlier contention that the first and primary law among nations is noninterference: "It is an evident consequence of the liberty and independence of nations, that all have a right to be governed as

---

[94] Vattel, *Law of Nations*, 490.   [95] Vattel, *Law of Nations*, 490.
[96] Vattel, *Law of Nations*, 105.   [97] Vattel, *Law of Nations*, 111, see also 105.
[98] Vattel, *Law of Nations*, 290.

they think proper, and that no state has the smallest right to interfere in the government of another."[99] And it is also despite Vattel's insistence that states have no right to judge one another's conduct. It is unclear how Vattel reconciles his hard view of noninterference with his endorsement of foreign intervention to support a just rebellion.

Vattel is threading a very fine needle here, working to acknowledge and bolster the Westphalian order of mutual noninterference and sovereign inviolability while still leaving room for the right of revolt and the right of aiding a just rebellion. He weaves back and forth, first stressing noninterference: "It does not then belong to any foreign power to take cognizance of the administration of that sovereign, to set himself up for a judge of his conduct, and to oblige him to alter it."[100] Then he tacks back to acknowledge the other side:

[But when] matters are carried so far as to produce a civil war, foreign powers may assist that party which appears to them to have justice on its side. He who assists an odious tyrant, – he who declares for an unjust and rebellious people, – violates his duty. But, when the bands of the political society are broken, or at least suspended, between the sovereign and his people, the contending parties may then be considered as two distinct powers.[101]

He then reverts and, like his predecessors, offers a strong caution against the potential abuse of this principle: "But we ought not to abuse this maxim, and make a handle of it to authorize odious machinations against the internal tranquility of states. It is a violation of the law of nations to invite those subject to revolt who actually pay obedience to their sovereign, though they complain of his government."[102]

Yet again, Vattel goes back to stress that there are crimes so great as to justify a violation of the principle of sovereignty and noninterference, in language strikingly similar to Grotius': "As to those monsters who, under the title of sovereigns, render themselves the scourges and horror of the human race, they are savage beasts, whom every brave man may justly exterminate from the face of the earth."[103] Vattel gives as an example the three figures from Greek mythology whom Grotius had cited, legendary for arbitrary murder, human sacrifice, and feeding victims to animals. Surprisingly, then, despite this passage, Vattel specifically criticizes Grotius in the course of warning against humanitarian imperialism:

But, though a nation be obliged to promote, as far as lies in its power, the perfection of others, it is not entitled forcibly to obtrude these good offices on them. Such an attempt would be a violation of their natural liberty. In order to

---

[99] Vattel, *Law of Nations*, 289.   [100] Vattel, *Law of Nations*, 290.
[101] Vattel, *Law of Nations*, 290–291.   [102] Vattel, *Law of Nations*, 291.
[103] Vattel, *Law of Nations*, 291.

compel any one to receive a kindness, we must have an authority over him; but nations are absolutely free and independent . . . .

What led [Grotius] into this error, was his attributing to every independent man, and of course to every sovereign, an odd kind of right to punish faults which involve an enormous violation of the laws of nature, though they do not affect either his rights or his safety . . . . Could it escape Grotius, that, notwithstanding all the precautions added by him in the following paragraphs, his opinion opens a door to all the ravages of enthusiasm and fanaticism, and furnishes ambition with numberless pretexts?[104]

Vattel has plainly contradicted himself, or at the very least has laid out contradictory arguments for and against intervention. Because of the principle of noninterference, states may not put themselves up as judges over other nations' affairs. At the same time, every nation has the right to fight against "monsters" who "render themselves the scourges and horror of the human race," as well as to intervene in a civil war to support rebels fighting a just cause. How will we recognize such monsters to fight against or rebels to support without peering into the affairs of other nations and judging them? Vattel takes issue with Grotius and disagrees with the latter's argument that sovereigns have a right to go to war against nations that violate the laws of nature, but then makes the same argument himself. And his critique of Grotius seems at odds with his own argument in favor of the right to revolt and the right to intervene. Either Vattel is contradicting himself or he is making a fine (and somewhat artificial) distinction: if a tyrant oppresses the people such that they rise up in revolt, other sovereigns may intervene to help them; but if a tyrant merely violates the laws of nature without provoking rebellion, no state has a right to intervene. That would seem to be the only way to square the circle, but Vattel's passage about "monsters" who "render themselves the scourges and horror of the human race" seems to close off even that possibility. Like Pufendorf, Vattel does not appear to have a consistent or coherent doctrine of revolt and intervention.

What accounts for Vattel's vacillations on interventions? Vattel, like Pufendorf and Wolff, was a subject of the Holy Roman Empire. The empire was a weak, fragmented polity, insecure in the face of the other great powers of Europe. In Pufendorf's day, the empire had been the site of much of the fighting in the Thirty Years War. By Vattel's time, the empire as a unity existed mostly on paper, increasingly overshadowed by the rise of Prussia, a supposedly subordinate kingdom, and by the rivalry between Prussia and Austria. The empire, tottering and weak, on the brink of civil conflict, secession, or fragmentation, constantly faced the

[104] Vattel, *Law of Nations*, 265.

question of sovereignty. It was the state most likely to be intervened upon by other states, and not in a position to intervene in the affairs of others. National insecurity likely shaped the outlook of the nation's intellectuals, who naturally would feel uneasy about expanding other states' license to invade and who might not feel safe from the authorities when writing about the just grounds of rebellion in a state where rebellion and secession were always possibilities.

The other major issue of interest is Vattel's treatment of the balance of power. Like Wolff, Vattel takes up the issue of the balance of power and the right of war against rising powers. His argument differs little from Wolff's: "an increase of power [by a rival state] cannot, alone and of itself, give any one a right to take up arms in order to oppose it." But when the rival state shows untrustworthy behavior, it increases our rights against it. "When once a state has given proofs of injustice, rapacity, pride, ambition, or an imperious thirst of rule, she becomes an object of suspicion to her neighbors, whose duty it is to stand on their guard against her," even to the point of "prevent[ing] her designs by force of arms."[105] This is even more the case in situations of danger and uncertainty: "On occasions where it is impossible or too dangerous to wait for an absolute certainty, we may justly act on a reasonable presumption."[106] When a rising power inflicts actual harm on some neighbor, the international community ought to band together to counterbalance the aggressor: "should that formidable power betray an unjust and ambitious disposition by doing the least injustice to another, all nations may avail themselves of the occasion, and, by joining the injured party, thus form a coalition of strength, in order to humble that ambitious potentate."[107] Prudence, therefore, leads us to a hair-trigger preparedness to defend the balance of power: "The safest plan, therefore, is to seize the first favorable opportunity when we can, consistently with justice, weaken that potentate who destroys the equilibrium."[108] It is interesting that Vattel and Wolff seem to believe that defending of the balance of power would require war, or at least ongoing preparation for war, in contrast to the British practice of stabilizing the balance of power through a network of alliances.

In this respect, Vattel (and Wolff) envisions an international system designed to protect the liberty and independence of its constituent nations:

Europe forms a political system, an integral body, closely connected by the relations and different interests of the nations inhabiting this part of the world . . . . The continual attention of sovereigns to every occurrence, the constant

---

[105] Vattel, *Law of Nations*, 492.   [106] Vattel, *Law of Nations*, 493.
[107] Vattel, *Law of Nations*, 494.   [108] Vattel, *Law of Nations*, 498.

residence of ministers, and the perpetual negotiations, make of modern Europe a kind of republic, of which the members – each independent, but all linked together by the ties of common interest – unite for the maintenance of order and liberty. Hence arose that famous scheme of the political balance, or the equilibrium of power; by which is understood such a disposition of things, as that no one potentate be able absolutely to predominate, and prescribe laws to the others.[109]

Again, the remarkable vision of a unified or universal commonwealth (at least among European powers) recurs, suggesting that even sovereign nations are responsible to one another. Because this continental republic is the highest conceivable authority, Vattel reserves his strongest language for aggressors who threaten it, against whom it is the duty of all states to rally together:

If then there is anywhere a nation of a restless and mischievous disposition, ever ready to injure others, to traverse their designs, and to excite domestic disturbances in their dominions, – it is not to be doubted that all the others have a right to form a coalition in order to repress and chastise that nation, and to put it forever after out of her power to injure them.[110]

Nations that are always ready to take up arms on any prospect of advantage, are lawless robbers: but those who seem to delight in the ravages of war, who spread it on all sides, without reasons or pretexts, and even without any other motive than their own ferocity, are monsters, unworthy the name of men. They should be considered as enemies to the human race …. All nations have a right to join in a confederacy for the purpose of punishing and even exterminating those savage nations.[111]

Again, like Wolff, Vattel uses language strikingly similar to Grotius' description of those who commit crimes against nature, but for Vattel and Wolff the greatest criminal is the aggressive state who threatens the balance of power. Like Wolff, Vattel may have had in mind Bourbon France, which was enjoying a period of almost unchecked dominance and prosperity in the mid-eighteenth century and whose power threatened much of the rest of Europe. France fought a long and mostly unsuccessful war against the Habsburg monarchy in the War of Austrian Succession (1740–8) before swapping loyalties to side with the Holy Roman Empire against Britain in the Seven Years War (1756–63), a classic case of seeing no permanent interest but the balance of power to preserve the independence of Europe.

If Wolff represents the Westphalian tradition at its most consistent and most extreme, Vattel represents the tradition at its most mature – confident enough to revise some of its own strictures and reevaluate some of the Augustinian inheritance it had cast off. Vattel returns some of the nuance

---

[109] Vattel, *Law of Nations*, 496.   [110] Vattel, *Law of Nations*, 289.
[111] Vattel, *Law of Nations*, 487.

and tension that had marked Pufendorf's treatment of sovereignty, rebellion, and intervention, at the cost of some apparent contradiction and inconsistency. Vattel also represents an endpoint of sorts: he is the last prominent thinker to work self-consciously within the just war framework until after World War II. It seems appropriate, then, that Vattel's work represents the closest we have to a synthesis of the Augustinian and Westphalian traditions, albeit with a definitive loyalty to the latter.

The Rise of International Law (1758–1948)

After Vattel, the Westphalian tradition is best represented not by an individual thinker but by the coalescence of a body of norms that eventually came to be known as *international law*. As we have seen, the conversation about justice and war gradually evolved into one about the rights of war; in the two centuries after Vattel, it further evolved in one about the law of war. From there, it was subsumed into the broader institutionalization of international law from the nineteenth century onwards. We saw the beginnings of this transformation when Gentili and Grotius, who were jurists, not theologians, moved the conversation onto new grounds. It was not yet a strictly legal conversation because international law was still embryonic; thinkers such as Grotius, Wolff, and Vattel would have thought of themselves as philosophers, jurists, or (often) government advisors. Being jurists did not mean there was a bar before which they could practice. It meant that they specialized in speculation about the reasonableness of law-like norms in an area that, in their day, lacked legal infrastructure or institutions.

Speculation about law among nations long predated Grotius. Ancient Roman jurists had spoken of the law of nations (*ius gentium*) in the pre-Christian era in two senses. It was, partly, an extension of Greco-Roman philosophical universalism. Because they believed in universal rationality, they also believed binding moral rules of conduct held across cultures and states. This sense of the law of nations was essentially synonymous with natural law. But the Romans also had some practical need for a law of nations because, as the commercial and political center of the Mediterranean world, they had regular intercourse with other peoples. They had to create norms of conduct to regulate trade, diplomacy, and war with other states, and they described these norms as elements of a "law" of nations, despite their difference from domestic law that could be made in the Senate, enforced by the consuls, and argued in the courts.[112] In this sense, the law of nations was the evolving body of customary behavior between nations.

---

[112] Sherman, "*Jus Gentium* and International Law."

Early Christian thinkers did not give the concept much weight, preferring to let natural law do the work instead. Augustine seems not to have used the idea at all, and Aquinas understood the law of nations to be derived from natural law and, consequently, to share in all the characteristics of it. The two were, in principle, separate, but in practice it is hard to understand how they differed for him.[113] As we saw in Chapter 3, Gentili was among the first in the early modern era to give significant weight to the idea, though he still sometimes treated it as a synonym for natural law. Suárez, in 1612, devoted a whole book of his treatise on law to a systematic treatment of the differences between eternal law, natural law, and the law of nations. He argued that natural law was derived from reason, the law of nations from customary usage (somewhat reflecting the two senses the Roman jurists had given to *ius gentium*). The first was discovered deductively, from logic, nature, and Scripture; the second empirically, by gathering data about different cultures and peoples. The two often overlapped insofar as common usage reflected universal reason but not necessarily.

Over the next century and a half, the law of nations gradually gained in authority as natural law changed from teleological to descriptive. If natural law was merely the description of customs that guided conduct in the state of nature, then it was a body of customary law, indistinguishable from the law of nations. The distinction between natural law and the law of nations broke down and there was no longer much use for two separate concepts. That is why the Westphalians defined the law of nations – understood as the received customary law and body of treaties that regulated conduct among nations – as the law of nature applied to nations. In effect, they were arguing that states had existed in the state of nature, and the rules they came up with over centuries of interaction in this state of nature must have been derived from reason and were therefore the laws of nature, which took the shape of customary law. The very titles of the Westphalians' works are indicative: Pufendorf's *Of the Law of Nature and Nations,* Wolff's *The Law of Nations Treated According to a Scientific Method,* and Vattel's *The Law of Nations.*

After Vattel, the law of nations evolved into international law, helped along by contemporary political and diplomatic events. The proliferation of commercial treaties, and their collection into compendia, provided a large body of cross-national legal texts in this early era of globalization. Following Napoleon's defeat, the Congress of Vienna and its successor, the Concert of Europe, styled themselves as bodies to speak authoritatively on matters of European and even global concern, codifying

---

[113] ST I-II, Q95, article 4, in Aquinas, *On Law, Morality, and Politics,* 62ff.

diplomatic norms along the way. The 1841 Straits Convention, the 1856 Declaration on Maritime Law, and the 1864 Geneva Convention (for the "amelioration of the condition of the wounded in armies in the field") established the idea of a binding multilateral treaty that could pass into customary law, even for nonsignatories. It would be followed by the Hague conventions of 1899, 1907, and 1923, founding texts of written, or positive, international law. In the twentieth century, of course, came the Geneva conventions, the UN charter and the UN's resolutions, various international tribunals, and several treaties on chemical, biological, and nuclear weapons.[114]

The late nineteenth century was the first great era of international organization, when institutions such as the International Meteorological Association (1873), the General Conference on Weights and Measures (1875), the Universal Postal Union (1875), and the International Telegraph Union (1908) were founded, adding to the growing network of global governance, cooperation, and rulemaking. The era also saw treaties on the protection of submarine cables (1888); the exchange of government documents, scientific and literary publications, journals, and legislative chronicles (1889); patents and copyright (1911); and assistance and salvage at sea (1913). Most significantly, the Association for the Reform and Codification of the Law of Nations was established in 1873 and changed its name to the International Law Association in 1895.

The term "international law" seems to have been first used in English in the early nineteenth century and the first efforts to compile and codify international law date from the same era, drawing on treaties, custom, and the early modern jurists. The terms *ius gentium* and "law of nations" had been widespread in the preceding century, but their use in English works declined precipitously as the Napoleonic Wars wound down, and again after the Crimean and American civil wars. In their stead, "international law" became more common, surging in the 1830s and surpassing the "law of nations" and its variants around 1890.[115] "The new feature of the writings on international law of this time is the decline in abstract discussions of principle in favor of consideration of state practice," according to one historian of the era. "State practice enters the literature and dominates it, while natural law speculations disappear."[116] International law reflected the optimism of the time: the later nineteenth century saw leaps and bounds in scientific discovery and the industrial revolution that persuaded many thinkers that every evil of the human

---

[114] Guelff and Roberts, *Documents on the Laws of War*.
[115] According to Google's Ngram viewer: https://books.google.com/ngrams.
[116] Scupin, "History of International Law, 1815 to World War I," paragraph 6.

condition, including war, could be ameliorated with the right application of reason and goodwill. A durable peace among the great powers
had held since 1815 (except for the brief Crimean War), which was
evidence to many observers that war could be tamed. English-language
commentaries on international law, mostly following this new approach,
appeared from James Kent (1826), Henry Wheaton (1836), William
Manning (1839), Archer Polson (1848), Robert Philimore (1861), and
D. D. Field (1876).

The new regime of international law largely reflected the Westphalian
ideas of sovereignty, war, and nonintervention. For example, Kent opens
his chapter on "the rights and duties of nations" with a strident reaffirmation that "no nation is entitled to dictate to another a form of government or religion or a course of internal policy; nor is any state entitled to
take cognizance or notice of the domestic administration of another state,
or of what passes within it between the Government and its own subjects." Consequently, "non-intervention in the internal affairs of a state is
a rule that admits of no exception whatever," and Kent goes so far as to
claim that nonintervention is a "cardinal" principal of international law.
Kent approvingly quotes another authority that states may not even
support the side in a civil war that is deemed to have just cause, for
"that would be constituting such foreign power a judge of the justice of
the war," a position forbidden by international law, which must view the
war as "just on both sides."[117]

Wheaton, similarly, reiterates a hard view of sovereignty and nonintervention. Sovereignty is autonomy, not a commission of responsibility for the
common good. He gives each state the authority to judge when war is
justified: "Each State is also entitled to judge for itself what are the nature
and extent of the injuries which will justify such a measure of redress."[118]
States are effectively unaccountable, the only rule being a prohibition
against the first crossing of international boundaries. He acknowledges
that states quite regularly practice intervention for a variety of reasons,
including "the interests of humanity," but judges no rule can be made of
such instances and, by and large, intervention must be considered illegal.[119]
Indeed, he seems far more concerned with the question of whether intervention might be justified to preserve the balance of power or prevent a rival
from taking destabilizing actions than for any other reason.

Wheaton seems to argue against himself in his lengthy discussion of the
legality of the British, French, and Russian intervention in the 1827

---

[117] Kent, *Commentary on International Law*, 40, 79, 82, 83.
[118] Wheaton, *Elements of International Law*, 404.
[119] Wheaton, *Elements of International Law*, 90ff.

Greek War of Independence, judging it legal because "the general inter-ests of humanity are infringed by the excesses of a barbarous and despotic government."[120] But he squares the circle by detailing the written treaty between the intervening powers by which they authorized themselves to intervene and, implicitly, avoided establishing a general principle of inter-vention. Wheaton's argument is not very persuasive, but it illustrates the lengths to which the international lawyers of the nineteenth century went to avoid weakening Westphalian sovereignty even if they had sympathy with specific humanitarian causes. It also illustrates how persistent were the echoes of Augustinian thought or, perhaps, how early the Liberal tradition began to emerge.

The Westphalian tradition was, of course, the major influence on the most significant developments in international law in the twentieth cen-tury: the establishment of the UN and its predecessor, the League of Nations. The League of Nations covenant (1919) expressly recognized international law as the "actual rule of conduct among Governments." It bound its members to forsake war, "to respect and preserve as against external aggression the territorial integrity and existing political inde-pendence of all Members of the League," and to submit disputes to international arbitration. It gave the league authority to "take any action that may be deemed wise and effectual to safeguard the peace of nations," effectively placing the right of intervention solely in the hands of the league and out of the jurisdiction of any individual state.[121]

The UN charter (1945), similarly, "is based on the principle of the sovereign equality of all its Members." It prohibits members from "the threat or use of force against the territorial integrity or political inde-pendence of any state," and calls on all states to settle disputes by peaceful means. It disclaims any authority for interfering in the domes-tic affairs of any state. At the same time, the charter gives the UN Security Council "primary responsibility for the maintenance of inter-national peace and security."[122] The establishment of the UN and the codification of international law in the twentieth century could be seen as the triumph of the Westphalian tradition, enshrining something close to an absolute principle of territorial integrity and mutual noninterfer-ence in international law and prohibiting the use of force in any case except self-defense.

---

[120] Wheaton, *Elements of International Law*, 103.
[121] Covenant of the League of Nations, full text available: https://avalon.law.yale.edu/20th/century/leagcov.asp.
[122] Charter of the United Nations, full text available: www.un.org/en/charter-united-nations.

Conclusion

If the common theme of the Augustinian tradition is the use of force as an act of love to defend public order and the common good, the common theme of the Westphalian tradition is sovereignty understood as the inviolability of borders and the principle of reciprocal noninterference. The Westphalian thinkers describe natural law in different terms to the Augustinians: it is rule derived from human nature that commands adherence to reason, as institutionalized in a regime of rights. The state exists by the consent of its members to safeguard those rights and may use force to enforce and defend those rights when violently threatened. At the international level, the rights in question are those of sovereignty and noninterference. States may use force to defend these principles, and for little else. The Westphalians were divided – sometimes each thinker seems divided against himself – about the right to revolt and the right to support rebels but universally agreed on the priority of international boundaries.

But that is not the end of the story of the just war traditions. Even as the Westphalian tradition was crystalizing in international law and international institutions of global governance, the Liberal tradition of just war thinking was emerging as a critique and a proposed revision of the Westphalian order. Liberalism itself had roots centuries earlier but began to make itself felt in international affairs during the nineteenth century, though not yet in the language of just war. Immanuel Kant's *Perpetual Peace: A Philosophical Sketch* appeared in 1795, arguing that republican government and international cooperation could lead to the end of war. The multilateral intervention in the Greek Civil War in 1827 and the French police action in Syria in 1860–1 showed that the idea of humanitarian intervention was alive. The proliferation of international institutions and treaties included some for expressly liberal causes: a treaty for the suppression of the African slave trade (1890), similar efforts against the "white slave traffic" (i.e., sex trafficking, in 1904 and 1910), and the Agreement for the Suppression of Obscene Publications (1910). The Hague and Geneva conventions were largely motivated to alleviate human suffering, as was the founding of the Red Cross.

And the UN itself reflected the tension between Westphalian and Liberal goals. While it contained strong reaffirmations of state sovereignty and the idea of nonintervention, it also provided one of the earliest (and certainly the most prominent) expressions of human rights in international law. The charter expressed its members' "faith in fundamental human rights, in the dignity and worth of the human person, in the equal rights of men and women and of nations large and small." It defined one of the purposes of the UN as "promoting and encouraging respect for human rights and for fundamental freedoms for all without distinction as to race, sex, language, or religion," among five other clauses affirming human rights. And it was followed in 1948 by the Universal Declaration of Human Rights. The charter and the declaration left unresolved the question of what happens when human rights and states' rights conflict.

That question was addressed in the 1948 Genocide Convention, which declared genocide a crime under international law punishable by international tribunal. The Genocide Convention, whose norms had already been affirmed by the Nuremburg and Tokyo war crimes trials in 1945–6, was an extraordinary development. It was the first major amendment of Westphalian sovereignty and legal support for the liberal principle of human rights in international law. By declaring some acts of sovereign governments to be criminal, it established that governments are not the exclusive judge of their own actions; there are norms of conduct external to states to which they are accountable; sovereign rulers and government officials may be held personally accountable for their official acts; and *in extremis* other states may collectively intervene to enforce these norms of conduct. In the case of the Genocide Convention, the specific standard was the crime of genocide, the systematic murder of an entire people group. Put another way, the standard of conduct by which states would be judged and by which they could be stripped of their sovereignty was how they treated human beings and whether or not they recognized the sanctity of human life. This is the essential feature of the Liberal tradition of just war thinking.

5   Competing Visions of a Liberal Tradition

Several events in the mid-twentieth century collectively renewed interest in just war thinking in what amounted to a critique of the Westphalian understanding of justice and sovereignty. The two world wars were seen as a breakdown and failure of the Westphalian order. The Holocaust presented an especially deep challenge because the Westphalian system had no real proposal for how to prevent or stop such atrocities in the future. "While the Westphalian system and its conception of sovereignty have undeniable strengths, there is this undeniable weakness: it has no conception of the positive responsibilities – even the most minimal ones – of the exercise of political authority," according to Johnson.[1] In addition, innovations in the technology of war – aerial combat and bombardment, submarine warfare, missile technology, tanks, and, of course, nuclear weapons – increased the scale of destruction by orders of magnitude and made the control of war more urgently necessary. The Cold War kept concerns about the destructiveness of war at the forefront of the public's attention. The major effort to restore the international system after the wars took the form of a significant innovation: the creation of the League of Nations and the UN. At the same time, while strong states continued their perennial practice of intervening in the affairs of weak states, the purpose and goals of some of these states' interventions started to evolve in lines with growing, liberal norms.[2]

Several thinkers took up the cause of reviving just war thinking in response to these developments, as I review in this chapter, but at the outset we should note that they paid relatively less attention to other major developments of the twentieth century: decolonization and the emergence of scores of new, fragile states governed by regimes of questionable competence or integrity; and the rise of the liberal international

---

[1] Johnson, *Ethics and the Use of Force*, 92.
[2] Finnemore, *Purpose of Intervention*, see especially chapter 3.

118

order. Just war thinking revived in the aftermath of the world wars, but it was uneven in choosing what topics counted.

At the same time, thinkers who were inclined to revive just war faced another challenge, one from the scholarly community: the rise of post-Enlightenment thought. Poststructuralism, postmodernism, and deconstructionism claimed that there were no grounds for objective moral judgment; truth-claims were masks for power; and we should take refuge in a universal distrust of metanarratives. The postmodern critique accelerated the loss of moral consensus in the public square begun by the Enlightenment. The Enlightenment made it impossible to appeal to authority or revelation as the foundation for justice and moral judgment, emphasizing reason and nature in their stead. Postmodernism did to reason and nature what the Enlightenment did to authority and Scripture, with the result that there were no grounds left on which to advance arguments capable of commanding a consensus in the public square. Just as just war thinkers needed to recover the idea of justice in, and limits on, war, postmodernism seemed to deny them the grounds to do so.

With the seeming failure of the Enlightenment project of founding public morality on universal reason, some thinkers, such as Ramsey, tried to reestablish the older, explicitly religious foundations for just war thought. Others, such as Walzer, did the opposite, trying to establish just war on the moral intuition of twentieth-century liberalism. Both sought to amend the Westphalian order to make greater room for human rights or the sanctity of human life, which is why I have characterized them as belonging to a "Liberal" approach. They operated within the broad tradition of classical liberalism, though from decidedly different corners of it. Ramsey's approach was more consistent with the Augustinian tradition of just war and has had an enduring legacy in religious and theological discourse. Walzer's approach found greater acceptance and popularity in the secular academy, military educational system, and popular discourse broadly, despite enduring philosophical problems. I review the oeuvre of Ramsey and Walzer in turn as rival versions of a reconstituted Liberal tradition of just war thinking. I conclude with a shorter review of two efforts to reinterpret just war thinking for contemporary security challenges: the US National Conference of Catholic Bishops' letter *The Challenge of Peace*, and the international commission on the Responsibility to Protect.

Paul Ramsey (1913–88)

Ramsey, an American Protestant theologian and ethicist in the Methodist tradition, is chiefly known in just war scholarship for his extensive critique of nuclear deterrence and qualified support for the American war in Vietnam. The first issue is outside the scope of this book, having more to do with *jus in bello*, though it is worth noting that Ramsey's views against counter-population nuclear deterrence and obliteration bombing provide a sharp contrast with Walzer, who gave qualified endorsement to both through his notion of a "supreme emergency." I will largely focus on Ramsey's broader political theology and the other emphasis of his work: his views of Vietnam and what they imply for the rights of revolt and intervention (in Chapter 8 I use Ramsey's work on nuclear deterrence for a discussion of North Korea). Ramsey sought to resurrect key elements of the Augustinian tradition of just war thinking and he described his project in explicitly Augustinian terms. However, he is also a major contributor to the Liberal tradition insofar as he emphasized the justice of the international common good, the importance of liberal goals in justified revolt and intervention, and the absolute value of human life.

In previous chapters I started by tracing each thinker's view of natural law. At the time Ramsey was writing, the concept of natural law had changed beyond recognition compared to what it had been for Aquinas and others in the medieval tradition. Ramsey argues that "the norm of Christian love, and not natural justice only," is the proper source of just war doctrine: just war is "not merely the result of an independent natural-law reason." He goes so far as to oppose an "alien natural law principle drawn from some source outside of Christian morals" against "what love requires."[3] Aquinas, for whom natural law encompasses Christian morals, would not have recognized this distinction. Because of his different understanding of natural law, Ramsey argues that natural-law principles are "inadequate" by themselves to ground just war and criticizes the "natural law optimism"[4] of Pope John XXIII's 1963 encyclical, *Pacem in terris*.

Instead Ramsey grounds just war in love, claiming Augustine's mantle and authority for his argument.[5] Ramsey argues that "Justice is the form of men's loves," which ends up getting at much the same thing that Aquinas and Augustine meant when they rooted justice in natural law. Ramsey similarly invokes an Augustinian idea of statehood, citing the

---

[3] Ramsey, *War and the Christian Conscience*, xviii–xx.   [4] Ramsey, *Just War*, 192.

[5] Johnson argues that Ramsey reads too much into Augustine: "This way of using Augustine exaggerated the connection between the thoughts contained in these diverse passages and Augustine's ethic of Christian love. He himself never made this connection explicitly; nor did the tradition which later coalesced during the medieval and early modern periods, which placed Augustine's various just war-related observations in a systematic frame defining the rights and responsibilities of government for ensuring and protecting the common good" (Johnson, *Ethics and the Use of Force*, 23–24). See also Johnson, "Just War in the Thought of Paul Ramsey," 189; Miller, "Love, Intention, and Proportion."

Augustinian notion that "in the State it is the form of that love or agreement to pursue in common the objects which a 'people' desire." Later, Ramsey summarizes his view of the just war tradition: "love for neighbors threatened by violence, by aggression, or tyranny, provided the grounds for admitting the legitimacy of the use of military force."[6] In keeping with Augustine's understanding of the *tranquilitas ordinis*, Ramsey argues that peace and justice are intertwined and cannot rightly be distinguished from each other: "Order is not a higher value in politics than justice, but neither is humanitarian justice a higher value than order. Both are in some respects conditional to the other … the only real political justice is an ordered justice." The policymaker, then, must "reckon order and justice both – and not justice only – as ends or the effects of responsible action."[7]

Rooting just war in love rules out a number of causes for war. Like older thinkers who denied vengeance or honor were just causes for war, Ramsey was keen to deny that proving the strength of one's will or resolve was a just cause for war: "Policies of extreme committal to irrational behavior are only one illustration of where one is driven when war is regarded as primarily or exclusively a trial of wills or a test of resolve." He criticizes the idea of war as "a test of resolve which has no other purpose than to prove who wins in a battle of wills."[8] This leads to Ramsey's famous denunciation of strategic nuclear deterrence – of total nuclear war, massive retaliation, or counter-population nuclear war – as "bizarre" and a form of "insanity" because of the obviously unloving nature of threatening civilizational annihilation.[9] He similarly dismissed the notion that the Vietnam War could be justified on "considerations of *mere* honor and prestige," though he found other reasons to support that war.[10]

Ramsey also differentiates between justice and international law. We saw in Chapter 4 that just war thinking evolved into, and was subsumed by, international law, and that international law largely reflected Westphalian notions of sovereignty and justice among nations. As a result, during the Westphalian era what was understood to be *just* was the same as what was understood to be *legal*. Ramsey disentangles the two: "The use of power should not always stick by the legal boundaries …. A responsible political action is never simply a legal act," because sticking by the law can be counterproductive if a lawful act does not pay attention to the realities of power and politics in the world, or to the ideals of justice that the law is supposed to serve.[11] This

[6] Ramsey, *Just War*, 144.   [7] Ramsey, *Just War*, 11.   [8] Ramsey, *Just War*, 222.
[9] Ramsey, *Just War*, 226–227.   [10] Ramsey, *Just War*, 491.
[11] Ramsey, *Just War*, 12–13.

means that just war is more than merely defending borders, insisting on self-defense, or adopting a principle of no-first-strike: "Western political thought did not until recently stand clothed only in an 'aggressor–defender' concept of warfare."[12] For Ramsey, a war might be just even if it was not strictly consistent with international law – which makes sense insofar as international law only reflects a Westphalian notion of justice. (This will be important for some of my case studies in Chapter 8.)

Ramsey positions his just war doctrine within a broader political theology in which power is inescapable, but justice is exigent: "The use of power, and possibly the use of force, is of the *esse* of politics." But this power is not blind or amoral. "Power without purpose and purpose without power and both equally non-political," by which Ramsey meant either alone were politically irresponsible because either without the other ignored the nature and demands of just political action.[13] Ramsey's emphasis on "purpose" is the guise in which teleology reappears in Ramsey's thought. Though he does not favor the language of natural law, he nonetheless understands political power to have a goal or purpose towards which it must be oriented. The goal of the statesman is to use power to advance the national and international common good – and, where possible, to increase the area of overlap between the two. The policymaker's responsibility is defined by "the national common good and by the international common good. These goods are not always the same." Policymakers ought to try to increase the overlap between them: "The Christian influence in our nation, it would seem, should be in the direction of including within the scope of national policy as much of the world common good as is realistically possible."[14] That the nation should seek to align its interests with the "international common good" is a key distinctive feature of the Liberal tradition, echoing Kant's *Perpetual Peace* and Wilsonian ideals of international cooperation.

Given these commitments, we can better understand the broader political theology from which Ramsey derives his just war thinking and its application to the Cold War context of his day. Ramsey was unhesitating in his condemnation of communism: "No Christian and no man who loves an ordered liberty should conspire with communism in coming to power."[15] Ramsey believed that the United States had unique responsibilities in the world because of its exceptionally powerful position and its commitment to liberty and human rights and, to the extent possible, it should use its power in the service of the global common good. Ramsey

[12] Ramsey, *Just War*, 151.   [13] Ramsey, *Just War*, 5, 8.   [14] Ramsey, *Just War*, 459.
[15] Ramsey, *Just War*, 449.

writes about the United States in a passage that faintly echoes how Cicero and Augustine spoke of Rome:

The United States always needs an environment or field of forces favorable to its power in the world, and we need always an environment favorable to our purposes in the world. Broadly speaking, the overriding goal of our foreign policy is to create and sustain a system of free and independent nations . . . . This understanding of the international common good is the *bene esse* of our political actions towards foreign powers.[16]

American security requires a benign environment, which in turn requires a system of free and independent nations. Ramsey thus supports the broader liberal project, albeit for distinctively Christian and American reasons. He believed that supporting the international common good meant supporting a system of liberty among nations – we can presume, given his condemnation of communism, among liberal democratic nations. Ramsey believed that the political expression of Augustinian love is liberal democracy and international cooperation.

Ramsey analogizes to Jesus' parable about the Good Samaritan (Luke 10:25–37). It was just to help the stranger waylaid and beaten on the road to Jericho; by extension, would it not be just "to resist by force of arms any aggression upon the ordering power or nation that maintains a police patrol along the road to Jericho?"[17] Ramsey is careful, however, to circumscribe the United States' responsibility for creating and sustaining this system of global order. He also emphasizes the limits of what is "realistically possible" and asks policymakers to recognize that they are "not called to office to aim at all the humanitarian good that can be aimed at in the world."[18] He recognizes the limits of the United States' capabilities: "The primary reality of the present age and for the foreseeable future is that the United States has had responsibility thrust upon it for more of the order and realized justice in the world than it has the power to effectuate."[19] He understands the United States to be trapped in an essentially inescapable position of global responsibility: "This nation has inherited both power and responsibility in imperial proportions. This means simply that we are one of the nations that has the power significantly to influence events beyond our borders. Whether we do or don't, we *do*."[20] But like a good Niebuhrian, Ramsey cautions as much against doing too little as against doing too much in the world. His understanding of America's role in the world and its inescapable duties played a large role in shaping his views of intervention.

[16] Ramsey, *Just War*, 8.   [17] Ramsey, *Just War*, 501.   [18] Ramsey, *Just War*, 9.
[19] Ramsey, *Just War*, 23.   [20] Ramsey, *Just War*, 488.

Ramsey on Vietnam and Intervention

Ramsey approaches the rights of revolt and intervention against the backdrop of the Vietnam War. He broadly supported the US military action against the communist insurgents and their North Vietnamese backers (with qualifications and an ultimate reversal, as I discuss below); as such, he was predisposed to focus on the justice of fighting against rebels, not the possible justice of rebellion. He rejects the notion that all national liberation movements are *ipso facto* just: "There are those among us whose single, overriding political norm seems to be the justification of radical social revolutions wherever they may be occurring, threatening to occur, or in need of occurring."[21] This reads almost like a preemptive rebuttal of Walzer, who a decade later will argue that national liberation is a just cause for rebellion. Ramsey criticizes this view as simply another version of treating God and "History" as the same thing, another version of *might makes right*.

Nonetheless, Ramsey does allow certain narrow grounds for revolt. He aligns himself with Calvinist resistance theory,[22] according to which lower political authorities might lead resistance against a higher authority if the higher overrides the basic principles or the constitution of the commonwealth. Ramsey acknowledges that it is only one further step to say that private citizens may take up the office if lower magistrates do not. He likens this to a citizen's arrest, in which "a private person clothes himself for a moment with the majesty of public order and he acts on behalf of society as a whole." Such an action is legitimate, but it comes with the necessary condition that the citizen also acts within the same limits and laws that govern the state, were it available: "In a similar fashion, justifiable revolution is revolution within responsible limits."[23]

Ramsey is at pains to circumscribe and limit the right of revolt: "This theory of 'constitutional' or 'official' revolution" has serious implications. It "means that an abstract and universal justice ... is never sufficient to warrant an appeal to arms." Allowing any violation of justice to trigger revolt "would lead to civil war for an infinite end, on an infinite number of occasions, and probably by the use of limitless means." Rather, would-be rebels "must wait – long past the point where simple justice began to be violated – until there arises someone or some group capable of bringing this to pass without letting worse befall."[24] Further, Ramsey seems to

---

[21] Ramsey, *Just War*, 462.
[22] Ramsey, *Just War*, 460. Ramsey invokes Calvin, but Aquinas had said much the same thing.
[23] Ramsey, *War and the Christian Conscience*, 123.
[24] Ramsey, *War and the Christian Conscience*, 124.

imply that only liberal or limited revolution could be legitimate revolution, although Ramsey's meaning is admittedly difficult to grasp. He writes of the Calvinist tradition that it "produced the politics of an ordered liberty that has prevailed to date in the Puritan political heritage." Given this heritage, "revolutionary violence was not more to be approved than international conflict," except when it met certain conditions as outlined within that heritage. I take Ramsey to mean that revolution is only legitimate if pursued with the intent of establishing (or reestablishing) the kind of polity dedicated to ordered liberty that was the inheritance of the Puritan political heritage; or, more simply still, only classical liberals can justly rebel, another illustration of Ramsey's liberalism.[25]

Ramsey is especially critical of the method of insurgency. He correctly understood insurgency to be the face of modern warfare: "the possibility of nuclear war has made the world safe for wars of insurgency," an insight that international relations scholars would belatedly recognize only decades later with the end of the Cold War.[26] He misunderstood the nature of insurgency, however, or at least he repeatedly blurred the distinction between insurgency and terrorism, claiming that insurgency necessarily involves attacks on civilians, which is why he claimed there was no possible just insurgency. "Guerilla war by its main design strikes the civil population .... This is an inherently immoral plan of war or revolution."[27] Given his premise that insurgency always involves deliberate attacks on noncombatants, his condemnation of all insurgency makes sense. But while the Vietcong certainly murdered noncombatants, Ramsey mistakenly takes them as the paradigmatic case of insurgency. Most contemporary security-studies scholarship defines the deliberate targeting of civilians as terrorism and characterizes insurgency as unconventional warfare against political and military targets; it does not define insurgency as necessarily involving the deliberate targeting of noncombatants.

The justice of intervention, however, receives more attention. Ramsey implies that nations have a presumptive right to intervene when he argues that "the right and duty of intervention to deal with breaches of peace and threats to a just peace can be withdrawn from the nation-state," only if a higher political authority, that is, a world government, were to assume that right and duty. This is a stark departure from the Westphalian tradition, and it follows from the relative ease with which Ramsey distinguishes the legal from the just. Intervention might contravene international law, but that does not overly trouble Ramsey if justice is at

---

[25] Ramsey, *Just War*, 460.   [26] Ramsey, *Just War*, 427.
[27] Ramsey, *Just War*, 507; see also 434, 480.

stake. For him, intervention is understood "sometimes as a responsibility, always as a possibility," unless and until a world authority takes it away.[28] Ramsey bases this belief partly on his judgment that noninterference is simply impossible: "It is simply an illusion to believe that there exists or can exist a system of impenetrable nation-states, founded upon an absolute principle of non-intervention."[29] Later, he is blunter: "non-intervention is not a principle of world order."[30] Attempting to solidify a universal and inviolable doctrine of nonintervention is an exercise in utopianism, the sort of abdication of political responsibility that Ramsey criticizes throughout his work. He also emphasizes the need to calculate the relative costs and benefits of intervention against nonintervention: "Anyone who is impressed only by the immorality and probably ineffectiveness of interventionary action should sensitize his conscience to the immorality and probably ineffectiveness of non-intervention."[31]

What are the just causes for a military intervention? Ramsey gives comparatively less attention to *jus ad bellum* throughout his work, but generally he starts by listing the same broad principles for just war: justice and order. "The statesman must make a decision about the politically embodied justice he is apt to sustain or increase by his choice to intervene or not to intervene," he writes. But by the same token, "A decision to intervene or not to intervene has, secondly, to be made in terms of an assessment of order as one of the ends power must serve."[32] Whose order and whose justice count in this calculation? "The justifiedness of intervention is to be measured in terms of the national common good and the international common good."[33]

Ramsey emphasizes the global scope and universal nature of this doctrine of intervention by rooting it in the same charity that grounds just war broadly. Against charity no other value could, in principle, limit the boundaries of action: "No authority on earth can withdraw from 'social charity' and 'social justice' their intrinsic and justifiable tendencies to rescue from dereliction and oppression all whom it is possible to rescue. This is why the traditional just war theory did not hesitate to justify 'aggressive war,' that is, initiative in the charitable extension of an ordered justice."[34] He uses similar language later: "it is the work of love and mercy to deliver as many as possible of God's children from tyranny, and to protect from oppression, if one can, as many of those for whom Christ died as it may be possible to save."[35]

---

[28] Ramsey, *Just War*, 25, 27.   [29] Ramsey, *Just War*, 36.   [30] Ramsey, *Just War*, 460.
[31] Ramsey, *Just War*, 23.   [32] Ramsey, *Just War*, 28.   [33] Ramsey, *Just War*, 29.
[34] Ramsey, *Just War*, 35–36.   [35] Ramsey, *Just War*, 143.

Ramsey's criteria for intervention are in principle very broad: any disruption of order or justice in the national or international environment, including tyranny and oppression. His language about saving people from tyranny and oppression suggests he would support what we call humanitarian intervention, although he seems not to have directly addressed the issue except insofar as he saw Vietnam in those terms. He circumscribes his principles, of course, by reference to what is actually achievable and politically prudent given the realities of power, which it is the duty of statesmen to calculate. Within those bounds, the United States should, from a sincere charity and a desire to lovingly extend ordered justice to those who lack it, recognize a responsibility to intervene militarily to combat those who would disrupt or undermine ordered liberty around the world. Ramsey's clearest description of the just cause he believed to be at stake in Vietnam was cast in these terms: he criticizes the 1954 Geneva Accords as "not likely to create just government in Vietnam," and argues that they would "mean acceding to the surrender of the South Vietnamese to a national communism as the only force capable of organizing the country."[36] He goes on to criticize the call for peace in Vietnam because "to call for peace and not for justice and order as equally ultimate political values would itself come close to being a political immorality."[37] The just cause in the Vietnam War was nothing less than the defense and creation of a just government and a just peace, which for Ramsey probably meant a government capable of defending its borders and upholding public order and broadly devoted to the protection of human life and human rights.

Ramsey further specified two "secondary justifications" for intervention: counterintervention and invitation. Writing months after the US Congress had passed the Gulf of Tonkin Resolution authorizing an expansion of US military operations in Vietnam (but without explicitly mentioning it), Ramsey argued that the United States had the "right to assist a people in its right of self-defense against insurgency forces" that were supported by foreign powers (as the Vietcong was supported by North Vietnam, the Soviet Union, and China). Ramsey criticizes the weakness of the Westphalian tradition: "The nineteenth-century doctrine of non-intervention across legal borders became a weapon" for those who would exploit it; in this case, for communist insurgents in Vietnam.[38]

And of course, for Ramsey, the United States was just in responding to the South Vietnamese government's request for help against insurgents and their international backers. Invitation is helpful because it means there is something to work with, which increases the chances of success

---

[36] Ramsey, *Just War*, 491.   [37] Ramsey, *Just War*, 522.   [38] Ramsey, *Just War*, 35.

and lowers the cost of intervention – both important in calculating whether the benefit of intervening outweighs the costs. To improve the chances of there being a responsible host government to work with, "one main objective will be to strengthen the acceptance by the people of a government that continues to express their general will," though Ramsey clarifies he does not necessarily mean democracy. If helping a government under those circumstances "may often be immoral and unfeasible, non-intervention may also immorally abandon a people, and tragically may be no more effective in accomplishing what politically ought to be done."[39]

Through to 1967, Ramsey was alarmingly permissive in what he allowed counterinsurgency forces to do in the course of a just campaign. He argues that because "the guerilla lives among the people like a fish in water, we may be justified in accepting the destruction of an entire school of fish." He repeatedly lays the blame for collateral damage on the insurgents who have "enlarged the target it is legitimate for counter-insurgents to attack" by hiding among the people. He places no extra burden on counterinsurgent forces to practice a higher level of discrimination in a type of war that would seem to demand and require it. He acknowledges that, while direct attack is permissible, it may be "the wisest policy" to refrain and instead rely on a "sanitary cordon" to root out the insurgents with greater discrimination.[40] This relatively lax attitude towards civilian casualties seems inconsistent with Ramsey's insistence on fighting with charity. Later scholars will make the practice of greater discrimination the minimum, not maximum, standard of just counterinsurgency.

Until his view changed, Ramsey justified this more permissive conduct of counterinsurgency war by appealing to the principle of proportionality, "which requires that the good achievable or the evil prevented be greater than the values destroyed or the destruction involved in any resort to arms."[41] In 1966, he believed the proportion in Vietnam was a net positive because of the larger issues at stake in the Cold War: "It is likely that to warrant the present scale of destruction one has to see the connection between South Vietnam and the independent development of all the people of Southeast Asia, and the balance of power in the world at large."[42] It is noteworthy that despite his explicit criticism of the Westphalian notion of sovereignty, he nonetheless uses Westphalian arguments about the balance of power. (To my mind, that is exactly right: it appropriates the best of the Westphalian contribution while correcting for its signature weakness.) To his credit, Ramsey repeatedly

[39] Ramsey, *Just War*, 38.   [40] Ramsey, *Just War*, 436, 435, 439.
[41] Ramsey, *Just War*, 504.   [42] Ramsey, *Just War*, 448; see also 510 and 524.

insists that such judgments about politics and the balance of power are prudential, based on the facts at hand, expert knowledge, and policymakers' experience. Judgments about the balance of power are not matters of first principles, and thus not best decided by churchmen or theologians. Ramsey was at pains to defer to statesmen for their judgment about the state of world politics – which shows admirable intellectual humility but also a deference to the state that others, more strongly aware of governments' proclivity for deceit and manipulation, would not grant. In 1967, he strongly criticized the bombing of North Vietnamese infrastructure as a wrongful and disproportionate attack "upon that society itself" that set the United States on the road to "total war" akin to the obliteration bombing of World War II, probably a turning point in Ramsey's view of the Vietnam War.[43] By 1976, Ramsey had changed his mind. His final assessment was that "the Vietnam war was disproportionate and *therefore morally* unjustified."[44] Ramsey apparently never wavered over the just cause at stake, only the means used to prosecute it and the net balance of good achieved against evil done. Had the United States and South Vietnam waged the war more discriminately and proportionately, Ramsey, it seems, would have continued to affirm its justice.

Ramsey was the first and most prominent thinker to rediscover the language of just war in the early postwar era. His influence was probably less than what it might have been because, instead of laying out his views systematically, he explicated them piecemeal over the course of his decades-long focus on nuclear deterrence and the Vietnam War. Subsequent thinkers, including William V. O'Brien, Johnson, Elshtain, Eric Patterson, and Nigel Biggar have broadly followed a similar path to Ramsey, with and without direct influence, working to recover and apply Augustinian insights to the problems of the twentieth and twenty-first centuries.

Michael Walzer (1935–)

At the same time as thinkers such as Johnson and O'Brien were beginning their work, Walzer was fundamentally reshaping the agenda of just war scholarship in a direction that was profoundly at odds with Ramsey's approach. Walzer, an American of Jewish background, is a professor emeritus at the Institute for Advanced Study, having taught and written on government, politics, philosophy, and ethics since finishing his doctorate at Harvard in 1961. Aside from his academic work, Walzer has been public in his advocacy for left-wing political causes and, in the 1960s

---

[43] Ramsey, *Just War*, 534.   [44] Ramsey, "Some Rejoinders," 206 (emphasis in original).

and 1970s, his opposition to the Vietnam War, which he credits for inspiring his contribution to just war scholarship, *Just and Unjust Wars.*

Just and Unjust Wars is by far the most prominent book on just war in print today, and has been for a generation, making engagement with his argument essential. His work has remained in print since its first publication in 1977 and is currently in its fifth edition. Walzer appears on virtually every one of the top results of a Google search for syllabi on just war. One search turned up over 1,100 journal articles devoted to aspects of the book over the past forty years. Walzer has come to be seen as the "dean of contemporary just war theorists," in the words of the Stanford Encyclopedia of Philosophy, which describes his work as "the major contemporary statement of just war theory."[45] One historian of the just war tradition concluded that "the philosophical reappropriation of Just War theory [in the twentieth century] is largely due to Michael Walzer's *Just and Unjust Wars.*"[46] Another scholar judges Walzer to be "the single most influential just war thinker of the last hundred years" and his book "the single most important modern work in the field."[47] Walzer's work has arguably become the preeminent representative of just war thinking among secular philosophers, ethicists, and military academies – though not among theologians or intellectual historians. Walzer is useful because he exemplifies the transition between the Westphalian and Liberal traditions and helpfully illustrates the weaknesses of both.[48]

Walzer's prominence is interesting because his work is unrepresentative of the broader just war traditions. Walzer departs from, and changes, just war thinking in important ways – but ways that he does not acknowledge in his work. Indeed, his work is almost entirely free of any reference to prior just war thinkers. While it is a profoundly historical work, saturated with reference to military history, it is detached from its own history, the history of just war thinking. In that sense, Walzer "is not, in any considered sense of the term, a just war thinker at all," because "his account of the just war ignores, or sometimes actually rejects, many features of the tradition. His approach to the tradition is *a la carte.*"[49] For example, in *Just and Unjust Wars* Walzer refers to both Augustine and Pufendorf just once, in his postscript, by way of explaining his choice to prioritize military history and soldiers' memoirs over moral theology. In the same passage, he criticizes scholars who are "preoccupied with the academic literature about moral philosophy and just war theory."[50]

The poverty of Walzer's historical understanding is evident in his claims that "the theory of just war began in the service of the powers" and that originally "just war was simply an excuse, a way of making war morally and religiously possible."[51] As we have seen, most just war thinkers, including Cicero and Augustine, have in common a proximity to, but also critical distance from, power. They used the language of just war to hold their powers to account and to criticize them for failing to live up to their own professed ideals. They emphatically were not interested in merely "making war morally and religiously possible" but were just as interested in critiquing and holding warmakers to account. Augustine's *City of God* was hardly an excuse for imperial power. To take another example, Walzer recounts how "political scientists and philosophers discovered the theory," of just war after the Vietnam War.[52] Walzer discovered it after Vietnam, but Ramsey and John Courtney Murray helped relaunch the just war tradition beforehand. The student who knows just war only through Walzer knows little of the debate Walzer has entered, and nothing at all about how Walzer has subtly reshaped the tradition or resolved debates in unorthodox ways. Walzer is using the language of just war, but he is not participating in the community of just war scholars or engaging in just war as "social practice."[53]

Walzer's Legalist Paradigm and Liberal Foundations

With that context in mind, we can engage with Walzer's argument. Walzer begins by summarizing what he calls the "legalist paradigm," his label for the Westphalian tradition. The legalist paradigm boils down to a prohibition on crossing borders with armed force, what he calls the "crime of aggression." He then seeks to amend this paradigm in favor of certain exceptions, the defining trait of the Liberal tradition. Scholars continue to debate these exceptions, and I will take up some of those debates in Chapters 6 and 7, but for my purpose here I want to note that Walzer also departs from the Augustinian just war tradition most prominently by framing the debate in secular terms. Walzer, in contrast to Ramsey, avoids religion. "I am not going to expound morality from the ground up," he says, because "I am by no means sure what the foundations are." He argues that, to proceed, we must recognize that in public life "practical morality is detached from its foundations, and we must act

---

[50] Walzer, *Just and Unjust Wars*, 336.   [51] Walzer, *Arguing about War*, 3.
[52] Walzer, *Arguing about War*, 7.   [53] Kelsay, "Just War Thinking as a Social Practice."

as if that separation were a possible. . .condition of moral life."[54] Walzer's abstention from theological argument reflects his mid-twentieth-century context. The secularization of public discourse had reached a high tide and it was thought that secular, supposedly objective reasoning could provide common foundations for political life and morality. In this respect, Walzer's project is of a piece with John Rawls' or Jurgen Habermas'.

Does it matter? Can't we carry on with moral reasoning without the theological trappings? We can, but removing theistic foundations changes the structure and content of moral argument in important ways, as we saw with Pufendorf and the other Westphalian thinkers. Because Walzer cannot appeal to God, church, or natural law to justify his arguments, he has to appeal to something else. In *Just and Unjust Wars*, he appeals to moral intuition, to our instinctive and common moral judgments. "I want to account for the ways in which men and women . . . argue about war," he says.[55] To that end, Walzer employs curious verbal constructions when pronouncing a conclusion. Often, he relies on emotive language ascribed to the first-person plural. He justifies his arguments on the grounds that "we worry" about a conclusion, or that "we praise," "we have (or ought to have) no hesitation in condemning," "we would still want to say," "we will want to say," "we may decide," "we feel badly in such cases," or we "have come to feel uneasy about," something. He appeals to "what we intuitively want war to be," "what we expect of soldiers," "our sense of what is right," "our sympathies," "our moral preference," "our common moral judgments," "our own deepest values," "our deepest moral commitments," "ordinary moral sense," "the right attitude," and "a principle that has been commonly accepted" (alternately, rejecting an argument because it is "not an attractive principle"). Sometimes he uses the passive voice to avoid specifying who possesses the intuition in question: "it is thought that," "it is presumed," "it seems important to say," "it has been said," "it is said," something is "generally thought to be," or "commonly thought to have been."[56]

To the extent that Walzer stays true to this approach, he substitutes moral sentiment or intuition for natural law. He argues that "the moral reality of war" is fixed by "the opinions of mankind" when those opinions are "plausible to the rest of us."[57] In doing so, he introduces serious

---

[54] Walzer, *Just and Unjust Wars*, xxiii. All references are to the fifth edition unless otherwise noted.
[55] Walzer, *Just and Unjust Wars*, xxi.
[56] Walzer, *Just and Unjust Wars*, 27, 38, 65, 67, 71, 79, 86, 106, 108, 110, 117, 133, 147, 154, 155, 162, 175, 179, 192, 199, 204, 209, 210, 261, 313, 315.
[57] Walzer, *Just and Unjust Wars*, 14.

weaknesses in his argument. For one, his argument is, on its face, descriptive rather than prescriptive. He denies this: "That's not to suggest that we can do nothing more than describe the judgments and justifications that people commonly put forward. We can analyze these moral claims, seek out their coherence, lay bare the principles that they exemplify."[58] Still, this appears to be little more than describing moral intuitions and judging them for their internal consistency.

This language is part of Walzer's agenda to defend the phenomenological reality and significance of moral language for human beings. And rightly so, because humanity's lived experience is of a moral reality. Walzer is here participating in an older debate against analytical philosophers, for whom moral statements had no reality or meaning whatsoever. But his argument with them is beside the point: our lived experience may be real, yet still mistaken – or, worse, immoral. That is to say, our moral intuitions are real, but they are also changeable, contingent, and thus sometimes unreliable and mistaken. Walzer appears to have no grounds from which to critique or judge changing or incorrect moral intuition. He recognizes the weakness in his position. That human beings "share a common morality is the critical assumption of this book."[59] It is not clear if this assumption holds up. Taken to its extreme, his argument would be a form of moral relativism.[60]

Walzer surely does not intend to make a case for relativism; the opposite is closer to the truth. But he does have a blind spot for an obvious reality: our moral intuitions change and thus cannot be a reliable foundation for moral judgment. Many of Walzer's conclusions have been contested by other scholars and thinkers in the just war tradition, but he gives us no reason to prefer his conclusions to theirs. He occasionally notices the difference between his judgments and past thinkers' conclusions, such as when he notes that "the Schoolmen [of the eleventh and twelfth centuries] were too accepting of contemporary notions about the honor of states." Walzer subsequently dismisses their conclusion about honor as a cause for war: "The moral significance of such ideas is dubious at best. Insults are not occasions for wars."[61] He similarly notes in a footnote that "It was once argued by jurists and philosophers that conquerors had a right to kill or enslave the citizens of a conquered state" but no longer.[62] Such older views, Walzer thinks, are wrong. But why? He offers no reason, no justifying principle. As it happens, I think Walzer is right – but his argument amounts to little more than a raw assertion, an assertion

[58] Walzer, *Just and Unjust Wars*, xiii.   [59] Walzer, *Just and Unjust Wars*, xxii.
[60] O'Driscoll, *Renegotiation of the Just War Tradition*, 93–99.
[61] Walzer, *Just and Unjust Wars*, 80.   [62] Walzer, *Just and Unjust Wars*, 124.

that brings to mind Johnson's critique about writers who use the language of just war "simply to cloak the author's own prior judgments in just war language."[63] To be more charitable to Walzer, perhaps he is implicitly arguing that times have changed. If so, this is "chronological snobbery,"[64] or the progressive idea that the unfolding of history has an inner logic which brings civilization to "higher" stages as time goes by. More is needed.

That is why Walzer does more, of course. He does actually make judgments and his argument is prescriptive, not narrowly descriptive. But in doing so, he smuggles in a new foundation to substitute for natural law, as suggested by his plan to "lay bare the principles that [arguments] exemplify." For him, there are better and worse principles; laying bare the worse sort is a way of defeating arguments that rely on them. The right sort is found by examining the "socially patterned" character of our collective judgments. That is, we must examine the "religious, cultural, and political, as well as legal," roots of our judgments; "The task of the moral theorist is to study the pattern as a whole, reaching for its deepest reasons."[65] The deepest reasons are clear: he treats "life and liberty as something like absolute values."[66] Later, he asserts that "individual rights (to life and liberty) underlie the most important judgments that we make about war."[67] In sum, "the defense of rights" is "the only reason" that can justify war.[68] Walzer's foundation is the moral intuition of classical liberalism. When he speaks in the first-person plural, the "we" he is speaking for is the epistemic community, not of all humanity but of twentieth-century American liberals. That is why Walzer is best understood as representing a new just war tradition, one based on classical liberalism.

Walzer, Nationalism, and Intervention

Does it matter? Liberalism is a workable ideology; if we are to use criteria to judge when war is justified, liberal principles may be the best available that can command a consensus. I will try in Chapters 6 and 7 to reconstruct a useable version of the Liberal tradition, coupled with Augustinian insights. But there are many variants of liberalism, and Walzer's liberalism comes with embedded assumptions about sovereignty and nationhood that critically undermine his ability to speak to some of the most prominent forms of warfare in the twentieth and twenty-first centuries. His work is best understood as a hybrid between the Westphalian and

[63] Johnson, *Ethics and the Use of Force*, 3.   [64] The phrase is C. S. Lewis'.
[65] Walzer, *Just and Unjust Wars*, 45.   [66] Walzer, *Just and Unjust Wars*, xxiv.
[67] Walzer, *Just and Unjust Wars*, 53.   [68] Walzer, *Just and Unjust Wars*, 72.

Liberal traditions, a hybrid that collides, rather than coheres, when it
comes to civil war, intervention, and the right of revolt. Walzer's moral
intuitions were shaped by two major influences: the celebration of
national liberation movements and the protest against the Vietnam
War. Both judgments deserve revisiting.

One of the most significant ways in which Walzer reflects the moral
intuition of his own time, in contrast to previous eras, is his uncritical
acceptance of nationalism and self-determination as just causes for war.[69]
This attachment, which surfaces in his discussion of interventions, was
typical of the era of decolonization in which he wrote. The problem with
Walzer's privileging of nationalism is that it betrays a lack of concern for
how to draw the boundaries of nations; for how to define who is and who
is not part of a nation; and for the destabilizing implications of national
self-determination. Worst, Walzer seems to endorse the view that war is
a positive contribution to constructing national identity.

In constructing his argument against most forms of intervention and in
favor of some exceptions, Walzer depends on a certain conception of self-
determination, sovereignty, and nationhood. Nations, in his view, have
a right to determine their own future. National self-determination means
that "the regime of a country should reflect the history, culture, and
politics of that country, and not of any other," which effectively serves
as Walzer's doctrine of sovereignty.[70] This is founded on "the rights of
contemporary men and women to live as members of a historic community and to express their inherited culture through political forms worked
out among themselves," as Walzer argues in a later essay.[71] Wars for
national liberation are just – a significant and novel change in the *jus ad
bellum* criteria that is not present in the Augustinian or even Westphalian
traditions. Previously, the right to revolt had been granted to people
suffering under oppressive tyranny. For Walzer, merely living under
a government that does not "reflect the history, culture, and politics" of
its people is reason for revolt.

Walzer's nationalism introduces a number of problems into his just war
framework. First is his emphasis on national self-determination instead of
individual liberty. National self-determination is the key that determines
when intervention is and is not permissible. Self-determination is not the
same as the right of individuals to determine their future, or even to
determine their form of government. Walzer, summarizing J. S. Mill,
argues that "A state is self-determining even if its citizens struggle and

---

[69] See Luban, "Romance of the Nation-State," for another version of this critique against
Walzer.
[70] Walzer, *Just and Unjust Wars*, 4th edition, xvi.
[71] Walzer, "Moral Standing of States," 211.

fail to establish free institutions, but it has been deprived of self-determination if such institutions are established by an intrusive neighbor." States are self-determining "whether or not the citizens choose their government" so long as the government is not beholden to a foreign power.[72] A nation might be considered self-determining even if a large majority has no say in the nation's governance or future. To state it baldly, in Walzer's view what matters is that a people's oppressors speak the same language, or share the same religion or culture, as those they oppress. Using Walzer's argument, we might conclude that the Chinese people enjoy self-determination because their authoritarian government is also Chinese, while the Japanese people in 1945 were presumably deprived of self-determination because their democratic constitution was written by an American general. The right of self-determination is, ultimately, the right of noninterference from foreign powers: "The government is bound to the citizens to defend them against foreigners," – not against violence, injustice, or disorder, but against foreigners.[73]

Second, Walzer's nationalism is ill-defined and ends up invoking uncomfortable ideas of national essentialism. His notion of self-determination rests on a distinction between those inside the "nation" and those without, who are "foreign." He leaves unstated how a nation gets defined – we are left to assume he is appealing to a vague notion of shared language, ethnicity, religion, or heritage – and thus leaves himself exposed to the standard criticisms of nationalism. Who counts as part of the nation? Who gets to determine the criteria? What do we do about ethnic, religious, or other minorities who live within a nation but do not exhibit its shared traits? For example, who is a Frenchman? Do the speakers of regional dialects, such as Picard, Gascon, Limousin, Franco-Provençal, and Occitan, count? It is precisely over these questions that many wars start. Who, then, can claim the mantle of the "self" whose determination is a just cause? Walzer assumes that any existing state enjoys presumptive legitimacy that other states should not question:

Foreigners are in no position to deny the reality of that union [of people and government], or rather, they are in no position to attempt anything more than speculative denials. They don't know enough about its history, and they have no direct experience, and can form no concrete judgments, of the conflicts and harmonies, the historical choices and cultural affinities, the loyalties and resentments, that underlie it.[74]

---

[72] Walzer, *Just and Unjust Wars*, 86. Walzer reiterates his belief that "the presumption against intervention is strong" almost twenty years later (Walzer, *Arguing about War*, 68).
[73] Walzer, "Moral Standing of States," 211.
[74] Walzer, "Moral Standing of States," 212.

If Walzer's claim is that we do not know enough about other nations to judge them, the answer is simple: learn about them. There is a large industry devoted to assessing other countries' performance across a wide range of metrics, including human rights, transparency, human development, and more. But Walzer may be making a deeper, epistemological claim – that we *cannot* know enough about another nation to judge it because we cannot enter into its experience of itself, and that somehow some peoples might be fit for their oppressive governments. This approaches a sort of national essentialism in which "a people" take on fixed, distinct attributes that mark them out as fundamentally different in ways that cannot be experienced, understood, or judged by outsiders. National essentialism brings in the same hints of moral relativism we earlier saw in Walzer's framing, one belied by his invocation of human rights as an ultimate standard. Either human rights are universal or national identity is inscrutable: both cannot be true, yet Walzer seems to rely on both claims. It is hard to take national self-determination seriously as a foundation for moral judgments or as a just cause for war given the imprecision of the concept and its routine abuse in historical cases.

Third, despite his deep historical understanding, Walzer does not address the troubling historical record of nationalism or self-determination, and his argument ends up endorsing a *might makes right* view of history. The first nation-builders were the absolutist monarchs of the seventeenth and eighteenth century. They treated regional and local diversity as a threat to national unity and implemented brutal forms of oppressive nation building in response. In the twentieth century, national self-determination was the occasion for countless wars of secession, civil wars, insurgencies, and terrorism. It is hard to make the argument that all these wars, and the failed states that emerged in their wake, were preferable to the alternative. Yet Walzer (and Mill, on whom he draws for this argument) might defend these as legitimate and justified wars because, in his view, war helps construct national identity:

The problem with a secessionist movement is that one cannot be sure that it in fact represents a distinct community until it has rallied its own people and made some headway in the "arduous struggle" for freedom. The mere appeal to the principle of self-determination isn't enough; evidence must be provided that a community actually exists whose members are committed to independence and ready and able to determine the conditions of their own existence. Hence, the need for political or military struggle sustained over time.[75]

---

[75] Walzer, *Just and Unjust Wars*, 93.

There is a chicken-and-egg problem here: does the nation create the revolution or the revolution create the nation? Walzer leans towards the latter, but if that is true it is unclear how the revolution – launched before the formation of a nation whose self-determination supposedly provided the just cause – could be justified. Sustained political and military struggle helps create a nation, a "distinct community," defined as a community that has "rallied its own people" to compete in an "arduous struggle." Earlier he argues that "It is the coming together of a people that establishes the integrity of a territory"[76] and that "Our common values are confirmed and enhanced by the struggle" against an aggressor.[77] But if the revolution makes the nation, then nations have no other justifying principle than that they successfully revolted, regardless of the cause for which they revolted or the reality of the "nation" doing the revolting. This doctrine appears to be little more than endorsement for a "might makes right" approach to war and peace: if a rebel faction succeeds in establishing itself and making headway, it is a nation and has therefore acquired rights. If it fails, it deserves to have failed because it was never a nation in the first place. He repeats the point later in connection with guerilla warfare: "Once the guerilla struggle has reached a certain point of seriousness and intensity, we may decide that the war has effectively been renewed," and the guerillas gain rights as combatants.[78] This view is too lax and uncritical towards wars of national liberation, heedless of the character of the movements in question, and serves to incentivize violence in the name of revolutionary struggle. Critics of Walzer would argue that the American Revolution, for example, was just not because it succeeded but because of the ideals of liberty that made the pursuit of independence necessary.

Fourth, the way Walzer applies these ideas to intervention and civil war is incoherent. He recommends that foreign powers may intervene in a civil war to offset one another but not to sway the ultimate outcome: "It is not true, then, that intervention is justified whenever revolution is; for revolutionary activity is an exercise in self-determination, while foreign interference denies to a people those political capacities that only such exercise can bring."[79] Fighting is a sort of education or a process of character-formation; through the revolutionary effort, people learn how to be a people and how to act as a nation, in this view. Intervening deprives a people of the opportunity to partake in a crucial stage in their national development. In other words, outside powers can only intervene up to the point that their efforts might actually count; outside powers

---

[76] Walzer, *Just and Unjust Wars*, 57.   [77] Walzer, *Just and Unjust Wars*, 71.
[78] Walzer, *Just and Unjust Wars*, 177.   [79] Walzer, *Just and Unjust Wars*, 89.

must above all be careful not to win. "Counter-intervention in civil wars does not aim at punishing or even, necessarily, at restraining intervening states. It aims instead at holding the circle, preserving the balance, restoring some degree of integrity to the local struggle ... *the goal of counter-intervention is not to win the war.*"[80] Put another way, outside intervention aims solely at prolonging the fighting to ensure that the outcome must be due to the efforts of the local population alone. He favors intervention to stop massacre or genocide but not to change the character of a barbaric regime (except and unless the latter is required for the former).[81] The defense of repressive regimes is as legitimate and just as the defense of liberal and democratic regimes, so long as they are locally controlled.

Walzer's argument about intervention is strategically, historically, and morally incoherent. While he is concerned to make a moral argument, not a strategic one, it is at least worth noting that no statesman would take seriously the idea that they may intervene unless and until the intervention might make a difference to the outcome. In terms of history, Walzer seems to believe that authentic nations develop in insulation from outside influence and that the international community must respect this insularity until such time as a people is established.[82] But no nation develops autonomously and in isolation. Cross-cultural borrowing is universal; indeed, it is one of the crucial pathways by which cultural development takes place. This is true in military affairs as in other respects: even the American Revolution depended on French assistance. Was the Marquis de Lafayette unjust to volunteer in the Continental Army, or Admiral Francois de Grasse wrong to blockade the British at Yorktown, or the new American nation illegitimate for relying on French aid? Was Greece not an authentic nation for having received British, French, and Russian aid in its war of independence against the Ottomans? Nor Kosovo, for having received NATO's assistance (an operation Walzer supported)? Walzer's view again seems to endorse violent struggle as an important step in national development and make the experience of political violence a positive and normative component of national identity. If the goal of just war theory is to limit war, Walzer's doctrine does the opposite.

Almost twenty years later, Walzer revisited the idea of intervention in an essay that considerably expanded the grounds for it and improved the

---

[80] Walzer, *Just and Unjust Wars*, 95, 99 (emphasis in original).
[81] See his discussion in the preface to *Just and Unjust Wars*, 4th edition.
[82] This is similar to the "Prime Directive" in the *Star Trek* TV series. The Prime Directive prohibits the United Federation of Planets from interfering in the cultural and scientific development of species that have not yet discovered faster-than-light travel, thus ensuring purely indigenous evolution up until they are technologically capable of interacting with the rest of the galaxy. The directive first appeared in a 1967 episode of *Star Trek*.

coherence of his argument while making it less uniquely Walzerian. "All states have an interest in global stability and even in global humanity," he writes. But uncivilized tyranny and oppression threaten global stability because "behavior of that kind, unchallenged, tends to spread, to be imitated or reiterated. Pay the moral price of silence and callousness, and you will soon have to pay the political price of turmoil and lawlessness nearer to home."[83] To that end, Walzer calls for reconsidering international trusteeships and protectorates. He seemed to have become far less concerned about sustaining the local purity of liberation movements and more concerned about defending human life, bringing him more closely in line with other scholars who have come to favor humanitarian intervention. Walzer's views thus became more consistently liberal – in the sense of defending human rights – and less statist, but to the same extent he also departed from his earlier work.

Regime Type and the Nazi Exception

Fifth, and most troublingly, Walzer seems curiously unconcerned about the particular character of regimes or national liberation movements, the causes for which they fight, and the governments they establish (something that is especially noticeable in his discussion of the Vietnam War). He argues that both guerilla resistance and the punishment of resistance is legitimate, and this "has nothing to do with our view of the two sides."[84] National self-determination was intended to end colonial oppression. In actual practice, it often ended up substituting local for colonial oppression in the name of brutal and dehumanizing socialist or fascist ideologies. Pointing that out is not a defense of colonialism; but ignoring it is hardly a defense of self-determination. Walzer casually dismisses the concern: "It is not our purpose in international society ... to establish liberal or democratic communities, but only independent ones."[85]

For example, Walzer later defended the international community's decision to reinstall the al-Sabah family in Kuwait after the Gulf War without compelling reform or liberalization because "what happened after [the war] was (is) the business of the Kuwaitis themselves, free from the coercion of foreign armies."[86] This is nonsensical, of course, because the reinstallment of the al-Sabah family and their autocratic

---

[83] Walzer, *Arguing about War*, 74.   [84] Walzer, *Just and Unjust Wars*, 177.
[85] Walzer, *Just and Unjust Wars*, 92. Walzer gives qualified and circumscribed endorsement to post-conflict democratic state building in the fourth edition preface (page xi). But he expands on his belief that nondemocratic regimes can be legitimate in Walzer, "Moral Standing of States." See an excellent response in Luban, "Romance of the Nation State."
[86] Walzer, *Just and Unjust Wars*, 2nd edition, xviii.

governance was never the business of the Kuwaiti people but of the al-Sabah family. This points to the incoherence at the heart of Walzer's preference for national self-determination. The "self" in question is, functionally, the strongest warlord, clan, family, or faction, not the people. Walzer insists that "a state is legitimate or not depending upon the 'fit' of government and community."[87] His defense of the possible legitimacy of autocratic states suggests, troublingly, that he believes some people are "fit" for authoritarianism and oppression. He claims in a hypothetical example that "the Algerian people have a right to a state within which their rights are violated,"[88] which surely cannot be right: it is not the Algerian people who "have" such a state, much less a right to one, but the tyrannical ruling clique, and no one would claim they have a "right" to it. Under Walzer's criteria, wars for national liberation, even if they aim at overthrowing some kind of representative democracy and erecting a fascist dictatorship, could still be just if dictatorship were a better "fit." He denies that he is defending the legitimacy of tyrannical states, only insisting that "foreign officials must act as if they were legitimate, that is, must not make war against them."[89] It is hard to see the difference.

This is a moral intuition that has clearly evolved since Walzer's day, and Walzer himself seems to have evolved. By the logic of his 1977 work, he ought to have opposed international intervention in the Balkan wars of the 1990s as violating the national self-determination of Croats, Serbs, and Bosniaks, many of whom preferred to continue fighting rather than live together. Similarly, he ought to have opposed the decade-long project to undo the effects of the wars by building a multiethnic, pluralistic polity in Bosnia-Herzegovina, much as he opposed liberalizing Kuwait after the Gulf War. Yet in the 1990s, he expressed support for the American and NATO interventions because of his greater concern for humanitarian principles, apparently no longer as concerned with keeping local liberation movements unpolluted from outside interference.[90] Nor can Walzer claim the Balkan wars were uniquely contemporary worries that did not enter into the historical examples he consulted in his earlier work. In 1977, he wrote of the Hungarian Revolution of 1848 that the Hungarians were not fighting a pure, idealistic war of national liberation because they were as keen to deny self-determination to Croats and

[87] Walzer, "Moral Standing of States," 214.
[88] Walzer, "Moral Standing of States," 226.
[89] Walzer, "Moral Standing of States," 216.
[90] Walzer, *Arguing about War*, chapters 5 and 7. His concern for national self-determination almost entirely disappeared when he revisited the issue in the third edition preface of *Just and Unjust Wars*.

Slovenes as they were to secure it for themselves: "But this is a difficulty that I am going to set aside ... [because] it did not enter into the moral reflections of liberal observers like Mill."[91] Walzer's choice to "set aside" such difficulties is regrettable, for it sets aside key moral dilemmas of self-determination, intervention, and the just use of force in times of civil conflict.

Against the obvious objection to his indifference towards regime type – what about the Nazis? – Walzer carves out an exception that functions *sui generis*, not as a generalizable principle. For Walzer, the Nazis represented an absolutely unique evil, against whom the rules of warfare are somewhat looser: "Nazism was an ultimate threat to everything decent in our lives, an ideology and a practice of domination so murderous, so degrading even to those who might survive, that the consequences of its final victory were literally beyond calculation, immeasurably awful."[92] In the face of the possibility that such evil might triumph, combatants may violate the normal rules of warfare, including by adopting a more lax standard of avoiding killing civilians and by demanding unconditional surrender and regime change: "Here was a threat to human values so radical that its imminence would surely constitute a supreme emergency."[93]

Does this exception work for any other regime? Walzer sometimes suggests that other states might be "Nazi-like" but, in practice, never identifies any. "Except when they are directed against Nazi-like states, just wars are conservative in character,"[94] he says; and, elsewhere, "Except in extreme cases, like Nazi Germany, [just wars] don't legitimately reach to the transformation of the internal politics of the aggressor state or the replacement of its regime."[95] But reading closer, it seems Walzer does not mean cases *like* Nazi Germany: he just means Nazi Germany. For example, in discussing the doctrine of unconditional surrender, he argues it was justified against Nazi Germany, but not against Imperial Japan. The right to demand unconditional surrender exists "only in cases where the criminality of the aggressor state threatens those deep values that political independence and territorial integrity merely stand for in the international order,"[96] which he believes did not characterize the Japanese regime. He similarly gives qualified endorsement to the Allied terror bombing of German cities (at least at certain times) but not to the atomic bombing of Japan.

The only regime Walzer ever identifies as falling into the "Nazi-like" category is Nazi Germany. One suspects the millions of Korean, Chinese,

---

[91] Walzer, *Just and Unjust Wars*, 92.   [92] Walzer, *Just and Unjust Wars*, 251.
[93] Walzer, *Just and Unjust Wars*, 251.   [94] Walzer, *Just and Unjust Wars*, 121.
[95] Walzer, *Just and Unjust Wars*, 2nd edition, xvii.
[96] Walzer, *Just and Unjust Wars*, 113.

and Filipino victims of Imperial Japanese aggression would differ, as might the victims of the Khmer Rouge, the Soviet Gulag, the Taliban, the Islamic State, and North Korea. But for all practical purposes, there are only two regime types in Walzer's theory: Nazi Germany and everyone else. Walzer's harsh binary approach to regime types is morally problematic because it gives license for regimes to be as murderous and tyrannous as possible, so long as they do not cross the line of actually espousing racialist National Socialism and replicating the Holocaust. His view is irrelevant to the real world in which Nazi Germany is long gone but a wide spectrum of neofascist, theocratic, terroristic, and totalitarian regimes thrive. And so, his view seems unable to give ethical guidance to policymakers confronted with such evils and wondering which rules of warfare are supposed to apply.

Walzer and Vietnam

Walzer's liberalism, and his disregard for regime types, is most evident in his treatment of the Vietnam War, to which he returns throughout the book. He opens the book by disclosing that "I did not begin by thinking about war in general, but about particular wars, above all about the American intervention in Vietnam."[97] He devotes four subsections of the book to Vietnam or examples from Vietnam. It would be unproductive to nitpick Walzer's other historical examples because he has written a book of moral philosophy, not a book of history, and we should take his historical anecdotes as illustrative of principle rather than exhaustive narratives. But because Walzer leaned so heavily on Vietnam, and because it was so formative in shaping his understanding of just war, it is worth revisiting.

Walzer characterizes the US position as being that its intervention was justified, first, "as assistance to a legitimate government, and second, as counterintervention, a response to covert military moves by the North Vietnamese." He denies the factual bases of these claims. The first claim depends on the existence of a local government "that could conceivably win the civil war if no external force was brought to bear," a criterion he restates later, saying, "The test, for governments as for insurgents, is self-help" and "A legitimate government is one that can fight its own internal wars," which he argues South Vietnam could not do and thus was not legitimate. This is a curious standard by which to judge the legitimacy of governments, one that is not present in international law or in most reflections on the nature of sovereignty. It again reflects the "might

[97] Walzer, *Just and Unjust Wars*, xix.

makes right" implications of Walzer's approach to self-determination (conflating *de jure* with *de facto* sovereignty) and his lack of concern for the type of regime in question: if a government is strong enough to put down dissent, it is legitimate. To push the case: If a fascist-led government just shy of overt Nazism crushed an anti-fascist resistance, it would be legitimate, and Walzer would presumably refrain from helping the prodemocracy rebels. But if a weak democratic government asked for international help to fight a powerful near-fascist resistance, Walzer would deny it aid because it was incapable of self-help.[98] It leads us to wonder, at what point does a government become legitimate? Was the Vichy regime of France legitimate by virtue of holding power? Was it just to put down the French partisan resistance? Were the partisans fighting for an unjust cause? Walzer might reject the analogy between South Vietnam and the French resistance, but the analogy between North Vietnam and a fascist regime is much closer. The Vietnam War did not feature one side with clear title to the moral high ground, but Walzer seems untroubled by this.

The second argument in favor of the US involvement is that it was countering foreign intervention. This argument "suggests that our own military operations followed upon and balanced those of another power."[99] Walzer simply denies that this was the case, apparently under the belief that the foreign power the United States sought to balance was North Vietnam, which he does not consider truly foreign. But the foreign powers the United States was most concerned about were the Soviet Union and the People's Republic of China, both of which were plainly "foreign" and gave substantial financial, logistical, and military support to North Vietnam and to communist insurgents in the South. Walzer never positions Vietnam in its Cold War context and thus never addresses the reality of foreign intervention in the Vietnamese civil war on behalf of the North. If he had, he might concede that there was a strong case that the US intervention met his criteria of a counterintervention, balancing against Chinese and Soviet intervention.

Walzer seems oddly keen to deny legitimacy to the South Vietnamese government, writing that "When the South Vietnamese government refused to permit" the referendum on unification as mandated by the 1954 Geneva Accords, "it clearly lost whatever legitimacy was conferred by the agreements."[100] It seems one-sided to blame the South and deny it legitimacy for its refusal to hold the referendum while making no mention of, and tacitly exonerating, the North for its violations of the same

---

[98] Walzer, *Just and Unjust Wars*, 97, 98, 100   [99] Walzer, *Just and Unjust Wars*, 96.
[100] Walzer, *Just and Unjust Wars*, 96.

agreement by supporting insurgents and later invading the South in conventional force. More to the point, Walzer is being inconsistent: he elsewhere argued that legitimacy was conferred by the ability to defeat insurgents or by an ill-defined "fit" between the government and the people; here he argues legitimacy is conferred by adherence to an international agreement or by holding elections. Walzer's shifting criteria of legitimacy confuse his arguments about intervention, but none of the criteria can make sense of his argument about Vietnam: both North and South fail virtually all of the criteria. The North was not known for its fidelity to international law or democratic norms, and the idea that the North's corrupt tyranny was a better "fit" for the Vietnamese people than the South's corrupt tyranny is belied by the millions of Vietnamese refugees who fled the North because they did not feel brutal communist tyranny was a good fit for them.

In his discussion of guerilla warfare, he claims that while guerillas sometimes commit atrocities and war crimes "they generally do less of them than the anti-guerilla forces," a sweeping and empirically unfounded assertion.[101] His endorsement of guerillas is yet another statement of his "might makes right" criterion of legitimacy, a criterion that does not consider the Vietcong's record of war crimes or the brutal, illiberal, and authoritarian cause for which it fought. Walzer elsewhere expresses disapproval of the "sliding scale" of morality by which combatants who have greater justice on their side are permitted greater latitude in how they fight. Yet Walzer tacitly adopts this same standard towards the Vietcong, passing over in silence their many crimes because of their success in embodying the true national identity of the Vietnamese people. Their just case – national self-determination (and Marxism–Leninism) – makes them legitimate rulers for Walzer, against whom no war can be just.

Walzer plainly believes the North was legitimate and the South was not because he thinks the North embodied Vietnamese national self-determination while the South was reliant on American aid. Against the argument that the North was the aggressor, Walzer responds that this "somehow misses the moral reality of the Vietnamese case." In fact, he says, the South lacked "a local political base" while the North supported insurgents "with deep roots in the countryside."[102] Aside from all the problems with nationalism I reviewed above, this is a restatement of his criterion of legitimacy – that strength and the ability to defeat insurgents is the test of nationhood – and it is striking for the way Walzer has to ignore the oppressive character of the North Vietnamese regime, its reliance on

---

[101] Walzer, *Just and Unjust Wars*, 180.   [102] Walzer, *Just and Unjust Wars*, 98.

Soviet and Chinese aid, its violation of the Geneva Accords, and its aggression against the South to make his argument. For Walzer, the fact of Vietnamese nationalism trumps all these criteria – but the full "moral reality of the Vietnamese case" would take these into account.

Instead, Walzer believes that at some unspecified point in the war, the "guerillas consolidated their political base in the villages. That victory effectively ended the war." At that point, the South Vietnamese government and its American patron had not only been defeated, they were no longer justified in resisting because they were engaged in fighting against what had become a "people's war."[103] That leads to Walzer's denunciation of wars like Vietnam:

The war cannot be won, and it should not be won. It cannot be won, because the only available strategy involves a war against civilians; and it should not be won, because the degree of civilian support that rules out alternative strategies also makes the guerrillas the legitimate rulers of the country. The struggle against them is an unjust struggle as well as one that can only be carried on unjustly. Fought by foreigners, it is a war of aggression; if by a local regime alone, it is an act of tyranny.[104]

Little of this description of the Vietnam War holds up in light of historical scholarship. The Vietcong were virtually wiped out in the Tet Offensive in 1968, somewhat limiting their opportunities to "consolidate their political base in the villages." Walzer falsely states that, "The US Army could not defeat the Vietcong."[105] It could, and it mostly did. The Vietcong did not win the war; the regular North Vietnamese Army did. The North won when it violated the Paris Accords and invaded the South in conventional strength, not by riding a wave of popular revolution. The war was not, then, a "people's war," a war against the mass of the South Vietnamese population, which in turn suggests that fighting an indiscriminate war against civilians was not "the only available strategy." There were other strategies, including options that the US started to move towards after 1969. There was a wide-ranging debate within the US government and among military officers about how best to adapt its strategy, and an effort to focus the intervention on state building, reconstruction, and pacification – which presumably would have been more just and surely more effective than what the United States actually did – was at least considered and partly implemented, albeit too late to make a difference.[106] Despite that, Walzer saw no reason to amend this view of Vietnam. In 2002, he wrote of Vietnam, "Here was a war that we should

[103] Walzer, *Just and Unjust Wars*, 194.   [104] Walzer, *Just and Unjust Wars*, 196.
[105] Walzer, *Just and Unjust Wars*, preface, Kindle location 328.
[106] Krepinevich, *The Army and Vietnam*. Sorley, *A Better War*.

never have fought, and that we fought badly, brutally, as if there were no moral limits."[107] This may have characterized the United States' main approach to the war from 1965 to 1969, but it bears little resemblance to the American strategy beforehand or afterwards. Even critics who share Walzer's view that Vietnam was a costly mistake should recognize that his characterization of how the United States fought it – "as if there were no moral limits" – is simply false.

Walzer has always been clear that his view of just war was shaped by his understanding of the Vietnam War. But Walzer's understanding of Vietnam is incomplete, at best, for having ignored its Cold War context, mischaracterized American strategy (or overlooking how it changed in its later stages), and unduly privileged North Vietnam's claims to legitimacy. These errors, in turn, rest on Walzer's approval of national liberation movements as a just cause for war, regardless of the regime type or ideology for which liberation movements or their opponents fight. It rests as well on Walzer's endorsement of national self-determination, despite enduring ambiguities about who constitutes the "self" of the nation. Finally, Walzer's view implicitly rest on the notion that "nations" should develop autonomously, without outside influence or intervention, a view that has little historical support. The result is that Walzer has no clear doctrine of intervention or rebellion. He starts with Westphalian sovereignty and explicitly seeks to amend it to make greater room for intervention to protect human rights, but his principles for doing so are inconsistent and unclear.

In the four decades since Walzer first published his work, the literature on just war thinking has exploded. A sizeable literature has emerged critiquing or expanding on Walzer's ideas, especially his notion of the "supreme emergency" that allowed combatants to set aside the normal rules of war. Though I have not dwelt on this aspect of Walzer's work, from the perspective of the Augustinian just war tradition it is easy to see the problem with the "supreme emergency": it is a moral loophole through which any number of otherwise objectionable practices might slip towards justification. Walzer himself uses it to give qualified permission for the Allied obliteration bombing during World War II, nuclear deterrence, and even, in a later essay, possibly terrorism.[108] It is striking that Walzer could see his way to permitting those acts of war while objecting to the more limited and discriminating wars in Vietnam and Iraq, while Ramsey's approach led him to exactly the opposite conclusions. Ramsey's views had stronger safeguards against exceptions and

---

[107] Walzer, *Arguing about War*, 8.   [108] Walzer, *Arguing about War*, 54.

loopholes; but from the same framework, he was more willing to permit actual wars to be fought, even with their messiness and ambiguity.

The Challenge of Peace

After Ramsey and Walzer, another major impetus for the revival of just war debate in the twentieth century came from the US Conference of Catholic Bishops' 1983 pastoral letter, *The Challenge of Peace*. The letter was animated primarily by the bishops' concerns about nuclear weapons and the Cold War, which is mostly outside the scope of this book, though I briefly touch on nuclear deterrence in my case study on North Korea in Chapter 8. Commentary on the letter, and further work based on its arguments, has been a major ongoing conversation in the just war literature.

Much of the debate sparked by the bishops' letter has focused on their claim that the just war tradition contains a "presumption against war." As many critics argued, the Bishops' position amounted to *de facto* pacifism cloaked in just war language. As a historical statement, the bishops' claim about a presumption against war has little foundation, though we can, of course, judge its merits as an ethical norm separately from its intellectual genealogy. I leave this debate aside; for my purposes, I want to note how the bishops' letter draws on past just war thinking but reformulates some of it with the language of liberalism.

Unlike some other twentieth-century just war thinkers, the bishops are comfortable with the language of natural law. "All activities which deliberately conflict with the all-embracing principles of universal natural law, which is permanently binding, are criminal," they write, understandably given their theological commitments and their reliance on Augustine and Aquinas.[109] Also similar to Augustine (and Ramsey), they define peace and justice in terms of each other, though they recognize there are often short-term trade-offs between them. "Peace must be built on the basis of justice in a world where the personal and social consequences of sin are evident," they write. "Justice is always the foundation of peace. [But] in history, efforts to pursue both peace and justice are at times in tension, and the struggle for justice may threaten certain forms of peace."[110] Augustine's influence is also evident in their understanding of war and their rejection of pacifism (even as they express respect for pacifist courage and conviction). "The fact of aggression, oppression and injustice in our world also serves to legitimate the resort to weapons and armed force

---

[109] US National Conference of Catholic Bishops, *Challenge of Peace*, paragraph 70.
[110] US National Conference of Catholic Bishops, *Challenge of Peace*, paragraphs 56, 60.

in defense of justice," they write. "War arose from disordered ambitions, but it could also be used, in some cases at least, to restrain evil and protect the innocent."[111]

But the bishops are not simply replicating the Augustinian tradition. In addition to their reliance on the prior Christian tradition, they also invoke the language of freedom, equality, and human rights drawn from the classical liberal tradition. Even as they use Augustinian language about peace and justice, they defend the ideal of peace, "which is indispensable for true human freedom." They quote Pope John Paul II that, "Unconditional and effective respect for each one's unprescriptable and inalienable rights is the necessary condition in order that peace may reign in a society." They cite the same pope's 1979 address to the UN in which he "articulated the human rights basis of international relations." In some of their most sweeping language, they offer as an ultimate principle of their political theology a defense of human rights: "The obligation for all of humanity to work toward universal respect for human rights and human dignity is a fundamental imperative of the social, economic, and political order."[112]

The bishops fuse their Augustinian and liberal commitments in their description of the global polity humanity inhabits: "The globe is inhabited by a single family in which all have the same basic needs and all have a right to the goods of the earth," they write. "The fundamental premise of world order in Catholic teaching is a theological truth: the unity of the human family rooted in common creation, destined for the kingdom, and united by moral bonds of rights and duties. This basic truth about the unity of the human family pervades the entire teaching on war and peace."[113] Their language echoes that used by Gentili when he writes about the whole world as a single body and a single home for a united humanity, language later echoed by Wolff and Vattel in their description of Europe as a united republic sharing a common customary law – but the bishops marry this language with the liberal notion of fundamental individual rights.

Their concern for human rights carries straight over into their understanding of the just causes for war. They write, "War is permissible only to confront 'a real and certain danger,' i.e., to protect innocent life, to preserve conditions necessary for decent human existence, and to basic human rights," illustrating how theologians who saw themselves as the inheritors of the Augustinian and Thomist mantle in the twentieth

[111] US National Conference of Catholic Bishops, *Challenge of Peace*, paragraphs 78, 81.
[112] US National Conference of Catholic Bishops, *Challenge of Peace*, paragraphs 67, 69, 238, 66.
[113] US National Conference of Catholic Bishops, *Challenge of Peace*, paragraphs 202, 236.

century believed the language of liberalism was the best idiom available to them to express their theological convictions.[114] They seem, briefly, to endorse the principle of a right of revolt. They do not focus on or explicate it, only noting that "Historically, the just-war has been open to a 'just revolution' position, recognizing that an oppressive government may lose its claim to legitimacy."[115] Their liberal commitments lead them to endorse a far-reaching agenda that includes nuclear pacifism, disarmament, multilateralism, qualified support for the United States in the Cold War, support for the UN, anti-poverty programs, and more. In a letter published in 1993, they also endorse humanitarian intervention, echoing their 1983 language about a united human family:

> Geography and political divisions do not alter the fact that we are all one human family, and indifference to the suffering of members of that family is not a moral option ... [S]overeignty and nonintervention into the life of another state have long been sanctioned by Catholic social principles, but have never been seen as absolutes. Therefore, the principles of sovereignty and nonintervention may be overridden by forceful means in exceptional circumstances, notably in the cases of genocide or when whole populations are threatened by aggression or anarchy.[116]

The bishops' letter, then, continued in Ramsey's line of resurrecting and reformulating just war language, adapted to incorporate the classical liberal concepts of liberty and human rights. In doing so they prepared the ground for the explosion of just war scholarship amid the apparent triumph of liberalism in the aftermath of the Cold War.

The Responsibility to Protect

The major focus of the just war literature since the Cold War has been on a set of related issues that include humanitarian intervention, state building, post-conflict operations, and justice after war. These have come to dominate the conversation so thoroughly as to constitute a defining feature of the Liberal tradition. Here I want to focus on the most recent, and most significant, contribution to this debate: the report *The Responsibility to Protect* (R2P). Following the worldwide failure to halt genocide in Rwanda in 1994, the UN and the government of Canada established the Commission on Intervention and State Sovereignty to study when, if ever, intervention is justified. The commission recommended in its 2001 report that the international community intervene to halt large-scale loss

---

[114] US National Conference of Catholic Bishops, *Challenge of Peace*, paragraph 86.
[115] US National Conference of Catholic Bishops, *Challenge of Peace*, paragraph 89.
[116] US National Conference of Catholic Bishops, *Harvest of Justice Is Sown in Peace*, section E.4.

of life and ethnic cleansing (criteria that would be clarified a few years later as applying to genocide, war crimes, crimes against humanity, and ethnic cleansing). The commission rested its argument on the idea that exercising sovereignty entails a "responsibility to protect" the people under one's care; if a state is unable or unwilling to protect its people that responsibility passes to the international community.[117] The international community unanimously endorsed a version of this norm at the 2005 World Summit.[118]

R2P is explicitly rooted in just war thinking. The authors of the original report wrote in *Foreign Affairs* that "on the core issues there is a great deal of common ground, most of it derived from 'just war' theory."[119] Much of their argument is structured within the familiar categories of the just war tradition: just cause, right authority, right intention, last resort, proportional means, and so on. A just cause for intervention is "serious and irreparable harm occurring to human beings, or imminently likely to occur," specifically, "large scale loss of life" or "large scale ethnic cleansing." Right intention is halting or averting human suffering. Right authority is the UN Security Council if possible, although other multilateral bodies or even a unilateral intervention are not ruled out.[120]

Another similarity between R2P and the older just war doctrine is in how the authors seek to limit intervention only to the most extreme cases. Just as the early modern thinkers had limited intervention to stop human sacrifice, piracy, cannibalism, and crimes against nature, R2P has defined four crimes – genocide, war crimes, crimes against humanity, and ethnic cleansing – that are perceived to be so appalling, so abnormal by all states in the current international system as to deprive states of their normal sovereign immunity and territorial inviolability. These are the violations of the law of nature that we recognize today, and their perpetrators are the "wicked" that the international community has agreed to punish. This appears to be a successful resurrection of the older just war doctrine, shorn of its religious particularity, and applied to the contemporary problem of humanitarian catastrophes.

Perhaps most significantly, the idea conveyed in the title of the report – that sovereignty means responsibility, not boundless authority – is deeply consistent with the Augustinian understanding of sovereignty. This points to a fundamental convergence between the Augustinian and

---

[117] International Commission on Intervention and State Sovereignty, *Responsibility to Protect.*
[118] UN General Assembly, Resolution A/RES/60/1.
[119] Evans and Sahnoun, "Responsibility to Protect," 103.
[120] Evans and Sahnoun, "Responsibility to Protect." See also Bellamy, *Responsibility to Protect.*

Liberal traditions that I will expand on in the next chapters. The Augustinians circumscribed sovereignty by norms drawn from Christianity; the Liberals drew from human rights – but the effect is much the same: governments are accountable to a standard outside of themselves and they can lose their legitimacy and thus their claim to statehood if they systematically flout those standards.

The Responsibility to Protect argues that the state is responsible "for the functions of protecting the safety and lives of citizens and promotion of their welfare." It is also responsible in the sense of being accountable "to the citizens internally and to the international community." Finally, saying that sovereignty is responsibility means that "the agents of state are responsible for their actions; that is to say, they are accountable for their acts of commission and omission," which echoes the Nuremberg and Tokyo trials and recent tribunals in Yugoslavia and Rwanda. Drawing on a 1999 speech by UN Secretary General Kofi Annan, the report justifies this way of conceiving of sovereignty by reference to human rights: "The case for thinking of sovereignty in these terms is strengthened by the ever-increasing impact of international human rights norms, and the increasing impact in international discourse of the concept of human security."[121]

However, there are two problems with R2P as described in its inaugural reports. First, while the norm purports to apply narrowly to four specific crimes, those crimes defy easy definition and might in fact capture a very broad array of behavior. A "war crime" could be understood as any act violating any of the laws of war, laws which have grown so numerous and detailed that simply tracking compliance with them is the full-time mission of multiple nongovernmental organizations. Some definitions refer to "excessive brutality in war" or the deliberate targeting of civilians, which begs the question of how to define "excessive brutality" and "civilian" and so forth. "Crimes against humanity" is even more vague, referring to any number of crimes – including murder, rape, and torture – that are perpetrated on a "widespread" or "systematic" scale. And, of course, we lack an agreed scale for judging when a crime has become "systematic" or "widespread." Genocide and ethnic cleansing suffer from similar ambiguity, albeit to a lesser degree. I am not arguing that these crimes lack definition – they have very specific definitions in international law – but that the application of those definitions to real-world scenarios is fraught with more difficulty than is widely appreciated. The reliance of R2P on legal definitions provides a false sense of precision that does not

---

[121] International Commission on Intervention and State Sovereignty, *Responsibility to Protect*, 13. See Annan, "Two Concepts of Sovereignty."

solve the problem of how to limit and define the practice of intervention with any clarity and consistency.

The second difficulty, somewhat counterintuitively considering my first criticism, is that R2P is not broad enough. While the definition of the four crimes at the heart of R2P may be ambiguous, the reliance of R2P on only those four crimes limits intervention only to the extreme cases when those crimes are actually happening, or are clearly about to happen, at which point intervention is extremely difficult, costly, and more likely to fail, and it is equally difficult to pinpoint what "intervention" really requires short of regime change and nation building. In practice, this is functionally useless. The UN Security Council's successful agreement to authorize an intervention in Libya in March 2011, typically cited as evidence that R2P is a useable norm, obscured deeper disagreements: Russia and China did not vote in favor of the resolution but merely abstained, while the broad coalition in favor of the resolution almost immediately collapsed in disagreement over what the resolution actually authorized and whether the outside powers were supposed to protect civilians or overthrow the Libyan government. The UN's subsequent paralysis in the face of a similar situation in Syria illustrated the problem.

R2P is not well-suited to describe whether, how, and when the international community might intervene in response to a broad array of other conditions unrelated to the four R2P crimes but which nonetheless often pose a threat to people in states too weak to protect them. Such scenarios might include cases of extreme privation or famine, mass refugee flows, institutional breakdown, natural disaster, pandemic disease, civil war, or cases in which illicit nonstate groups grew more powerful than the state, such as organized criminal networks, drug traffickers, cyber criminals, pirates, and terrorist organizations. Simply put, R2P fails to grapple with the problem of state failure. One might argue that this is an unfair criticism because the commission did not set out to address such issues. But the commission claimed to establish "when, if ever, it is appropriate for states to take coercive – and in particular military – action, against another state *for the purpose of protecting people at risk* in that other state."[122] It was the commission's decision – arbitrary, in my view – to limit itself to cases in which people are at risk specifically from genocide, ethnic cleansing, war crimes, or crimes against humanity that narrows and weakens R2P as a normative framework. The just war tradition was never so narrow.

On the other hand, the commission rightly included a "responsibility to rebuild" as part of its concept of intervention. If and when an intervention

---

[122] International Commission on Intervention and State Sovereignty, *Responsibility to Protect*, vii (emphasis added).

takes place, in the aftermath "there should be a genuine commitment to helping to build a durable peace, and promoting good governance and sustainable development. Conditions of public safety and order have to be reconstituted by international agents acting in partnership with local authorities." Rebuilding must include security, justice, reconciliation, and development under UN auspices. The report rightly stresses the importance of local ownership of the rebuilding process and cautions against fostering dependency.[123] This parallels the simultaneous emergence of *jus post bellum* in the just war literature, which I address in the next chapter.

The norms of R2P were given an endorsement of sorts at the 2005 World Summit. The summit's outcome document, unanimously approved by the nations of the world, affirmed that each state has a "responsibility to protect its populations from genocide, war crimes, ethnic cleansing, and crimes against humanity." It affirmed that the international community has a responsibility to help states carry out this duty through peaceful means under normal circumstances. But, it added, "should peaceful means be inadequate and national authorities are manifestly failing to protect their populations," the international community has a duty to take "collective action" under chapter VII of the UN charter, the chapter which authorizes the UN and member states to use force against threats to international peace and security.[124] The World Summit document fell short, however, of endorsing the full R2P report and all its implications. The underlying theory of sovereignty – that it entails ultimate responsibility, not merely ultimate autonomy – was thus not fully recognized. It might be considered a matter of *lex ferenda*, what law ought to be, rather than a fully operative measure of international law.

Finally, R2P suffered a fatal setback in 2011. NATO and its member states invoked R2P as their justification for intervening in Libya to prevent its government from massacring civilians in Benghazi. As mentioned above, Russia and China abstained from the UN Security Council vote authorizing the action, thereby avoiding endorsing the R2P justification. NATO and its partners subsequently used the UN authorization not only to halt the Libyan military but to overthrow the Libyan regime, seemingly vindicating Russian and Chinese fears that R2P was a Trojan horse for

---

[123] International Commission on Intervention and State Sovereignty, *Responsibility to Protect*, 39. Patterson rightly criticizes R2P on a number of grounds, including that it does not stress the moral character of political order. However, his criticism that the report does not adequately emphasize the importance of local responsibility for reconstruction misses the mark. See Patterson, *Ending Wars Well*, chapter 7, and compare with International Commission on Intervention and State Sovereignty, *Responsibility to Protect*, 44–45.

[124] UN General Assembly, Resolution A/RES/60/1.

regime change and Western hegemony, effectively killing any possible international consensus around R2P. While individual states might still use the language of R2P, the UN is almost certain to avoid endorsing any further international intervention on the basis of R2P in the foreseeable future.

Conclusion

The emerging Liberal tradition of just war thinking has significant internal variance. Ramsey approached the subject from an explicitly theological perspective but still supported key Liberal tenets, such as democracy, human rights, and the "international common good." In arguing for the "international common good," Ramsey suggested that a just foreign policy, including just war, would aim at defending and building ordered liberty among nations. Ramsey's emphasis on love as the cornerstone of just war meant human life was an absolute value, more important than Westphalian sovereignty. Walzer was more explicit about his liberalism, but he built it on weaker foundations. He sought to amend the Westphalian tradition to allow for intervention for humanitarian purposes, a position he strengthened in later work, but he also maintained a preference for national self-determination without concern for ideology or regime type that was in tension with his commitment to human rights.

Since the end of the Cold War and the emergence of new and unfamiliar security dynamics, scholars have continued to try to adapt and expand just war thinking and apply it to contemporary security challenges. According to one search of published peer-reviewed journal articles in English, there are about 1.6 million on "just war" in the past century; remarkably, fully half of them have been published since 1990. By another measure, we are currently living through the peak of interest in just war scholarship: Google's Ngram viewer, which tracks the frequency of terms in its library of scanned books going back centuries, shows clearly that the term "just war" in English was fallow throughout the eighteenth and nineteenth centuries, picked up in the interwar period, spiked in the 1960s and 1970s following the work of Ramsey, Johnson, and Walzer and the experience of the Vietnam War, and dramatically surged after the Cold War in a movement that is still ongoing.

Two aspects of the contemporary renaissance of just war scholarship limit its usefulness. First, much of it tends to be narrow in scope, focusing on only one new or emergent problem in the contemporary security environment (e.g., nuclear weapons, humanitarian intervention, or terrorism). But the contemporary security environment is best understood not as a set of disconnected, disparate phenomena. There is a close connection between the nature of sovereignty, the right of revolt, and the right of intervention; or, another way of putting it, a close connection between state failure, nonstate actors, humanitarian crises, and intervention. Treating each separately is unnecessarily complex. Just war thinking should respond to the underlying reality – the reality of, and threats to, the ordered liberty within and among nations – more than to its various symptoms.

Second, some contemporary just war thinking is ahistorical in its treatment of the just war tradition. There is a tendency to treat the just war tradition as a set of categories – just cause, right authority, right intention – while overlooking the specific content that past thinkers have argued should fill those categories. The result is that some recent writers, following Walzer's example, virtually reinvent just war thinking from scratch and write at length without any sense of the foundations from which they make their moral judgments and without reference to what Augustine or Vitoria or Suarez argued about just war. I empathize with Johnson's "impatience with contemporary Christian" – and secular, for that matter – "thought on the ethics of war that misunderstands, misuses, or sometimes completely ignores the historical Christian tradition on just war and its placement in theology, moral teaching, and the interrelation between religion and its social context."[125]

The ahistorical approach is problematic on several grounds. It can give readers that are new to the subject an inaccurate understanding of what the just war tradition is. It implicitly asserts that the criteria of just war are whatever the current generation says they are, which is essentially the opposite of what past thinkers argued, considering their commitment to a transcultural and timeless natural law. The ahistorical approach also deprives contemporary thinking of the benefits of insights from past thinkers. And by implicitly acting as if the past had little to say about the present, this view exaggerates the newness and uniqueness of some challenges of the contemporary security environment. In fact, some of the current challenges have ample precedent in past eras and were directly addressed by pre-twentieth-century just war thinkers. I seek to reappropriate the just war traditions and apply them to the contemporary security environment in the next chapters.

---

[125] Johnson, "Thinking Historically about Just War."

6   Augustinian Liberalism

When is war just? What does justice require? The just war traditions have offered a range of answers to these questions over the preceding millennia, yet we have no public consensus on how to answer these questions for our time. The Augustinian tradition in its original form cannot fully answer these questions for us because it was crafted to speak to the world of Christendom. The conditions of modern pluralism and liberal democracy preclude a public consensus around the Augustinian vision – at least, around an unrevised version of it, given Christendom's blurring of lines between church and state. The Westphalian tradition is equally insufficient for different reasons. Its emphasis on noninterference and the sanctity of borders leaves it unable to make a meaningful contribution to debates over some of the key security and humanitarian challenges of our time. Its vision of justice is too thin and it does not give us tools to combat the grave injustices of genocide, state failure, or terrorism that its vision of sovereignty enables. The Liberal tradition has attempted to correct for these problems but has yet to cohere around any central organizing principle in a way that preserves the balance between human rights and national sovereignty. It perhaps came closest through the R2P effort, though that seems to have passed its zenith. In some hands, the Liberal tradition glosses over the meaningfulness of national particularity and becomes a Trojan horse for universalism and liberal imperialism. In Walzerian hands, it lurches too far in the opposite direction, in which national self-determination trumps other claims.

If each of the three traditions is insufficient by themselves, what then? The answer lies in a partial – though not even – synthesis among them. In this chapter and the next I offer a reinterpretation of the just war traditions for today. The next chapter is the heart of the argument, in which I offer my answers to the questions of this book: *When is war just? What does justice require?* Before I can get there, I spend this chapter developing the philosophical foundations on which I base the claims of the next. For the sake of clarity, I will be candid about my own philosophical and theological commitments. As a Christian, I broadly agree with Augustinian cosmology and with Christian and biblical ethical norms, including those about the nature and purpose of government. I was originally drawn to the just war framework because it gave me a theological language with which to think about my experience in war. As an American, I believe democracy and human rights are the closest approximation in this world to a just regime, warts and all (though it remains a far cry from the perfect justice of the City of God). These two sets of beliefs – Christianity and some kind of liberalism – are fundamentally compatible, or at least the versions I hold to are. I describe my preferred version of Christian liberalism in this chapter.

I am skeptical of the hard claims of Westphalian sovereignty, though I recognize it was responding to a genuine need. While I endorse most of the Augustinian tradition, the political theology of Christendom, seeking to establish a close partnership between church and state, was fatally flawed for theological as much as for practical reasons. Johnson rightly notes that "the conception of sovereignty as responsibility for the common good was employed to justify internecine war over contrary religion in Europe and the destruction of indigenous cultures and civilizations in the New World."[1] We cannot and should not go back to an unrevised Augustinian vision.

But the secular response from Hobbes and Pufendorf – creating the Westphalian state, exiling moral claims from statecraft, setting the table for realism, and paving the way for absolutism and nationalism – clearly has problems of its own and, more importantly, was not the only possible path out of Christendom. Liberal institutions and ideas were another possibility, including liberal ideas arrived at by a few Christian thinkers, such as John Milton, Roger Williams, and John Smith, before John Locke. I am interested in this blend of Christian and liberal principles, which I will define and defend in this chapter as *Augustinian Liberalism.* The synthesis I argue for is mostly between the Augustinian and Liberal traditions, with a few nods in the direction of some Westphalian principles.

I am especially drawn to natural law and human rights because they provide a language with which to make moral claims about the common good across the boundaries of culture and religion. This language has the greatest chance of overcoming the postmodernist challenge in contemporary public discourse and winning the widest agreement possible in a diverse, pluralistic polity. Ordered liberty is as close to a universal value system as the world has yet seen. In the Augustinian Liberal perspective,

[1] Johnson, *Sovereignty*, 155.

the principles of ordered liberty, human rights, and human flourishing do much the same work that natural law and justice did for the Augustinian tradition as an external standard above the state, to which the state must be accountable. Justice requires the vindication of rights but is not exhausted with rights because, for rights to be meaningful, we must also sustain the conditions required to promote human flourishing – which is a long way of saying that justice requires ordered liberty. Sovereignty means responsibility for the common good, which means responsibility for establishing, sustaining, and defending a system of ordered liberty at home and abroad.

What Is Augustinian Liberalism?

Terms like "liberalism" and the "liberal international order" are contested. Using them in sweeping statements as I do in this chapter – claiming that liberalism is just and the defense of the liberal order is a just cause – is sure to get me in trouble because it is easy to impute vast, diverse, and contradictory meanings to them, most of which I do not intend. If possible, I would avoid the word altogether and use instead the phrase *ordered liberty*. Alas, the label is inescapable, and so this is as good a place as any to define my terms – and here I should acknowledge that I have written my books out of order. My argument about just war would be clearer if I had already written the book that I intend to write about liberalism, specifically defining and defending one kind of liberalism against other versions of it. For now, I will note in brief that I am most in sympathy with the kind of liberalism Reinhold Niebuhr defended in *The Children of Light and the Children of Darkness* and that I call "Augustinian Liberalism."[2] Importantly, Niebuhr defended liberal institutions even as he critiqued the conventional Lockean, Kantian, or Enlightenment justifications for them because of their naivete and utopianism.[3] Augustinian Liberalism believes in liberal institutions for Augustinian reasons.

---

[2] See also Leeman, "Not a Augustinian Liberal"; Miller, "Augustine of Hippo" and "Augustinian Liberalism"; Owen, "Retrieving Christian Liberalism"; Walker, "Eschatology and the Defects of Liberalism."

[3] The distinction I am drawing has some similarities to that between republican and liberal paradigms in Onuf, "Normative Frameworks for Humanitarian Intervention," in Lang, *Just Intervention*. For just war arguments rooted in something like Kantian or Lockean liberalism see Frost, "Ethics of Humanitarian Intervention"; Luban, "Just War and Human Rights"; Nardin, "Moral Basis for Humanitarian Intervention." None explicitly invoke Locke and only Nardin appeals to Kant, but their arguments are premised on an Enlightenment version of liberalism. This is especially interesting in Nardin's case considering that he prefaces his argument with a history of the Augustinian tradition.

Every kind of liberalism, as I understand it, begins with the belief that human beings possess equal and inherent dignity and moral worth. Crucially, our moral worth resides in our essential humanity – which we share equally with everyone else. No one of us is inherently superior by virtue of birth, lineage, rank, wealth, or any other attribute so as to merit special treatment by the government or special access to power. If none of us merits political power by virtue of our birth, then we all deserve an equal say in how we are governed. Unless we live in a city-state small enough for participatory, direct democracy, this situation leads us to collectively entrust power to a subset of people who govern on our behalf. And so we arrive at some form of representative rule, accountable governance, and majoritarian decision-making under law – law to which governors and governed are equally subject. At the same time, since even those in the minority are equal under law, there are limits to what the majority can do to them. And so we also arrive at a concept of inviolable and individual rights that fundamentally limit the state's jurisdiction. These basic starting points are what distinguishes liberalism from monarchy, aristocracy, oligarchy, dictatorship, theocracy, and other forms of hierarchical, illiberal government. If you believe in human equality and its political consequences, you end up supporting some notion of an open society and human liberty. We might call this the lowest common denominator of liberalism. Liberalism is a system of *ordered liberty* – not the unrestricted liberty of anarchism nor the total order of tyranny but the median between the two.

To this positive case for human liberty, we should add the negative case against concentrations of power because of human fallibility, a longstanding feature of liberal thought that leads to checks and balances within government to keep it within its proper sphere. This brings us to the distinctively Augustinian version of liberalism. Augustine understood the impossibility of achieving true justice in this world and, thus, the need to temper our aspirations for the state. "Every human society from the family to the empire is never free from slights, suspicions, quarrels, and war, and 'peace' is not true peace but a doubtful interlude between conflicts," according to Deane's interpretation of Augustine.[4] Or in Augustine's own words, "True justice, however, does not exist other than in the commonwealth whose Founder and Ruler is Christ."[5] True peace and true justice are not possible in the earthly City of Man.

This is why Augustinian liberalism is, at heart, a constrained vision of political and society life *par excellence*. Augustinian liberalism does not

---

[4] Deane, *Political and Social Ideas of St. Augustine*, 62.
[5] Augustine, *City of God*, II.21, 78.

pretend we are able to definitively solve social and political problems, eradicate evil, eliminate all poverty, or enable flourishing for every person. Augustinian politics is the comparatively humbler task of adjudicating disputes peacefully, allocating power in a roughly fair way, enforcing agreed-upon rules, and upholding the best approximation of justice we can expect in this world. We will never, through political action, build the Kingdom of Heaven, achieve the perfected American ideal, or revive the fabled organic *polis* of antiquity. As Deane says, "Rebirth and salvation come through Christ and the Church that He established, and not through the activities or instrumentalities of the state."[6] Augustinian liberalism is not merely anti-utopian. It is anti-utopianism: it is principled opposition to utopian politics. All illiberal movements are utopian because of the boundless faith they invest in some leader or group of leaders.

We strongly need Augustine's dose of political humility and anti-utopianism. One way of understanding illiberal movements is that they stem from Romantic-era nostalgia for the city-states of ancient Greece, an arrangement in which city, state, community, and church were essentially merged. They yearn for an organic, whole polity in which citizens share a common heritage and a common sense of loyalty and the state instills virtue into its model citizens. Augustine recognized that this is impossible because of the realities of sin. "The Christian view that the principal function of the state is the repression and punishment of the wicked is at the opposite pole from the classical, and especially the Greek, conception that the purpose of the state is to promote the good life and to train and educate its citizens so that they become good and virtuous men," as Deane argues.[7]

Augustine made the distinction between the two sharp and clear. In Deane's interpretation, the Greek (and, later, the Enlightenment) view that the state "was the highest and noblest form of human association, which existed to make possible the good life for its citizens and to form and educate them so that they might become truly human, that is, good and virtuous men who had realized their fullest potentialities," was wrong.[8] Of course, Augustine kept some of the classical idealism: he simply transferred it from the state to the church – or, more accurately, to the City of God. "In that city alone can men realize the noble aims proclaimed by the philosophers of Greece and Rome – complete and unbroken peace, perfect concord and harmony, true self-realization,

---

[6] Deane, *Political and Social Ideas of St. Augustine*, 8.
[7] Deane, *Political and Social Ideas of St. Augustine*, 7.
[8] Deane, *Political and Social Ideas of St. Augustine*, 11.

and perpetual happiness," according to Deane.[9] That is the vision and purpose of the City of God and the church, not the City of Man and its government.

Deane argues that the Augustinian state "does not seek to make men truly good or virtuous. Rather, it is interested in their outward actions."[10] Government "does not change, and does not attempt to change, the basic desires and attitudes of the men whose conduct it seeks to regulate."[11] These lowered ambitions make sense because the rulers are themselves sinners and could not be trusted to rule in the name of virtue. The state with lower ambitions "does not *require* good and just men as its legislators, judges, jailers, or executioners."[12]

This is the version of liberalism that I want to defend as the rightful aim of the state, the just purpose of statecraft, and the legitimate goal of a just war. It is a pared down, humbler, and more achievable liberalism than some others in currency today, and thus evades accusations of imperialism and utopianism. In particular I am very keen to differentiate Augustinian Liberalism from both progressivism and nationalism (including Christian nationalism), both of which indeed are utopian and, when manifested in foreign policy, quasi-imperialistic. Nationalism is far more consonant with realism than with liberalism because it privileges the state and elevates national interests and national power as ultimate principles (and that is true whether or not the particular nationalism in question cloaks itself in Christian rhetoric), and can lead to the conventional imperialism that rests on assertions of racial, national, or cultural superiority. On the other side, some progressives advocate for a thicker version of liberalism and the liberal international order that comes close to denying the legitimacy of national sovereignty and national borders and that makes sweeping assertions about the moral authority of the UN and other institutions of global governance. This leads to a different kind of imperialism, a sort of imperial nanny made up of intergovernmental institutions and international law.

The distinction I am drawing is similar to the split between "pluralist" and "solidarist" views of international society, as defined by Hedley Bull. In the solidarist perspective, states can achieve a large degree of solidarity around human rights, international law, and notions of justice, derived from an overarching natural law – similar to the progressive internationalist viewpoint I warned against above. In the pluralist viewpoint – roughly parallel to a nationalist viewpoint – states lack the ability or inclination to achieve that consensus and international law is

[9] Deane, *Political and Social Ideas of St. Augustine*, 11.
[10] Deane, *Political and Social Ideas of St. Augustine*, 117.
[11] Deane, *Political and Social Ideas of St. Augustine*, 140.
[12] Deane, *Political and Social Ideas of St. Augustine*, 142 (emphasis in original).

comparatively thinner or small in scope.[13] Bull leaned towards the pluralist viewpoint but tried to split the difference, acknowledging the virtues of both perspectives. As I understand the two viewpoints, unrestricted solidarism would lead to progressive internationalism and liberal imperialism; unrestricted pluralism would lead to nationalism and realism. Bull's effort to split the difference is intuitively attractive. The viewpoint I advocate is what I called in my previous book "conservative internationalism."[14] It is unapologetically internationalist, and thus a thicker vision of international society than a mere pluralist or nationalist vision; however, it is *conservative* internationalism, founded on pessimistic Augustinian liberalism, not the optimistic Enlightenment kind, and thus it is a thinner, more tempered internationalism than the unalloyed solidarist perspective. Augustinian Liberalism leaves states as the primary actors responsible for the common good without fetishizing international borders or the moral authority of the state. This aspect of my argument is important because it guards against accusations of liberal imperialism and keeps faith with principles of subsidiarity, federalism, and localism.

Augustinian Liberalism on Natural Law, Liberty, and Sovereignty

How does Augustinian Liberalism view the nature, purpose, and responsibilities of statehood? I want to begin by noting an overlooked relationship between the just war traditions and classical liberalism. From the foregoing survey of the intellectual history of just war thinking, it should be apparent that the Augustinian just war tradition prefigured the rise of liberalism in important respects, and the Liberal tradition has an obvious connection with it. The late Augustinian just war tradition took its mature shape in the sixteenth century in explicit opposition to the "holy war" theories that had wide circulation during the Wars of Religion (as did the Westphalian tradition, for that matter).[15] Similarly, the Liberal tradition took shape in part to rebut what amounts to the holy war claims of fascist, communist, and jihadist political religions. In other words, just war thinkers of all stripes argued that the state may not coerce in matters of

---

[13] Bull, "Grotian Conception of International Society."
[14] Miller, *American Power and Liberal Order.*
[15] See Johnson's discussion in chapter 2 of *Ideology, Reason and the Limitation of War.* He argues that the holy war doctrine was a version of just war thinking, albeit one that fundamentally changed the tradition's emphasis by allowing, rather than forbidding, war for religion and for church. Here I simply note that the version of the just war tradition that we appropriate for our purposes today is the "modern" just war tradition that decisively rejected the holy war arguments.

Table 6.1 *Mapping just war traditions and their views*

	Augustinian tradition	Westphalian tradition	Liberal tradition	Augustinian Liberalism
Ideological alignment	Christendom	Nationalism	Enlightenment liberalism, progressivism	Augustinian Liberalism
Purpose of sovereignty	The common good	Autonomy, defense of borders, mutual non interference	Protection of rights	Ordered liberty
View of balance between universal and particular	Religious universalism	Particularism	Cosmopolitanism	Subsidiarity
View of international society	Solidarity around Christian principles and natural law	Pluralist perspective	Solidarist perspective	Solidarity around principles of ordered liberty, with allowance for pluralism
Foreign policy guiding framework		Realism	Liberal internationalism	Conservative internationalism

belief abroad. When applied domestically, the same argument is a cornerstone of liberal thought and liberal institutions. Another way of putting it: there is a limitation to the state's jurisdiction; there are things the state may not do. Just war is precisely the field of inquiry about the state's rightful authority regarding the use of its most distinctive instrument, that of lethal force. It asks what the state's responsibilities, rights, privileges, and obligations are, questions that imply there are meaningful answers. It is meaningful to ask about what the state may and may not do; both just war and classical liberalism presume some notion of *limited* or *accountable sovereignty* to make room for some degree of liberty. The Augustinian tradition predated liberalism with this insight, stemming from debates over the Reformation a century and a half before Locke's *Essay Concerning Toleration.*

Just war was never an isolated exercise in military ethics; it is an argument about political theory and political theology, about the rights and purposes of the state, about natural law, and about justice. It is a body of political theory opposed to theocracy, universal empire, and unlimited sovereignty because (in the Augustinian version) it argues that such ambitions violate the state's God-given jurisdiction and are utopian, inconsistent with humanity's sinful nature, and doomed to achieve the opposite of the justice it professes. The state is commissioned for a specified purpose; sovereignty is not a plenary grant of power to do whatever the prince wants to do. The state's authority has limits. In the Augustinian tradition, those limits come from natural law, obligations to which supersede the state itself; in the Liberal tradition, those limits come from human rights and the consent of the governed. In both cases, just war thinkers argued that the purpose of the state is to provide for something higher than the state itself, whether understood as the security of the body politic, the common good, the *tranquilitas ordinis*, human rights, the conditions of human flourishing, or the conditions of a just and lasting peace. These ideas were the measure of justice and, subsequently, of the legitimacy of states. The standard of justice judged the state; the state did not define justice – not, at least, until the Westphalian tradition and, even more so, when just war as a whole gave way to the stark realism of the "long nineteenth century." As Johnson has argued, "Modern liberal democratic states … have managed to hold on to the core values of the older conception of sovereignty as responsibility for the common good: that good rule means concern for others, namely, the people governed, rather than oneself."[16]

That is how the Augustinian just war tradition (and, partially, the Westphalian as well) anticipated some of the arguments which classical liberal thinkers would use. (In a few cases, including Grotius and Pufendorf, there was direct overlap insofar as they relied on the notion of the social contract for their understanding of sovereignty.) The same body of political theory – the political theory of secularized Christendom – is implicit in both the just war traditions and in classical liberalism. Even the Westphalian tradition reflected this same intent to prevent universal empire or theocratic totalism, albeit only in relations between states, not within them. The key flaw of the Westphalian tradition is that it has no response to the tyrant who scrupulously adheres to jurisdictional limitations on the international stage while violating them at home.

Classical liberalism is an improvement over Westphalian realism because it is more consistent about what governments may do at home and abroad. Liberalism argues that there are limits on the state's jurisdiction; sovereignty is not unlimited; there should be no coercion in matters of belief; and universal empire and ideological totalism are dangerous,

---

[16] Johnson, *Sovereignty*, 112.

illegitimate ambitions. Classical liberalism even described the source of these rules in similar terms as the just war traditions had, as coming from the "self-evident" truths about human nature and human rights that derive from the inherent dignity of human beings. In this respect, human rights claims are a contemporary appeal to natural law (though few explicitly use the idiom of natural law) and they play a similar role in the just war discourse as an ultimate justifying principle. "If there is no natural moral law or basic moral reality, then the now widely popular rhetoric of universal human rights is just that: rhetoric," as Biggar rightly argues.[17] Both classical liberal rights and the just war traditions teach the universal equality and dignity of all humankind. For example, if Spain could not conquer the Indians because of the latter's moral equality, then by the same logic no sovereign could conquer another, use force in matters of belief at home or abroad, or try to impose a universal dominion on nonconsenting peoples.

Rengger makes a similar point about the relationship between liberalism and just war from a different direction. Just war "is a tradition that emphasizes reflection on moral and political purposes and choices," he argues. "Inasmuch as it does this, it is closer in fact to liberal thinking on politics than often appears to be the case. The just war tradition emphasizes choice; the freedom, indeed, even perhaps the requirement, to make choices for ourselves about moral and political issues."[18] While I would not emphasize choice as the point of similarity between the two, I concur with the conclusion. Rengger also astutely observes that without a standard external to the state, such as natural law, just war thinking will "take on the moral coloring (as it were) of the institutions that provide legitimacy in its given context," namely, "the state and the conception of politics dominant in the state."[19] Just war deteriorates into Westphalian statism and realism without an anchor, such as natural law or liberal norms, to preserve its integrity.

The kinship between just war and classical liberalism is interesting for the intellectual historian, but is it relevant for our purposes? I believe it is. I argue that if we are to be faithful to the political theology of the just war traditions (at least, to the Augustinian and Liberal versions and to the Westphalian tradition's concern to prevent universal empire), we should by the same logic be faithful to the political theology of classical liberalism. Similar principles animate both. Just war is, by definition, opposition to universal empire, theocracy, and ideological totalism – and so is classical liberalism. If it is a just cause to oppose universal empire, we might as

[17] Biggar, *In Defence of War*, 160.   [18] Rengger, "On the Just War Tradition," 363.
[19] Rengger, *Just War and International Order*, 92.

well say it is a just cause to defend liberalism. It is just to defend a system or a set of institutions designed to prevent universal empire, guard against theocracy or ideological totalism of any kind, and safeguard limits on a government's jurisdiction. These ideas were behind the just war traditions' arguments against wars for religion; today they are manifest in the institutions of ordered liberty at home and abroad.

This claim rests ultimately on the Augustinian Liberal perspective on justice, order, and liberty, which are closely connected concepts. I am drawing on the Augustinian idea that peace and justice are conditions of each other, neither can be fully achieved without the other, and justice is to provide for the common good of all. I add to it the liberal idea that ordered liberty is the essential precondition for the common good of all. Thus, to *do justice* is to uphold a framework of ordered liberty that enables the equal flourishing of all. That framework requires both order and liberty: flourishing is not possible under a regime of total order, such as autocracy or totalitarianism, because it lacks any semblance of justice or liberty. It is equally impossible, and equally unjust, under a regime of total liberty, such as anarchy or state failure, which is not true freedom because it lacks the order that enables human community. Sovereignty, taken to mean responsibility for the common good, thus means responsibility for establishing, sustaining, and defending a system of ordered liberty at home and abroad. Put another way: if the ancients spoke of peace, justice, and order as the preeminent virtues of public life, I would add liberty to the list. Ordered liberty is the rightful purpose of statecraft, the just aim of the state – which means it is also the just purpose of warfare.[20]

A critic may respond that the Augustinian tradition took shape during the era of Christendom and did not correspond to the rise of classical liberalism. The latter developed after the Augustinian just war tradition had been succeeded by the Westphalian tradition. Classical liberalism was, historically, accompanied by Westphalian sovereignty, while the Augustinian tradition was more closely associated with preliberal regimes of the medieval era. As a matter of chronology, this is indisputable – but it is beside the point. I am not arguing that just war thinking *caused* liberalism (I do suspect there may be a stronger connection than is widely recognized, but it is beyond the scope of this book to establish that claim). For the purposes of this argument, I am merely noting a family resemblance, a similarity of worldviews, a shared set of concepts. Although Westphalian sovereignty developed in parallel with classical liberalism, they are a poor fit for each other. Liberalism makes universal

---

[20] I recognize the claims in this paragraph need much greater exposition and defense. These ideas are essentially the abstract of the book I hope to write on Augustinian Liberalism.

claims about human dignity, freedom, equality, and political legitimacy without respect to borders that stand in tension with the statism and sacrosanct international borders of Westphalia. Though Westphalian thinkers claimed the state was to govern a community of common values, in practice it led more naturally to the absolutist regimes of the seventeenth and eighteenth centuries and the nationalist movements of the nineteenth and twentieth centuries than to liberal democracy. The rise of the liberal international order, and the rise of the Liberal tradition of just war thinking, are the long-gestating but logical consequences of the rise of classical liberalism in the eighteenth century.

Liberalism is the contemporary idiom in which very old arguments based on natural law present themselves; appeals to "self-evident truths," "human dignity," and "human flourishing" are appeals to a universal, natural, transcultural standard of justice. (Terry Nardin similarly invokes the idea of a "common morality" among all humans based on the Kantian notion of respect for all individuals and their ability to think and choose.)[21] In the same way, liberalism is the contemporary ideology in which the insights of just war have been institutionalized. The Augustinian and Liberal just war traditions and classical liberalism are cut from the same cloth, siblings born of the same mother, secularized offshoots of Christendom. That is why just war has fit so well as the war doctrine of the liberal state. Just war explains and justifies the use of lethal force in terms that are consistent with, and bolster, the liberal state's claims about itself.

Johnson argued that natural law was of limited use today because "for such appeals to gain general assent, there must be a common value-consciousness in all those persons for whom the argument from nature is intended to speak."[22] But liberalism now effectively serves as a "common value-consciousness" among much of the world, as aspirational documents such as the Universal Declaration on Human Rights illustrate. Of course, we lack unanimity on these principles, much more so on their application, but their extraordinary success around the world has made them the default ordering principles of the public square and, consequently, they can order our judgments about war and peace as well.

Just War and the Liberal International Order

With all the definitions and caveats in mind, I can state my main argument more concisely. If it is just to defend a system of ordered liberty, it is

---

[21] Nardin, "Moral Basis for Humanitarian Intervention."
[22] Johnson, *Just War Tradition and the Restraint of War*, 111.

also just to defend ordered liberty among nations.[23] The arrangement of institutions and relationships that comprise ordered liberty among nations today is what we call the liberal international order, the maintenance of which is a rightful goal of statecraft and the defense of which is a just cause. The liberal international order is a culture of ordered liberty among the states of the world; it is world order defined and shaped by the ideas, habits, and institutions of liberalism. As I argued in *American Power and Liberal Order*, liberal order emerges from, and reinforces, a community of sovereign and independent liberal democracies dedicated to the rule of law and civil liberties at home and nonaggression and territorial inviolability abroad (with limited exceptions for humanitarian intervention). Economically, liberal order is a system of regulated capitalism, relatively free trade and low trade barriers, freedom of the seas, neutral rights, the sanctity of contract, and peaceful, rule-based dispute adjudication. Institutionally, liberal order favors intergovernmental cooperation on issues of global concern, especially cooperative security among liberal states (such as through NATO). While imperfect, the liberal international order is largely responsible for an extraordinary flourishing of peace and prosperity around the world in the twentieth and twenty-first centuries.

The liberal order is certainly flawed, and I do not mean to gloss over those errors or treat the liberal order as the perfect embodiment of justice. (And I do not mean that any violation of any liberal principle justifies war in response, as I describe in the next chapter.) Augustine wisely kept a firm distinction between the City of God and earthly approximations of justice. There is an important distinction between abstract principles (ordered liberty) and their necessarily flawed embodiment in history (liberal democracy and the liberal international order). For example, I concur with Ramsey's attitude towards international law. Insofar as it reflects exclusively Westphalian notions of justice and sovereignty, it can sometimes be more of an impediment than a servant of (Augustinian and Liberal) justice and human flourishing. If it were possible to make the argument without unnecessary hairsplitting, I would argue for the justice of *a* liberal international order, rather than the actually existing order, to emphasize that I am more interested in the principles of order and liberty among nations than the world order founded after World War II. But concision has its merits and pedantry has none, so I will reluctantly speak

---

[23] I prefer "ordered liberty" to Luban's emphasis on "socially basic human rights." Though I think human rights exist and are an important part of a system of rightly ordered liberty, I do not think they exhaust the meaning of ordered liberty. Luban's formulation, in particular, invokes social contract theory, which I do not think is a helpful way to think about the legitimacy of states. See Luban, "Just War and Human Rights."

of *the* order, though I still want to stress the principled argument (my last book was concerned with how to revise and adapt the liberal order to make it more effective and more just). Just as the Augustinians argued that the achievement of the *tranquilitas ordinis* was the animating purpose of the state and the purpose of any just war, and just as the Westphalians argued that the preservation of the balance of power was necessary for international peace and the liberty of each sovereign state, so I argue that sustaining a system of ordered liberty between and among nations is essential for securing a just and lasting peace in our age.

In my previous book I argued that the United States can and should uphold the liberal international order because it is pragmatic grand strategy: liberal order is the outer perimeter of American security (and the security of liberal states around the world).[24] Here I argue that statesmen can and should uphold (and revise) the liberal international order because it is just. We can draw elements from all just war traditions to support this idea. Augustinian and Liberal support for the liberal international order is easiest to see on the issue of humanitarian intervention. The Augustinians and Liberals were remarkably candid and explicit in their endorsement of interventions to suppress and punish crimes against nature, reflected ultimately in the twentieth and twenty-first centuries in moves to recognize a category of crimes – including genocide, ethnic cleansing, and war crimes – so heinous that they required international action. This has developed into a pillar of the liberal international order, one clearly supported by the Augustinian and Liberal approaches to just war.

But that does not exhaust the ways in which we can draw upon the Augustinian tradition: humanitarian intervention was just a single application of a broader argument about the ethical duties of sovereignty. The liberal international order is the best available institutional mechanism today for securing something like the tranquility of order. In other words, the liberal international order is a political tool for a just and lasting peace among nations and for human flourishing. We love our neighbors politically when we support ordered liberty at home and abroad. As Johnson summarizes:

I think it is suggestive that historical just war tradition does not speak of *self-defense* in this way [i.e., as mere territorial defense] but of *defense of the common good*, implying a moral decision as to what constitutes that common good. This concept is also one that includes not only defense of one's own community's good but also that of the larger community of responsible societies . . . . Thus thinking of defense of the common good as a just cause for resort to armed force returns us to

---

[24] Miller, *American Power and Liberal Order.*

the conception of sovereign authority as an exercise of responsibility to establish a good society and the conditions within which such societies can flourish.[25]

Patterson concurs: "'Self-defense' is not the only sufficient criteria for considering employing the military instrument. The victory of tyranny, the enslavement of human beings, torture, the systematic incarceration and extra-judicial killing of people based on race or creed ... these are horrors worth fighting against."[26] I take Oliver O'Donovan to be saying something roughly similar when he describes war as "a provisional witness to the unity of God's rule in the face of the antagonistic praxis of *duellum*," that works "in service of international justice, rather than in national self-defense or self-aggrandizement."[27] War is an act of judgment; judgment depends on a criterion of justice; the criterion of justice comes from outside the state and stands above the state; justice then stands in judgment over both combatants, the criminal aggressor and the one who acts as the agent of judgment; and justice demands, not mere victory by the latter, but restoration of the former to a common life of ordered peace together. The point of commonality between the Augustinian and the Liberal traditions is the belief that there is something above the state to which the state must be accountable. We justly fight against violent disorder and injustice; we fight for the norms, institutions, and rules of ordered liberty.

This argument amounts to a rejection of the most distinctive part of the Westphalian tradition: absolute territorial autonomy, inviolable borders, and mutual noninterference with no exceptions, which also entails a rejection of some parts of contemporary international law. However, we can still draw on some elements of the Westphalian tradition, albeit with a different emphasis. The Westphalians were right that the balance of power is necessary to preserve the freedom and independence of states, which is rightly seen as a just cause. The Westphalians erred by stressing too much the defense of the state and its territory regardless of the character of the regime or the causes the state might pursue. For them, the defense of the state elided into the security of the state, which in turn evolved into the power of the state under the guise that power was necessary for security. In that way the Westphalian tradition gave birth in the eighteenth and nineteenth centuries to the doctrine that states should pursue power for its own sake: just war turned into realism, just cause into *raison d'état*.

But the Westphalian doctrine has some truth to it. Power is the *sine qua non* of politics; political power does indeed often flow from the barrel of

---

[25] Johnson, *Ethics and the Use of Force*, 93 (emphasis in original).
[26] Patterson, *Just War Thinking*, 106.   [27] O'Donovan, *Just War Revisited*, 7.

a gun; and the justice of just wars can only be achieved by very large and well-aimed guns. Power is an essential tool for any state to achieve any purpose, just or unjust. Ramsey was right that power is the *esse* of politics. If a state is just in defending itself, it is just to use power for that end. If liberal states are to pursue just ends, such as constructing a liberal international order, they must use power. When the Westphalians insisted on the *justice* of the balance of power, they were saying something quite proper, or at least something that we can put to proper use. If certain tools are required to achieve a just end, the use of those tools is just, and maintaining the sharpness and viability of those tools is just. When liberal states are opposed by large and powerful illiberal states, as the United States and its allies face opposition from Russia and China today, they must seek a favorable balance of power to protect their independence and sovereignty – and to protect the liberal international order they have constructed. Liberal order does not exist by fiat, good intentions, or institutions; it exists because powerful states have liberal ideals and liberal ideals are backed by powerful states. If we recognize the justice of the liberal international order, we must also recognize the justice of the balance of power necessary to bring it about and defend it. In *American Power and Liberal Order,* I argued that the United States should use two different approaches to two different types of states: it should invest in democratic peace between democratic nations and it should maintain a favorable balance of power against rival autocratic states. I conceived of democratic peace and the balance of power as complementary mechanisms or tools for upholding the liberal international order (and thus American security): the first to deepen it among its member states and the second to protect it against its rivals and enemies.

In the same way, we can conceive of the Augustinian doctrine of loving our neighbors politically by upholding the ethical obligations of sovereignty as one tool; the Westphalian doctrine of preserving the independence of nations through the balance of power is another. They work together to accomplish the same goal: the tranquility of order. The Westphalians would not have said it that way, of course. They would stress the equality and independence of states, but that was what they (mistakenly) thought justice and peace meant. Today, statesmen seeking to use power for just ends will defend ordered liberty among nations. That means they will defend the liberal international order as the best available institutional mechanism for securing the tranquility of order; they will also defend that order by seeking and preserving a balance of power favorable to liberalism.

There are, of course, tensions and conflicts between the Augustinian and Westphalian traditions, especially around the issue of humanitarian

intervention and international law. I do not claim that these traditions
dovetail seamlessly or that they were really saying the same thing all
along; they quite clearly were not. Rather, I am selecting the parts of
their arguments that seem to fit together best and, more importantly,
speak to the needs of our day. We can appropriate the best of their
insights and reformulate just war for the needs of the twenty-first century. In this way, we stay true to the broader community of discourse
that defines just war thinking while applying its insights to new and
evolving challenges.

Some examples from contemporary statesmen help illustrate what I am
getting at. British Prime Minister Tony Blair formulated what he called
the "doctrine of the international community" in 1999. "Now our actions
are guided by a more subtle blend of mutual self interest and moral
purpose in defending the values we cherish," he said. "In the end values
and interests merge. If we can establish and spread the values of liberty,
the rule of law, human rights and an open society then that is in our
national interests too. The spread of our values makes us safer."[28] Blair
was conflating liberalism, national interest, and justice: it was in the
British interest to invest in the liberal order, and it was also just to do
so. This is a precise echo of Ramsey's call for statesmen to align the
national interest with the international common good.

President Barack Obama was getting at something similar in his Nobel
lecture a decade later: "For peace is not merely the absence of visible
conflict. Only a just peace based on the inherent rights and dignity of
every individual can truly be lasting ... peace is unstable where citizens
are denied the right to speak freely or worship as they please; choose their
own leaders or assemble without fear."[29] A just peace is defined as one
that protects liberal rights, and only this is a stable peace. In this vision,
justice, stability, peace, human rights, national interest, and international
comity go together. Despite much criticism, President George W. Bush
said essentially the same thing in his second inaugural address: "The
survival of liberty in our land increasingly depends on the success of
liberty in other lands. The best hope for peace in our world is the expansion of freedom in all the world. America's vital interests and our deepest
beliefs are now one."[30]

The liberal international order is a corporate self whose defense is just,
and we can and should use the available mechanisms – institutions,
political stratagems, instruments of statecraft, and military force – to
defend it. The Westphalians focused on one particular stratagem that

---

[28] Blair, "Doctrine of the International Community."   [29] Obama, "Nobel Lecture."
[30] Bush, "Second Inaugural Address."

was new to them: the balance of power. They were right; but they were wrong to see it as an end in itself or as the only or most important stratagem. Among the other stratagems or mechanisms are democratic peace, intergovernmental institutions, and the practice of cooperative security. While liberal states must rely on the balance of power in their relations with illiberal rivals, they can and should rely on cooperative security and reciprocal trust among themselves. In effect, liberal order actually accomplishes among democracies what Wolff and Vattel believed the balance of power would accomplish everywhere.

The idea of the self-defense of the liberal international order is admittedly expansive. But the contemporary security environment justifies such an interpretation. States have grown more interdependent thanks to technology, globalization, and a deep network of international institutions from which they benefit and to which most have voluntarily subscribed. This interdependence means that it is easier for a threat against one to translate into a threat against all; some threats are truly global because there is an international order that can be threatened. The terrorist attacks on 9/11 killed citizens of seventy-seven nations, including twenty-eight South Koreans, forty-one Indians, and forty-seven citizens of the Dominican Republic. This interconnectedness is why much of the world has gravitated towards a "cooperative security system, in which states identify positively with one another so that the security of each is perceived as the responsibility of all. This is not self-help in any interesting sense, since the 'self' in terms of which interests are defined is the community; national interests are international interests" according to Alexander Wendt.[31] Or, as Blair said in in his 1999 speech, "we are mutually dependent, [and] national interest is to a significant extent governed by international collaboration."[32]

These realities justify a new application of just war thinking, one that recognizes collective self-defense of the liberal order against transnational threats. Threats to the liberal international order – terrorism, piracy, territorial aggression, or proliferation of weapons of mass destruction – are threats to the states that benefit from that order. Ramsey, Niebuhr, and others rightly recognized that the United States has a special duty in this context. American policymakers have long recognized that because the United States is the leading power, architect, and beneficiary of the liberal international order, America has a unique responsibility to organize international efforts to sustain it. America's duty is not due to a special

---

[31] Wendt, "Anarchy Is What States Makes of It."
[32] Blair, "Doctrine of the International Community."

moral status, which it does not have, but because of its unique magnitude of power. This also means the use of American power requires special scrutiny, much as Cicero and Augustine scrutinized Roman power and held it up for critique precisely because of its potential to achieve a unique degree of good in the world.

7   Just War and Ordered Liberty

In this chapter I draw from the history of the just war traditions and offer a reinterpretation for thinking about contemporary security challenges. In doing so I am trying to respond to the challenge with which Johnson concludes his seminal 1975 work. Johnson argues that the effort to limit war had, by the nineteenth century, become an effort to create a "non-ideological" basis for just war. Such efforts aimed to "exclude the possibility of an ideological just cause," that is, to disallow causes rooted in "particularist ideology," such as war for religion. This "led inexorably to the concept of war for reason of state [and] the doctrine that there are no restraints on a sovereign's power to make war for what he deems to be the national interest."[1] The search for nonideological limits led, in practice, to fewer and fewer limits at all. It deteriorated into the doctrine of no first use and a general prohibition against crossing international boundaries in force. But "that doctrine is too simplified to be any help in clarifying right and wrong" in contemporary conflicts that involve genocide, ethnic cleansing, war crimes, and other atrocities.[2]

Johnson argues that humanitarian considerations might support the first use of force and suggests the "classic" just war tradition would endorse such an argument. He argues that "only a minimum level of restraint on war can be provided" by the "non-ideological" approach to just war and that "ideological constraints on war hold out a hope as well as a threat," that is, a threat of a new kind of holy war.[3] The hope is that a new ideology grounded in humanitarianism can avoid the pitfalls of liberal imperialism while offering more substantive and meaningful limits on the occasion and conduct of war. Johnson drew hope from the embryonic international community to ground his belief that "a universal value system is not so far off as it was throughout the intervening centuries. We are now at a good point in history to try again the limitation of war by

[1] Johnson, *Ideology, Reason, and the Limitation of War*, 266.
[2] Johnson, *Ideology, Reason, and the Limitation of War*, 270.
[3] Johnson, *Ideology, Reason, and the Limitation of War*, 273–274.

restraints based in ideological standards, with the hope and intent that a new and *just* war doctrine can result."[4]

I attempt to develop this new just war doctrine on the basis of a universal value system of ordered liberty, one that is inspired from its predecessors yet postured for the security challenges of this century. I draw insights from the Augustinian and Liberal traditions and, to a lesser extent, the Westphalian tradition to offer *ordered liberty* as a central organizing concept for just war thinking. As I argued in the previous chapter, ordered liberty is the rightful purpose of statecraft, the just aim of the state – which means it is also the just purpose of warfare. This helps answer the two questions animating this book: *When is war just?* The violent disruption of ordered liberty is the "injury" in response to which force may be used and war may be justly waged. *What does justice require?* Justice requires the vindication and restoration of ordered liberty in, through, and after warfare.

When Is War Just? Sovereignty, Rebellion, and Intervention

The Augustinian Liberal view restores an older conception of sovereignty as care for the common good, updated to mean the maintenance of ordered liberty. This way of thinking about just war simplifies a number of issues and helps answer the question, when is war just? The violent disruption of ordered liberty is the "injury" in response to which force may be used and war may be justly waged. That obviously includes cases of territorial defense when attacked by an aggressor, but it also clarifies the complicated questions around intervention. Sovereignty, rebellion, and intervention are all tightly connected. Johnson captures the difference between Augustinian and Westphalian sovereignty perfectly. The former includes

a conception of sovereignty not in terms of the state and its territorial inviolability but in terms of the moral responsibility of the ruler for the common good of the people governed . . . . Here the right to use force is tied explicitly to the obligation to protect and preserve justice by restoring it when it has been violated and by punishing those persons responsible for the violation. The sovereign ruler, on this conception, has the obligation to establish an order in which justice is the norm, and thus to establish peace in his (or her or in some cases their) own domains and in relation to other political communities. Thus would the common good be served.[5]

Johnson elsewhere draws the logical conclusion that responsibility for the common good does not stop at one's borders. The "idea that

---

[4] Johnson, *Ideology, Reason, and the Limitation of War*, 274 (emphasis in original).
[5] Johnson, *Sovereignty*, 2. See also Johnson, "Humanitarian Intervention after Iraq."

sovereignty implies responsibility for the common good extends beyond the sovereign's own society to the order, justice, and peace of other societies as well."[6] I would add that this extended or extraterritorial responsibility is exceptional, not normal: it holds only when there is no effective sovereign in another society, or when events in another society threaten to disrupt the peace and order of one's own society. Johnson continues, "thus it is both a right and a responsibility of legitimate sovereigns to put down and punish tyranny, and to assist in establishing order, peace, and justice in societies that had been oppressed by tyranny."[7] The crux of the matter is the idea of sovereignty as responsibility for human life and ordered liberty: "The argument for intervention seems importantly to depend on the idea that there is a general responsibility both for individual states and for the international community to maintain and nurture respect for fundamental human rights."[8]

Normally, states are responsible for upholding ordered liberty for their own territory and for their own citizens. But when a state fails in this responsibility, either from lack of capacity or lack of will – through state failure or through exceptional, heinous tyranny – that responsibility passes to the only other actors capable of receiving it: the people in that state (i.e., rebels) and other states (or the intergovernmental organizations they create).[9] That the citizens would have a right to replace their state under conditions of anarchy or extreme tyranny seems to need no further justification. Do other states have such a right? Biggar invokes a "fraternal" model of international society in which states are indeed equal but not in a Hobbesian sense. They "are originally sociable, originally subject to the natural law, and originally their brother's keeper. Therefore equals may and should judge one another in the exercise of fraternal correction."[10] Equality does not mean nonjudgmentalism or even noninterference: one must sometimes stage an intervention to save a brother from himself. Other scholars have come to the same conclusion. Boyle argues that what he calls the "traditional" (i.e., Augustinian) just war tradition "does not mean that a state is limited to defending itself or to defending its allies. In that theory it is human beings' welfare and interests, not simply the welfare and interests of a given polity's

---

[6] Johnson, "Moral Responsibility after Conflict," in Patterson, *Ethics beyond War's End*, 20.

[7] Johnson, "Moral Responsibility after Conflict," in Patterson, *Ethics beyond War's End*, 19.

[8] Johnson, "Moral Responsibility after Conflict," in Patterson, *Ethics beyond War's End*, 26.

[9] The authority to intervene lies primarily with states, not the UN (which derives whatever authority and responsibility it has from the states which created it), though the UN can be a convenient tool for coordinating action. For a different view, see Bellamy, *Just Wars*, 208ff.

[10] Biggar, *In Defence of War*, 166.

subjects or allies, that is rightly defended from injury." For that reason, "morality demands that we consider not only the good of a single polity but also the more embracing good of the human community."[11] The implications for cases of state failure are clear. When a state collapses or ceases functioning, as in Haiti after the 2010 earthquake, other states or intergovernmental institutions should step in temporarily to help reestablish order.

The implications for unusually brutal tyranny – totalitarianism, genocide, and enslavement – are equally clear, if more controversial. When a government declares war on its own people, it is no longer acting as a rightful sovereign caring for the common good. Augustine quips that a government without justice is indistinct from a gang of criminals, and we have too many literal examples to doubt it. Governments engaged in mass murder or enslavement are not governments, they are criminals. Nations run by criminals exist in a vacuum of legitimate authority, an absence of just order, as evidenced by mass violence, civil war, insurgency, genocide, or totalitarian enslavement. A criminal regime's behavior constitutes a violent disruption of ordered liberty to which others might justly respond (to be very precise, it is the regime's deeds, not its character, that constitute its crime). People inhabiting that nation are justified in seeking to reestablish just order by forming a new government by force of arms. Other states are also justified to intervene for the same reason. Right authority passes downward, to the people, and outward, to other states, until they meet back in the middle, in the construction of a new state. The right of revolt and the right of intervention are triggered by the same thing: the absence of a legitimate, functioning, and just sovereign authority. This avoids the muddle and inconsistency that often characterizes discussions of intervention and rebellion (e.g., in Pufendorf or Walzer).[12] There are not two distinct discussions, one about rebellion and one about intervention, nor is there one doctrine of intervention for a civil war and a separate one for humanitarian intervention. There is a single discussion about sovereignty and what to do when it is absent.

---

[11] Boyle, "Traditional Just War Theory," 45, 48.

[12] Walzer specifically insists there are two separate debates. "It is not true, then, that intervention is justified whenever revolution is: for revolutionary activity is an exercise in self-determination, while foreign interference denies to a people those political capacities that only such exercise can bring" (Walzer, *Just and Unjust Wars*, 89). This partly accounts for the incoherence of his doctrine of intervention. I do not view self-determination as sacrosanct, and certainly not as something that must happen in isolation from other nations for it to be legitimate.

Objections

How do we limit this principle and avoid liberal imperialism? Does this view of sovereignty obligate us to advocate for world government? Defenders of Westphalian sovereignty argue that is the case. For them, sovereignty is all or nothing; it is either an absolute, inviolable principle or functionally meaningless. Nardin, in critiquing what he calls "humanitarian imperialism," suggests that humanitarian intervention rests on the idea that "only morally legitimate states have rights, and international politics gives way to transnational or supranational modes of global governance," a world he characterizes as "a world without sovereignty."[13] And, indeed, he is right that it would be a world without Westphalian sovereignty. Because the Westphalians have defined sovereignty as the absolute inviolability of international borders, the qualified, conditional, and accountable nature of the Augustinian and Liberal visions of sovereignty renders Westphalian sovereignty inert. If we accept the Westphalian definition of sovereignty but reject its practice, we are left with no other option than world government. But we do not have to accept it. We might advocate for a world without Westphalian sovereignty that still makes room for an Augustinian-Liberal understanding of it.

What would that look like? The midway point between Westphalian sovereignty and world government is variously called federalism, subsidiarity, or devolution. If the sovereign is responsible for the common good, it stands to reason the sovereign ought to know the people whose good he or she is caring for. That implies a closeness, a proximity, and mutual recognition between governor and governed to allow genuine relational knowledge to grow between them. Governments should be close to the people they govern, should know them, and should govern with their input and under their accountability.[14] World government fails to do any of these things. Sovereigns, to be truly effective at their core function of caring for the common good, must be plural, responsive, and local. A plurality of states enjoys presumptive favor as the most effective and legitimate tool for governing human beings. Augustine rightly argues, "If men were always peaceful and just, human affairs would be happier and all kingdoms would be small, rejoicing in concord with their neighbors.

---

[13] Nardin, "Humanitarian Imperialism," 23.

[14] I am not arguing in favor of Walzer's notion that there should be a vague "fit" between people and government. I am more concerned with responsiveness and accountability than with cultural affinity. Cultural affinity may be useful because it makes governance easier and more efficient, but efforts to manufacture cultural homogeneity fall afoul of the typical problems of nationalism.

There would be as many kingdoms among the nations of the world as there are now houses of a city."[15]

Coates has developed this way of thinking about sovereignty and its implications for humanitarian intervention. Coates starts with the idea that human beings are naturally social and political creatures. We need community to fully realize our human potential and achieve our greatest flourishing. This way of understanding human life "sees the process of moral formation (or malformation) taking place in, and largely through, the moral and political communities to which all individuals belong."[16] These communities, starting with the family, the neighborhood, and the church but extending up to the nation, are thus morally significant and intrinsically good because of their role in sustaining and enriching the life of humanity. We should seek to sustain these communities. Any effort to override the integrity of our local, particular, or national communities in the name of efficiency, cosmopolitanism, or universal principles requires special justification. That means humanitarian intervention must meet a high standard.

[B]y conceiving universality as a plural and concrete unity (grounded in the ethical role of the state and the political nature of human beings), the tradition is able to affirm and do justice to cultural and political differences in a way that is foreign to more abstract (cosmopolitan) versions of universality. This dual aspect has a beneficial impact on the treatment of humanitarian intervention. As a result, the tradition is less eager to endorse intervention in the first place and, when interventions are called for, more sensitive to the circumstances and requirements of the communities affected by the intervention.[17]

It is a high standard – but it can be met. As opposed to the Westphalian standard of sovereignty, in which nothing stands above the state and nothing can judge its conduct, Coates recognizes the necessity of "moral universalism" that "upholds the primacy of a moral community that transcends states and embraces all humanity," because "it is this community that generates the rights and the duties that apply across borders and that provide the moral basis of humanitarian intervention." We have to have standards outside and above the state lest we fall into the amorality of Westphalian order. But states still enjoy a presumption in their favor. The "ethical privileging of the state in the Thomist–Aristotelian tradition has a further, naturally restraining effect on intervention."[18] Biggar similarly argues that "Christian just war reasoning

---

[15] Augustine, *City of God*, IV.15, 159.   [16] Coates, "Humanitarian Intervention," 74.
[17] Coates, "Humanitarian Intervention," 71–72. I am uncomfortable with Coates' notion of the state's role in "moral formation," but the rest of his argument can still stand.
[18] Coates, "Humanitarian Intervention," 78.

about rebellion is critically conservative. It is conservative in its recognition that peaceful order is basic to all other forms of human flourishing, and so should not be disturbed needlessly," which gives national states a presumption in their favor. "Nevertheless," he continues, "it is morally critical in its awareness that sometimes peaceful order can be tyrannical or repressive to an extent that should not be borne."[19] Johnson, too, argues that the responsibility to prevent atrocities must be balanced against other responsibilities, among them the preservation of international order.[20]

Understood this way, intervention actually serves to bolster and defend (Augustinian and Liberal) sovereignty in two ways. It is a rightful exercise of the intervening power's sovereignty to care for the common good, failure in which would be a dereliction of duty. Second, intervention should aim at the restoration of true sovereignty in the target of intervention. Intervention thus violates Westphalian sovereignty, recognizing that doing so is the price of restoring Augustinian Liberal sovereignty of both the intervener and intervened-upon.

What Does Justice Require? *Jus Post Bellum*

If an intervention happens, what then? What are the obligations of the intervening state? This raises the second main question of this book: *What does justice require?* Justice requires the vindication and restoration of ordered liberty in, through, and after warfare. Perhaps the largest implication of my argument is for *jus post bellum*, or justice after conflict. If the purpose of war is to do justice, restore sovereignty, care for the common good, and defend ordered liberty, the outcome of a war matters greatly in seeing this done. Combat does not accomplish much on its own: at best, successful combat removes obstacles to peace and justice and *gives the victor an opportunity to reestablish a just order.* "The end of peace that just war tradition sets as the proper goal in order for the use of armed force to be just is not in fact a goal that such force by itself can bring into being: All it can do is help to establish the conditions," as Johnson argues.[21] The adversary's military defeat is only the beginning of a process, a process that must extend through combat and continue after it is concluded. In that light, *jus post bellum* is almost the whole ballgame: it is where the moral purpose of war is actually accomplished, not merely thought of, intended, or pursued. The justice of the US Civil War was consummated

[19] Biggar, "Christian Just War Reasoning," 399.
[20] Johnson, "Humanitarian Intervention after Iraq."
[21] Johnson, "Moral Responsibility after Conflict," in Patterson, *Ethics beyond War's End,* 28. The famous strategist Thomas Schelling made a similar point about "the diplomacy of violence" in 1970.

by the Thirteenth Amendment – before it was marred by the botched and incomplete reconstruction of the southern states. The justice of World War II was accomplished at Nuremberg and Tokyo and by regime change and the democratization of Germany and Japan – before it was marred by the Soviet occupation of Eastern Europe. That the military might play only a supporting role during this phase does not excuse us from thinking through statesmen's responsibilities in it. A war might be initiated on just premises, conducted justly, yet fail to achieve just order in the aftermath of the fighting. It is hard to understand how we could characterize such a conflict as a just war. Patterson is exactly right to remind us of the "morality of victory" and the importance of vindicating the values for which we fight: "If it is just to go to war in the first place ... then is it not just to win?"[22] Ending wars conclusively with a just victory means ending cycles of violence and establishing a new status quo. In this light, the emergence of *jus post bellum* as a category of just war thinking is perhaps the best development within just war scholarship since its revival almost a century ago.[23]

It is a development authentically rooted in the Augustinian tradition. Just warriors motivated by love do not use victory as license for vengeance, murder, or rapine in the aftermath. Vitoria and Grotius counseled magnanimity in victory – as did Cicero, illustrating that this is not a distinctively Christian concern and does not require Christian theological commitments for its foundation. Vitoria, Gentili, Grotius, and others wrote extensively on peace treaties and the treatment of the conquered, beginning a conversation about the justice of war's aftermath that the Westphalians did not follow. Johnson suggests that *post bellum* issues are captured by the older tradition's understanding of peace. "Peace, as conceived here, is not simply the absence of war," he argues, "it is a state of affairs interconnected with the establishment and maintenance of a just order."[24] War fought for true peace will concern itself with the "establishment and maintenance of a just order," a quintessentially *post bellum* task. Biggar goes so far as to reject the category of *jus post bellum* because he thinks it is superfluous: these issues "are already implicit in the *ad bellum* requirements of right intention," as described by Aquinas.[25] If combatants have right intention, they will naturally work after the war

---

[22] Patterson, *Just American Wars*, 166.
[23] Brian Orend has been instrumental in this development, see *Morality of War*; *Michael Walzer on War and Justice*; *War and International Justice*; "Justice after Wars"; "Jus Post Bellum." For a critical appraisal of *jus post bellum*, see Bellamy, "Responsibilities of Victory"; Evans, "Moral Responsibilities."
[24] Johnson, "Moral Responsibility after Conflict," in Patterson, *Ethics beyond War's End*, 20.
[25] Biggar, *In Defence of War*, 3.

to ensure the goals of the war are met through the aftermath. Biggar is correct that right intention, properly accounted for, should capture intentionality regarding the aftermath of a war. But that is precisely the point: right intention has not been properly accounted for. The Westphalian tradition demoted right intention into a functionally useless category. The explicit addition of *jus post bellum* into the tradition helps recover these issues, albeit under a new label, which should be a welcome development.

What I want to emphasize is that doing justice through war requires keeping the ideals of justice and peace in mind as polestars throughout the process: as one gets into war, by ensuring the war is aiming at a just peace; in the conduct of war, by using appropriate means with discrimination and proportionality; through the end of a war and into the aftermath, by investing in the conditions that lead to long-term stability and reconciliation. If the Augustinians got at this idea by talking about right intention and today we categorize this as a matter of *jus post bellum*, the basic idea is the same: war ought to aim at a better peace. As I demonstrate in the next chapter, this has significant consequences for how governments should plan for war and how scholars should evaluate the justice or injustice of wars.

I also want to highlight how this view operates as a severe restriction on war to counterbalance my expansive interpretation of just cause. The upshot of this chapter is that just cause is broader than is conventionally understood but justice after war carries far greater responsibilities. (Though I do not discuss *jus in bello* in this book, I would also add that the restrictions on how we fight should be extraordinarily strict, in keeping with the moral responsibilities of fighting for a just peace.) It is worth belaboring this point because, while it may seem obvious, it is one that policymakers have repeatedly failed to incorporate in the post-9/11 era. Boyle wrote in 2006:

Since undertaking warfare for humanitarian purposes without serious expectation of some concrete outcome to which the rescuing state is seriously committed is likely to further harm those who are to be rescued, to weaken international stability, and to impose considerable expense and probable loss of life on the rescuing state, it seems wrong to fail to face this motivational problem fully before intervening.[26]

Boyle probably had the United States' failure to plan for post-invasion Iraq in mind, but another example suggests itself. It is remarkable that five years after Boyle wrote this, NATO did exactly the same thing in Libya.

---

[26] Boyle, "Traditional Just War Theory," 47.

Whatever the justice of saving the citizens of Benghazi from Muammar Gaddhafi's avowed aim of ethnic cleansing, the moral and strategic idiocy of overthrowing the Libyan regime without subsequently doing anything to replace it was breathtaking. Walzer similarly wrote in 2010, "Imagine a humanitarian intervention that ends with the massacres stopped and the murderous regime overthrown; but the country devastated, the economy in ruins, the people hungry and afraid; there is neither law nor order nor any effective authority. The forces that intervened did well, but they are not finished."[27] It is because of examples like this that the emphasis on *jus post bellum* in contemporary just war scholarship is welcome.

What specific principles guide *jus post bellum*? Orend, the first to systematically treat *jus post bellum* as a separate category, suggests at a minimum that justice after war must vindicate whatever rights were violated by the war, roll back aggression, demilitarize aggressors, punish leaders through war-crimes trials, exchange prisoners of war, publicly declare peace terms, and get an apology from the aggressor. Beyond that, Orend rightly argues that the "rehabilitative" model is superior to the "revenge" or retributive model. Instead of compensation and punitive damages from the aggressor and sanctions until it meets its obligations, Orend argues for reconstruction and even regime change, if the latter is necessary to prevent war from recurring.[28]

Elshtain similarly suggests that the intervening state must accept the appropriate level of responsibility, repair physical and political infrastructure (which can include regime change), uphold order, and deter the reemergence of the causes that led to war in the first place. Crucially, she argues that states accrue more responsibility the larger their role in the war, an important standard for assessing the United States' responsibilities in its global counterterrorism campaign (and which also helps us understand the place punitive raids or airstrikes have in just war).[29] Mark Evans, in a more critical treatment that rightly recognizes that *jus post bellum* looks different for different kinds of wars, suggests that just combatants should ensure a "just and stable peace" while also redressing "the injustices that prompted the conflict." They should be prepared to help rebuild after the physical devastation of war. Finally, they should participate in conflict prevention and in reconciliation. In cases of regime change or occupation, the intervening state should work to restore sovereignty to the target state.[30]

---

[27] Walzer, "Aftermath of War," in Patterson, *Ethics beyond War's End*, 20.
[28] Orend, *Morality of War*; Orend, "Justice after War," in Patterson, *Ethics beyond War's End*, chapter 9.
[29] Elshtain, "Just War and an Ethics of Responsibility," in Patterson, *Ethics beyond War's End*, chapter 7.
[30] Evans, "Moral Responsibilities."

Patterson has developed probably the best framework for thinking about *jus post bellum* because it is elegant, simple, and focused on broad principles rather than a laundry list of specific policies. He argues that *jus post bellum* requires order, justice, and conciliation, in that order.[31] Patterson's prioritization of order over justice makes sense as a pragmatic concession to the realities of policymaking and the messiness of war and its aftermath, not as a matter of theological or philosophical principle. Augustine, recall, insists that peace and justice are tightly connected: "In comparison with the peace of the just, the peace of the unjust is not worthy to be called peace at all."[32] A postwar military occupation that reestablishes order without justice has not fulfilled the requirements of *jus post bellum*. Ramsey echoes Augustine when he argues that "Order is not a higher value in politics than justice, but neither is humanitarian justice a higher value than order. Both are in some respects conditional to the other."[33] True peace and true justice cannot be separated: the true end of statesmanship is a just peace, the tranquility of order. *Jus post bellum* should aim at this inseparable blend of peace, justice, and order together.

But Patterson has a point when it comes to the day-to-day realities of policymaking and policy implementation. In the aftermath of a war, or in the conditions of an irregular conflict in which violence is still periodic, order has a good claim to priority if only because it is nearly impossible to make meaningful progress towards any more aspirational goals unless and until order is reestablished. If I am hesitant to endorse the notion that order is more important than justice, it is because too often policymakers take "security first" as license for "security only," and leave justice aside. Patterson's own definition of order avoids this pitfall: he includes a "governance dimension," in his understanding of order, covering the rule of law, sovereignty, and "the fundamental tasks of governance, including over the economic sector."[34] But when we go so far as to include governance and the rule of law as part of order, we may as well say that the first principle of *jus post bellum* is not order, but *just order*.

After his discussion of order, Patterson rightly argues that justice is a vital component of bringing a war to a conclusion. Done right, justice should "reinforce the political order and the moral order," provide an accounting of and some punishment for past wrongdoing, acknowledge victims, and deter future wrongdoing. Conciliation, Patterson's third criteria, is probably the hardest to define and the rarest in implementation. It involves

---

[31] Patterson, *Ethics beyond War's End*; *Ending Wars Well*.
[32] Augustine, *City of God*, XIX.12, 934.   [33] Ramsey, *Just War*, 11.
[34] Patterson, *Ending Wars Well*, 47.

coming to grips with the past for the sake of moving forward in a new direction and could include amnesty, truth-seeking, disarmament, demobilization, reintegration, and even forgiveness.[35] Evans has helpfully highlighted the importance of democracy in consolidating justice after war: "If one believes that democracy is most conducive to peace, the case for it in the postwar domestic order of the occupied state could be very compelling."[36] This will be particularly important in my case studies in the next chapter.

There are some common themes among these different treatments of *jus post bellum*. Generally, the victor must, first, make right whatever wrong prompted the war; second, make right the wrongs *of* war (the death and destruction of combat); and third, prevent the recurrence of those wrongs in the future (all while continuing to observe the same rules of discrimination and proportionality that guide *jus in bello*). In the first category – making right the wrongs which prompted the war – are vindication of rights, reversal of aggression, and formal apology from the aggressor. These are paramount, even before the restoration of order, because without them the war has not really ended and order cannot be restored. (This is one sense in which some aspects of justice could have both chronological and conceptual priority over order.) In the second category – making right the wrongs done during war – we see the complete restoration of order and the beginnings of justice: reestablishment of public safety and stability, exchange of prisoners, war-crimes trials, and reconstruction to undo the effects of combat. The third category – preventing the recurrence of wrongs – includes demilitarization, other forms of transitional justice, a peace treaty, and (when necessary) regime change. The third category is where we finish the work of justice and see its evolution into conciliation.

These criteria will look different in different kinds of military operations. At the low end, I suggest that there are no *jus post bellum* obligations in the wake of a simple punitive strike or a one-off military reprisal against a terrorist attack, such as the US strike against al-Qaida training camps in Afghanistan in 1998 following that group's bombing of two US embassies in Africa. Such strikes are often the only realistic option available to policymakers when large-scale war and large-scale reconstruction seem unlikely to succeed, and plainly should not impose a large reconstruction burden on the state carrying out the punitive action. I do not mean to imply a blanket permission for punitive strikes or to comment on

---

[35] Patterson, *Ending Wars Well*, 70; for the full argument see chapters 4 and 5, esp. 70ff and 106ff.
[36] Evans, "Just Peace," in Patterson, *Ethics beyond War's End*, 213.

the prudence or efficacy of such strikes. I can envision circumstances in which punitive strikes are appropriate, but I suspect policymakers are drawn to them precisely because they wish to avoid the broader commitments that come with war, which, if true, could be an immoral avoidance of responsibility masquerading as prudent restraint. (I take up this issue in more detail in the next chapter's discussion about drone warfare.)

In limited, conventional war, *jus post bellum* is straightforward: restoration of the status quo ante, perhaps with reparations. If Ukraine successfully defeats the Russian-backed insurgents fighting in the Donbas region and reestablishes control, its obligation would be simply to consolidate that control and govern in a way that sustains its local legitimacy. Russia, were it ever to acknowledge its role in the conflict, should pay reparations for the damage done during the war. The same would be true if Ukraine were ever to regain control of Crimea.

Jus post bellum is considerably more complex in cases of total war and, on the other end of the spectrum, in unconventional war, civil war, insurgency, and low-intensity conflict. In cases of total war, the obligations of *jus post bellum* will be commensurately greater, to include reconstruction, nation building, and probably regime change. In cases of unconventional war, counterinsurgency, and low-intensity conflict, the responsibilities of *post bellum* do not change, but they do merge with those of *jus in bello*. Just combatants have to pursue war-ending justice and conciliation as part of an unconventional war strategy. Failure to do so means either defeat or stalemate, neither of which is a just outcome. This is the crucial interpretive key of my analysis of the war in Afghanistan and the war against al-Qaida in the next chapter.

Objections

One of the hardest questions for *jus post bellum* is about where the limits of *post bellum* responsibility lie. Once we acknowledge that victors incur moral obligations, we have to describe when those obligations are discharged. Otherwise, *post bellum* justice becomes a blank check that both imposes impossible and infinite obligations on the victor but at the same time can become license for the victor to stay forever and justify any policy. Evans has questioned whether "just peace" is a useable concept, given its inherent vagueness, and warns that a concept ostensibly designed to end wars well might instead serve to prolong them indefinitely. He recognizes a key dilemma, rightly arguing that "it cannot be the objective of a just war to make another society just," while at the same time acknowledging that we "cannot dispense with some view of what constitutes a just society" in our efforts to advance justice after war.[37] Advocates of *jus post bellum* must answer these questions: Where are the limits of the victor's responsibility? When is our duty discharged? These are related to the questions: What are the limits of our responsibility for humanitarian intervention? Are we *obligated* to intervene whenever there is an emergency?

There is a useful analogy here with domestic laws regarding the "duty to rescue" and "Good Samaritan" laws protecting volunteers from liability during emergencies. There are differences between the Anglo-American common law system and the civil law systems in the rest of the world, but in general there is no absolute or binding duty to rescue those in danger, though there is a duty to call for aid. There is, however, a binding obligation to rescue those with whom we have special relationships, such as parents to children, spouses to each other, employers to employees, and so on. Some jurisdictions impose steeper obligations but never oblige a stranger to put themselves in danger for others. Good Samaritan laws encourage bystanders and passersby to volunteer aid by protecting them from liability for civil damages. The Good Samaritan is not deemed responsible for any damage done in the course of good-faith efforts to render aid – but that protection does not extend to damage done as a result of gross negligence or recklessness. Importantly, once a volunteer has gotten involved, the law requires him or her to remain at the scene until the victim is stabilized, the volunteer is relieved by a professional emergency responder, or it becomes unsafe.

We can apply these principles to cases of international behavior. There is no universal, binding obligation on every state to intervene in cases of humanitarian emergency, and certainly no obligation to risk one's national independence, impose a high cost on one's nation for the sake of others, or volunteer for *post bellum* reconstruction after a war to which one was not a party. There is, however, an obligation for states to "call for aid" by raising awareness, drawing attention to the emergency, and raising it on the agendas of international and nongovernmental organizations. Ignoring emergencies for the sake of political expediency or convenience is plainly immoral. In short, for most states and under most circumstances, intervention is permissible but not obligatory. Grotius and others explicitly emphasized these limitations in their discussion of intervention. The exercise of sovereignty is a weighty moral responsibility. Its abrogation or dereliction is a grave moral injury, the rectification of which is urgent. That does not tell us who may, much less who must, do the rectifying, the determination of which requires other considerations.

[37] Evans, "Just Peace," in Patterson, *Ethics beyond War's End*, esp. 208ff.

What other considerations? Importantly, the same analogy leads us to recognize that there *is* an obligation on states to rescue states with whom they have a special relationship. There are a number of circumstances that constitute a special relationship. We should clearly include allies and those to whom we have explicitly promised aid through treaty or repeated assurance. We should also include neighbors who share proximity to and interest in crises, such as Vietnam in Cambodia in 1979 and India in Bangladesh in 1971, because humanitarian emergencies routinely spill over borders. In those cases, the obligation to intervene is self-interested as much as other-interested (which does not obviate the moral quality of intervention since states rightly pursue their own security). President Franklin Roosevelt's famous analogy of lending one's firehose to a neighbor whose house is aflame is a good illustration of an intuitive point: in the neighborhood of nations, what happens elsewhere is sure to affect us. We can also include under the category of "special relation-ship," a unique kind of obligation on the most powerful states when faced with a crisis that they uniquely could address and that could be averted with a relatively low-cost intervention. I have in mind the genocide in Rwanda in 1994, the great powers' nonintervention in which was rightly regarded as shameful.

Perhaps we can also recognize special obligations between states with a shared history, especially a history of wrongs for which one wants to make symbolic recompense (as with imperial powers to former colonies, or Germany to Israel). Finally, I would add further that we incur obliga-tions to states against whom we have gone to war, which is a unique kind of special relationship. The act of warring together means a commitment to finding a shared peace together afterwards; combatants incur an obli-gation, not merely permission, to build peace afterwards. The longer and more destructive the war, the greater the obligation; wars of regime change incur the greatest obligation.

Though I started by asserting there is no general or universal obligation to intervene, these considerations taken together add up to a substantial obligation for many states under many conditions. This, I hope, is a Goldilocks doctrine of intervention: neither obligatory on everyone all the time nor prohibited under all circumstances but permissible under extreme conditions and, sometimes, obligatory for some.

What about limiting the responsibilities we incur during an interven-tion? How do we judge when the obligations we have taken upon our-selves are discharged? When are we allowed to leave? This is a tricky question because we want to avoid two errors. If we limit responsibility too much, the intervener is off the hook and can leave too soon, before the work is done. If we define responsibility too expansively, the intervener never leaves and is burdened with an impossible task, or they could use "responsibility" as a pretext for a neo-imperial presence. Broadly, we should want states to volunteer to help in cases of humanitarian emergency, just as we should want states to stay and build *post bellum* peace after the wars they fight, and so the principles of the Good Samaritan laws should apply. Barring gross negligence, intervening states should enjoy some measure of presumption in favor of their good faith and exemption from liability for what happens during a crisis. But given the history of botched reconstruction operations, our tolerance for gross negligence should be low.

However, I want to be cautious in using this argument to limit what obligations we incur when we decide to intervene. The law also says that Good Samaritans must remain at the scene until the patient is stabilized. The analogy is not perfect because Good Samaritan laws apply to private citizens acting temporarily until higher authorities can show up. There are no higher authorities in cases of international intervention. Good Samaritans' responsibilities are limited because they can be relieved by professional emergency responders, state authorities, doctors, and insurance companies to see the rest of the work done. International interveners end up acting as all of those things together. They are not just passing citizens. Stabilizing a sick nation takes a long time, especially because there are no higher authorities or professional responders that specialize in nation building to whom we can hand off responsibility. If I help a stranger in a car wreck, I am not obligated to pay their medical bills and buy them a new car. But if I overthrow a government to save a nation from genocide, I do have obligations to remain and rebuild.

To be more specific, our obligation is discharged when we have made right the wrongs of war in all three senses I discussed above. I argued that victors should make right whatever wrong prompted the war; make right the wrongs committed during the war; and prevent the recurrence of those wrongs in the future. The responsibilities of *jus post bellum* are discharged when we have accomplished these things. The most difficult and important, and hardest to measure, is the third task because that is where we "stabilize the patient." In a previous book I argued that success in post-conflict operations means sustainably changing a nation's trajectory for the better. That means that "stabilizing the patient" does not require restoring them to full health, to some objective or global standard of development; it requires seeing their indices of development on a sustainable trajectory of improvement over a period of time.[38] To critics who think this argument increases international authority for intervention

[38] Miller, *Armed State Building*, 14–16.

and thus increases the danger of imperialism, I respond that it *increases international responsibility for what intervention entails* and thus should dampen any enthusiasm for intervention that might otherwise exist.

What about Liberal Imperialism?

This discussion about how to limit responsibility so that it does not become an excuse for liberal crusading raises a broader set of objections. A critic may argue that I am defining just cause in extraterritorial terms, which threatens to undo the Westphalian system of independent states. Such a move defines just cause in global terms, unrestricted by national borders, opening the door to imperialism and crusading. A war for liberalism might be, on this understanding, strikingly similar to a war for religion. Both entail waging war to defend abstract beliefs, ideals, and the institutions, rules, and practices that embody and enforce those ideals. This might lead, in tragic irony, to the paradox of liberal imperialism. My argument could be seen as merely the latest in a long line of self-serving justifications for the use of force and imperial expansion: liberal order is the new *mission civilisatrice*, the new "white man's burden," an updated standard of civilization, the Mandate of Heaven, or the writ of Nature, God, or Scripture. In this view, the liberal international order does not guard against universal empire and ideological totalism; it *is* a universal empire with ideologically totalistic ambitions.

Critics regularly raise these objections. For example, when I made an early version of my argument in the pages of *First Things* in 2013 by way of defending the justice of the war in Afghanistan, Andrew Bacevich objected (somewhat hyperbolically) that "A state is not a church. A state exists not to redeem humankind or to do God's work but to provide for the security and wellbeing of the people who reside within its boundaries," refuting an argument I had not actually made. Mark Henrie accused me of using just war to expand the opportunities for war rather than limit them. Paul Griffiths characterized the argument as "interestingly wrong-headed." He objected to my use of the parable of the Good Samaritan as a metaphor for the humanitarian possibilities of military intervention, calling it "confused and repellent" (Ramsey used the parable long before I did, though I had not read Ramsey yet). He and Bacevich both wondered where the limiting principle was; that is, if we accept that defending a norm is just, what stops us from conquering the world in the name of defending our values? How is this not a moralistic fig leaf covering the ambitions of an American empire? Griffiths claimed my "position is an imperial one, at least by aspiration, and that means blood and violence and darkness, as utopian imperial aspirations always do."[39]

Separately, David Chandler warns against the "empire in denial" of humanitarian and state-building interventions.[40] Yoram Hazony characterizes liberal internationalism as "an imperialist ideology that incites against nationalism and nationalists."[41] He claims that the liberal international order "is incapable of respecting, much less celebrating, the deviation of nations seeking to assert a right to their own unique laws, traditions, and policies."[42] Imperialism and universalism engender hatred towards "nations or tribes that refuse to accept its claim of universality," a hatred "found among imperialists of every stripe," including liberal internationalists.[43] Neta Crawford takes issue with the expansive view of the self that is implied in the internationalist project: "If the self is defined so broadly and threats to this greater 'self' are met with military force, at what point does self-defense begin to look, at least to outside observers, like aggression?"[44]

Just war thinking and humanitarian intervention, for some critics, are complicit in this new kind of imperialism. Rengger warns that just war thinking, by emphasizing punishment of injustice, undermines its own attempts to restrict war and limit its destructiveness. "Where injustice is everywhere, the reason to use force to oppose it are not hard to find," he argues, stressing that any effort to "expand the *provenance* of war," necessarily means increasing our trust in the exercise of power by government, which should always be viewed skeptically.[45] Nardin insightfully notes the parallel between justifications for imperialism and arguments for today's liberal order:

In the old literature of empire, humanitarianism was invoked to justify the supposed responsibility of an imperial power operating at the margins of the civilized world to uphold the standards of civilized morality by suppressing cannibalism,

---

[39] Bacevich, "Limiting Moralism"; Griffiths, "Good Samaritan's Burden"; Henrie, "War without End"; Miller, "Afghanistan, Justice, and War."
[40] Chandler, *Empire in Denial*.   [41] Hazony, *Virtue of Nationalism*, 219.
[42] Hazony, *Virtue of Nationalism*, 39.   [43] Hazony, *Virtue of Nationalism*, 191.
[44] Crawford, "Just War Theory and the US Counterterror War," 14.
[45] Rengger, *Just War and International Order*, 67, 175 (emphasis in original); see chapters 2 and 3 for his discussion of just war. Rengger focuses his discussion on the just war tradition in the modern age, meaning after Westphalia, and he critiques the overemphasis on *jus in bello* at the expense of *jus ad bellum* and the functional marriage between just war, statism, and realism. To that extent, I agree with Rengger's critique and my argument can be seen as an attempt to rescue just war from these tendencies. But Rengger's contention that just war, even the Christian version of it, has been fatally compromised by "teleocratic" views of the state is unpersuasive. The Christian (and Liberal) versions escape this tendency because they have their own *telos* outside the state and are thus not captured by the state.

human sacrifice, and other barbaric practices. In today's rhetoric of empire, it is the barbarity of tyranny and terrorism that threaten these standards and that must be countered, in the name of humanity, by the exercise of imperial power.[46]

Nardin's observation is at least partially correct: my argument for liberal order uses past arguments about imperial responsibility. This argument takes on especially sharp form when tied to the specific case under consideration: the United States and its relationship to the liberal international order. Given the United States' record of hypocrisy, how can anyone take its claims to defend the principles of liberal order seriously?[47] Even more damning for my argument, some enlist Augustine in their case against American empire, insisting that the liberal order is a form not of the *tranquilitas ordinis* but of the *libido dominandi*, the lust for dominance, that Augustine so clearly warned against. Given this line of critique, is my argument is fatally compromised by the specter of empire? Or is it possible to affirm similar basic principles – about sovereignty, responsibility, and intervention – without tacitly endorsing imperialism?

I think it is possible. I have responded to some of the objections in this chapter, and I believe that my definition of Augustinian liberalism defangs many of these criticisms. (In fact, I agree with many of these criticisms insofar as they highlight the problems with progressive and nationalist versions of liberalism.) Here I add that, first, the liberal international order is not imperialism. Second, there is an obvious but important difference between defending the liberal international order and coercively expanding the liberal international order. Third, I affirm the principle that military intervention should always be a matter of last resort and subject to the criteria of proportionality and having a reasonable chance of success. Fourth, justice has often been defined in extraterritorial terms in the just war traditions.

First, the liberal international order is not imperialism. One can only confuse the two by redefining "imperialism" to mean something drastically other than what is historically meant. In the present liberal order, no global body dictates what language we must speak or what religion we must practice. No global body practices permanent administrative or

---

[46] Nardin, "Humanitarian Imperialism," 25. See also Zolo, *Cosmopolis*; Chesterman, *Just War or Just Peace?*

[47] For more critiques of just war as a cover for American empire, see Blumenwitz, "Future of World Order" and Tompkins, "Question of Just War Theory," both in De Paulo et al., *Augustinian Just War Theory*. Some critics are sure to make this criticism more personal: how can I, given my record of public service in the United States government, be objective in answering these questions? Of course, my participation in an American war no more disqualifies me from scholarly analysis of it than Walzer's political activism against another one disqualified him.

military control over overseas colonies. The various military interventions by liberal powers since the end of the Cold War have been more notable for how eager the intervening states have been to leave and for their recognition of the sovereignty of the intervened-upon state than for any supposed neo-imperialistic ambitions. The inequities of global capitalism are real, but there is no moral equivalence between them and the physical violence that undergirded historical imperialism. The most nakedly neo-imperialistic actions by any state in the past quarter-century – Russia's invasions of Georgia and Ukraine – were roundly condemned by the organs of the liberal international order. (As was the US invasion of Iraq, for those inclined to count it as an example of imperialism, which I do not.) The principal pillars of the liberal international order – the United States, Europe, Japan, and India – are the freest societies in the world, as regularly measured by objective, third-party institutions such as Freedom House, the World Bank, and the Polity IV Project.

To be clear, as I said above, I am more comfortable defending *a* liberal order, which is precisely the arrangement of institutions that maximize human flourishing and individual and national freedom, than *the* liberal order, which is of course flawed and fallible in practice. There are some versions of internationalism that come closer to imperialism insofar as they deny the legitimacy of national boundaries and national sovereignty; that is why I have been at pains to distinguish my argument from them. An Augustinian, classically liberal internationalism – what I have called conservative internationalism – is not imperialistic. In practice, I do think the liberal international order built in the aftermath of World War II has been a net positive for ordered liberty among nations despite its flaws, more anti-imperial than neo-imperial. For example, the United States and the UN were the principal engines of decolonization and the end of formal empire in the twentieth century, and the liberal order has, on the whole, helped encourage accountable, representative governance and respect for human rights.

Second, I reaffirm the obvious but important distinction between defensive and offensive war. Despite its problems, the conventional aggressor–defender distinction has some applicability here. It is just to defend the liberal international order; it is not just to wage offensive war for the sole purpose of expanding the liberal international order. This is a fine distinction because oftentimes in defending against a threat to liberal order we are presented with an opportunity to expand liberal order by fostering democracy in the aftermath of war. Such was the case in Germany and Japan after World War II, in Afghanistan after the fall of the Taliban, and in the aftermath of some two dozen civil wars that came to an end after the Cold War. To help foster democracy in post-conflict conditions is not unjust and is not a species of offensive warfare.

To belabor the point: it would obviously be unjust to preemptively invade Iran or North Korea and seek coercive regime change and democratization on the sole grounds that either is governed by an authoritarian government. But if either state initiated an aggressive war against a neighbor, embarked upon genocide, threatened international security through state sponsorship of mass-casualty terrorism, or threatened international security through the proliferation of weapons of mass destruction; and if the international community successfully and justly waged war against them in response; and if their governments fell in the aftermath of such a war; then the international community has an obligation to facilitate democratization in the aftermath. Democratization should be the effect, not the cause, of a just war to defend the liberal international order.

This distinction almost breaks down in cases of humanitarian intervention. NATO waged war against Libya in 2011 to prevent Gaddhafi's forces from carrying out their threat of ethnic cleansing or genocide. From one angle, it was an offensive war by mostly European nations against an African dictator who had not attacked them first. What gave the Europeans the right to attack him? The fact that while Gaddhafi had not attacked Europe, he had attacked his own people and, thereby, abrogated his own sovereignty. To defend the Libyan people and the liberal order, NATO acted offensively against one regime. (The injustice of the aftermath – of the western powers' failure to help rebuild – is another question.) Is this a loophole by which the defense of the liberal international order could become a license for liberal crusading? It might be abused for that end but might not be, and in any case, any good principle can be abused, but abuse does not delegitimize the soundness of the principle itself.

Third, I affirm that military intervention should always be a last resort, have a reasonable chance of success in creating a better peace, and outweigh the evil it seeks to redress. I have not dwelt on these prudential criteria in this book, but they are valuable for judging specific cases. That means the evils against which we intervene must not be slight. The mere existence of a normally autocratic government that is not totalitarian or genocidal is not a just cause for intervention. I am comfortable in going quite far in asserting that illiberal regimes, merely by existing, harm the rights of their subjects, and that all such regimes are less legitimate than liberal regimes because the latter protect a system of ordered liberty to maximize human flourishing. However, that does not mean that illiberal regimes thereby lose all sovereign rights or that outside powers have just cause to invade them, a standard which would obviously, and foolishly, require the United States to conquer the world in the name of saving it. If sovereignty is understood as care for the common good, we have to recognize that, occasionally, nondemocratic regimes can succeed at some level, even if less consistently and less well than their democratic counterparts. Illiberal regimes span a very wide spectrum from relatively benign, enlightened monarchies to brutal but orderly military autocracies and theocracies to totalitarian and genocidal regimes such as North Korea, the Taliban's Afghanistan, Bashar al-Assad's Syria, and Saddam Hussein's Iraq. Normal oppression, corruption, inequality, and oligarchy are sadly the standard in human government. Organized, systemic mass violence or terror by a government against its people is not. When illiberal regimes are peaceful and generally orderly, we should advocate for liberalism through diplomacy and friendly suasion: that is what the criterion of last resort requires. The right of revolt and the right of international military intervention exist when a government wages war on its own people through mass murder or enslavement. That is how we avoid the temptation to "humanitarian imperialism" that Nardin warns against – by recognizing that "Intervention is called for by the specific crimes committed (or permitted) by a regime, not the character of that regime."[48]

This is important because it is a response to a typical criticism: war, because of its evils, cannot effectively serve a good end. The view I have outlined above has often been criticized for endorsing war as an instrument for protecting the innocent. War brings a host of evils: how can we save others from suffering through more of the same? This is essentially the argument Bartolomé de las Casas brought against Juan Ginés de Sepúlveda in their famous Valladolid debates in 1550–1 over the Spanish conquest of the New World, and it is the argument las Casas' modern interpreters often echo against contemporary humanitarian intervention. Despite the good intentions of a humanitarian intervention, it brings suffering and misery to the countries it purports to help. Daniel Brunstetter and Dana Zartner warn that "a return to the Sepúlveda-style rhetoric is a return to a just war paradigm without safeguards: an interventionist, proactive *jus ad bellum* that recognizes moral righteousness and power as a political license to enforce justice against evil."[49] More, humanitarian war risks delegitimizing the very principles it purports to defend by association with the evils of war.

---

[48] Nardin, "Humanitarian Imperialism," 22. Nardin wrongly argues that advocates for the war in Iraq argued for intervention based on the autocracy of the Iraqi regime. As Biggar's argument makes clear, it was the crimes of the Iraqi regime that justified the invasion; see Biggar, *In Defence of War*, chapter 7.

[49] Brunstetter and Zartner, "Just War against Barbarians," 746.

My argument, and that of others who have argued in favor of humanitarian intervention and counterterrorism operations, is crucially different
from Sepúlveda's. Sepúlveda defended the Spanish conquest of the New
World by invoking Aristotle's concept of the "natural slave." He effectively argued that barbarians do not have natural rights and thus civilized
countries may wage war on them even absent any injury received.
I disagree: I do not argue that barbarians (or tyrants, terrorists, or slavers)
lack natural rights because of who they are. I concur with Sepúlveda's
later argument – more consistent with Vitoria and Grotius and others –
that outsiders may intervene in response to barbarians' specific actions if
those actions rise to the level of a "crime against nature." And I reiterate
that revolt and intervention should, of course, aim at a better peace and
should only be undertaken if such a peace is achievable. In that sense, the
criterion of proportionality is crucial: only if an intervention might achieve
more good than evil is it worth pursuing.

The harshest critics of humanitarian war seem to assert that it is impossible *in principle* to achieve a positive proportion, that any evil in war
invalidates any good it might achieve. That amounts to functional pacifism
by absolutizing the evils of intervening while minimizing the evils of not
intervening. Brunstetter and Zartner are unfair when they argue that
"linking humanitarian goals to war also requires a leap of faith that war
will succeed in creating a better world."[50] It is not a leap of faith: it is
a prudential judgment based on the evidence at hand on a case-by-case
basis. It is, rather, a leap of faith to assert beforehand, *a priori*, a general rule
that no possible war could ever create a better world that outweighed the
cost of war. In contrast to this functional pacifism, I try to illustrate how to
make these difficult judgment calls through a series of case studies in the
next chapter.

Fourth, I respond that just cause has often been understood in extraterritorial terms. Augustine argues that the establishment and defense of
the tranquility of order was a just cause for war. Gratian emphasizes
"violations of justice rather than violations of territorial integrity," in his
understanding of just cause. That is why, regarding humanitarian intervention, "When viewed from the wider, universalist, moral perspective,
what looks like an act of unjustified aggression in the state-centered
context is defending the innocent, upholding justice, and vindicating
the universal moral community to which all states belong and to which
all are subject," according to Coates.[51] But even in the Westphalian
tradition, Wolff and Vattel argue that the defense of the balance of

[50] Brunstetter and Zartner, "Just War against Barbarians," 748.
[51] Coates, "Humanitarian Intervention," 64.

power is a just cause. The balance of power, they believed, is the crucial mechanism by which each state secures its own independence; justice, therefore, is not only a matter of territorial inviolability, but of an equitable distribution of power across territories. In all these cases, the just war traditions argue that the "self" of self-defense is not the territorial sovereign state. To reject an understanding of just cause because it is cast in extraterritorial terms is not merely to bias the understanding of justice in Westphalian terms; it is to reject virtually all conceptions of just cause except that advocated by the international lawyers of the nineteenth century.

In this chapter I apply the Augustinian Liberal just war framework to contemporary cases of war and conflict: Iraq, Afghanistan, terrorism, Syria, North Korea, and selected cases of cyberwar and autonomous weapons. The just war traditions have long relied on a case study approach to help students reason through real-world examples, grapple with the nuance and complexity that statesmen face, and weigh different principles and approaches against one another. I hope these case studies illustrate in more concrete terms what I mean when I say that the defense of ordered liberty is a just cause.

These cases collectively cover a wide range of contemporary security issues. First, I discuss Iraq because it is the largest recent war and has animated a huge amount of commentary from just war scholars. I contrast my approach with that of several other thinkers to show what I hope are the original insights of my approach. Second, I discuss Afghanistan and the War on Terror because they are conflicts I know intimately, having personally participated in them, and because the wars illustrate some features of the moral reality of contemporary war that I hope will shape our understanding of just war in the future. Third, I use Syria to discuss humanitarian crises, the use of weapons of mass destruction, and the costs of nonintervention. Fourth, I use North Korea to discuss nuclear war, nuclear deterrence, and preemptive and preventive war – issues that have been with us since the dawn of the Cold War and are still with us. Fifth, I discuss cyberwar and autonomous weapons as novel forms of conflict whose moral dimensions are still coming into focus.

Iraq (2003–11)

In this section I walk through arguments for and against the Iraq War by engaging with prominent just war scholars who have written on the subject. I do so not out of any great desire to dwell on Iraq, which has been more than exhaustively debated, but because it is the most prominent just war debate of the twenty-first century. Engaging with these debates is thus an excellent opportunity to highlight how my argument overlaps and differs with other contemporary just war perspectives. Walzer concludes that the Iraq War was unjust because it lacked just cause and was not truly a last resort. I disagree on both counts. Biggar constructs a persuasive case for just cause, with which I agree, but he also defends the coalition's right intention and what I would call the *jus post bellum* of the war, judgments with which I disagree. The through line of my engagement is whether the war in Iraq served the purpose of justice, peace, and ordered liberty. I believe it could have but did not, and thus started on just premises but was ultimately unjust in effect.

Jus Ad Bellum

Walzer judges the Iraq War unjust, though for odd reasons. He grants that the cause of disarming Iraq was just but argues that war was probably unnecessary to achieve that goal. Walzer's argument against the Iraq War rests on timing. Walzer argues there "was a just and necessary war to be fought [against Iraq] back in the 1990s" because it "would have been an internationalist war" whose justice "would have derived, first, from the justice of the system it was enforcing."[1] Later, after the invasion, he argues it was a war "before its time," as if the war would have turned out to be just and necessary at a later date.[2] So Walzer agrees it was just to disarm Iraq and that war would have been just in, say, 1995 and again in 2025, but for some reason not in 2003.

Part of the reason is the United States' "unilateralism." The war of 2003, in contrast to the hypothetical wars of 1995 or 2025, was initiated by the United States and the United Kingdom and undertaken almost entirely by troops from those two countries. (The war was, strictly speaking, bilateral not unilateral and there were, in fact, over fifty nations participating in the coalition, though the American and British militaries predominated.) They purported to be fighting for principles the international community had affirmed – disarmament and humanitarianism – but the rest of the world's dissent from the war made hollow, for Walzer, the principled internationalist case for it even granting that the United States and the United Kingdom were sincere. But whose fault is this? And does it render the war unjust? Walzer is right that "other states besides the United States [must] take responsibility for the global rule of law and . . . be prepared to act, politically and militarily, with that end in view."[3] But

---

[1] Walzer, *Arguing about War*, 144.   [2] Walzer, *Arguing about War*, 160.
[3] Walzer, *Arguing about War*, 156.

does other states' failure to uphold internationalist principles make the United States' fidelity to them immoral? The United States might act unilaterally (or jointly, with the United Kingdom and other coalition partners) because it is the only state willing to take such responsibility. The fact that the 2003 war was less than fully "internationalist" in character and lacked full legal authorization from the UN was not solely the United States' fault and surely could not deprive it of whatever responsibility – whatever right authority – it had to uphold liberal order. Walzer might insist that the war was simply illegal under a straightforward reading of international law and the UN charter, against which I would agree with Ramsey that legality is not the same as justice. The multilateral intervention in Kosovo also did not have UN authorization, yet Walzer supported it.

Confusing the issue, Walzer concedes that Israel may have had a strong case for preemptive war against Iraq, given Iraq's open enmity to Israel, yet he does not extend this right to the United States or the international community, who were comparatively less threatened.[4] But this should be a simple matter of cooperative security: if indeed Israel was justified in preemptively attacking Iraq, any other state might come to Israel's aid in doing so. This would be a clear reaffirmation of internationalist principles of the kind Walzer favors. Just as the international community banded together to aid Kuwait against Iraq in 1990–1 to defend the principles of sovereignty and territorial inviolability, might it not have done the same for Israel in 2003, given Walzer's judgment that Israel faced an imminent threat from Iraq? That this did not figure prominently in the public case for the war in 2002–3 does not render the cause impotent (though it may illumine whether or not the combatants had right intention).

More confusingly still, Walzer recognizes the timing dilemma facing the Bush administration in 2002–3, yet that earns US policymakers no charity from him. He accepts that delay would have been dangerous because Iraq would be stronger later and possibly armed with weapons of mass destruction, in which case not acting would be a dereliction of duty. But Walzer still argues that delay was nonetheless morally necessary because up until the moment that Iraq actually had the weapons, or was "literally on the verge" of acquiring them, inspections would be preferable to war.[5] Walzer's argument depends on there being an unidentified sliver of time when Iraq was close to having weapons of mass destruction but not too close; when the danger was imminent enough to justify the *threat* of war to compel inspections but not war itself, and also not so imminent as to render inspections meaningless or war too costly. But if the threat of

<hr>

[4] Walzer, *Arguing about War*, 147.   [5] Walzer, *Arguing about War*, 146.

war is justified, so is war (otherwise threats are meaningless), and so Walzer's endorsement of the threat of war but refusal to countenance its execution is incoherent. On the best reading, the timing issue is surely a prudential judgment, the kind Ramsey insisted was within the province of statesmen and should not be second-guessed by churchmen (or by scholars). And it is surely understandable that the actual policymakers' risk tolerance is naturally far lower than scholars', since they would be the ones blamed if they got the calculation wrong, and they would want to act sooner rather than later. In any case, Walzer's alternative proposal in late 2002 – threaten war to compel inspections – is in fact precisely what the Bush administration ended up doing, subsequently judging it needful to act on the threat, which Walzer then condemned. For Walzer, the United States was damned if it did, damned if it did not go to war.

Walzer dismisses the humanitarian case for war against Iraq, which we will see is one of Biggar's primary arguments in favor. Walzer argues that the war cannot count as a humanitarian intervention because it was not in response to "an actual, ongoing massacre."[6] It seems artificial to insist that a massacre be presently occurring to justify an intervention and to disregard massacres that happened in the past, such as the massacre of Kurds at Halabja in 1988. It is equally artificial to disregard other atrocities, such as the general character of totalitarian rule through terror, torture, and extrajudicial executions that typified the Ba'athist regime. Walzer uses that distinction to claim that the war in Iraq was not a humanitarian war but a preemptive war for regime change. "Change of regime is not commonly accepted as a justification for war," he writes, once again relying on an unspecified subject who is "commonly accepting" his judgments.[7] Vitoria, Suarez, and Grotius did accept humanitarian intervention and regime change to stop "crimes against nature." Walzer acknowledges that aggression and massacre are "legitimate causes of war" and laments that we have failed so far to learn to respond to them "in a timely and forceful way,"[8] but he gives no thought to the possibility that the invasion of Iraq was just such an effort to respond in a timely and forceful way to a regime that had proven itself hell-bent on aggression and massacre over many decades. Walzer identifies a problem, calls for a solution, and damns those who assume the responsibility to respond to his call. He is guilty of Monday-morning quarterbacking, criticizing the decisions made in the moment by those who are charged with that responsibility but who lack the hindsight with which Walzer judges them and finds them wanting.

---

[6] Walzer, *Just and Unjust Wars*, 4th edition, xiii.   [7] Walzer, *Arguing about War*, 148.
[8] Walzer, *Just and Unjust Wars*, 4th edition, xiii.

Walzer also specifically denies the legitimacy of the humanitarian motive in Iraq since the Kurds were already protected from possible humanitarian crimes by a no-fly zone. In January and March 2003, in fact, he called for expanding the no-fly zone to the entirety of Iraq as an alternative to war. But a nationwide no-fly zone is not an alternative to war: it *is* war. The no-fly zone was a standing violation of Iraqi sovereignty and an ongoing state of war against the Iraqi air force and air defense systems. Walzer preferred this "little war" to the big one that actually happened, but the little war was a war with no end, no peace, and no justice. (Walzer developed a concept of *jus ad vim* for this and related cases, against which I argue later in the context of drone operations.) Walzer's willingness to keep a no-fly zone indefinitely indicates a striking lack of concern for the requirement to end wars and achieve some kind of peace at their conclusion; his call to expand it ignores the realities of what that policy actually entailed. That war should result in a stable peace afterwards is precisely the criticism Walzer rightly brings against the occupation of Iraq, yet he ignores how the same criticism should apply to the no-fly zone before the invasion. If just wars aim at peace, just no-fly zones must do the same.

By contrast, Biggar judges the Iraq War just.[9] He rightly argues that the coalition had two just causes: Saddam Hussein's regime was characteristically atrocious and it was reasonably thought to be pursuing weapons of mass destruction.[10] He places far greater weight on the humanitarian case than Walzer. But the key distinction between Biggar's argument and Walzer's is Biggar's characterization of the Iraqi regime and Saddam Hussein's intent. Because the regime had proven itself "atrocious" over many decades of aggression, oppression, and tyranny, and because Hussein had a demonstrable long-term intention to build weapons of mass destruction and evade the UN inspections regime, Biggar dismisses the idea that the international community could contain Iraq indefinitely through no-fly zones, sanctions, inspections, and a permanent threat of war. (He acknowledges that, given the realities of Iraq's WMD programs as discovered after the invasion, the coalition could have afforded to wait a bit longer but also that the coalition's preinvasion fears of Iraq were rational.) Biggar, I think, is right, and not just for practical reasons. The containment regime amounted to a permanent state of siege warfare

---

[9] Biggar, *In Defence of War*, chapter 7. Elshtain makes almost an identical case for the war in *Just War against Terror*, epilogue; and in "Terrorism, Regime Change, and Just War." I choose Biggar as my interlocutor because his treatment is far longer, more exhaustive, and written in 2013, with the benefit of hindsight, compared to Elshtain, writing in 2004.

[10] For an extended justification of the war as humanitarian intervention, see Teson, "Ending Tyranny in Iraq."

against Iraq with no path or plan for bringing itself to conclusion and building some kind of just peace. Among the options available in 2002–3, containment had no prospects for creating the "tranquility of order" in Iraq or between Iraq and the world.

Walzer has taken issue with the idea that the character of a regime can be a just cause for war. He argues, rightly I think, that whether a state is "autocratic or democratic, secular or religious . . . whether its bureaucrats acted arbitrarily or were legally constrained" should not weigh in our decisions about whether to go to war against them, and insists that the US government's policy of regime change "was arguing for a significant expansion of the doctrine of *jus ad bellum*."[11] Walzer's first claim is true, but it is also a non sequitur in the debate about Iraq, the argument for which Walzer seems to misunderstand. The United States did not invade Iraq because Iraq failed to hold elections, and Biggar does not judge the Ba'athist regime "characteristically atrocious" because of its constitution or its method of choosing rulers. Biggar rightly judges the Iraqi regime to be atrocious based on what those rulers did once in office – which included a pattern of international aggression, arbitrary rule, extrajudicial executions, torture, imprisonment of political opponents, denial of basic freedoms, and more – and what those actions said about their (mis)use of sovereignty and their intentions and capabilities towards their people and their neighbors. Recall from Chapter 4: Wolff argued in the seventeenth century that rulers should evaluate the character of other regimes to judge their intentions, and he counseled rulers to take precautionary action if a regime with a proven track record of aggression appeared poised to upset the balance of power. Biggar's argument makes use of the same idea: our prudential calculations in the moment about Iraq should consider what we know and what we can estimate about the Iraqi rulers' intentions, drawn from their histories and their character.

Johnson makes a parallel or complementary argument to Biggar. The strongest justification for the war, in his view, was that it was to enforce international law. The Iraqi regime was an international scofflaw, having evaded and flouted UN Security Council resolutions, international sanctions, and International Atomic Energy Agency inspections from 1991 onwards. In a sense, the 1991 Gulf War never ended. Hussein never fully accepted or abided by the peace terms of the earlier war, which demanded disarmament and transparency. "It has long been a principle of customary international law that breaking a truce reopens hostilities . . . given the repeated and egregious violations of the terms of the [1991] truce, this principle justified the removal of the Saddam Hussein regime," according

---

[11] Walzer, *Just and Unjust Wards*, 4th edition, xii–xiii.

to Johnson.[12] In that sense, the war was a response to existing conditions that were a standing affront to international order, not a preemptive use of force, and most of the debate about whether or not preemption was justified missed the point. Similarly, critics who object that the invasion violated Iraq's sovereignty overlook, or deny, that Hussein's own actions abrogated his government's sovereignty. Hussein "forfeited the right to sovereign immunity and, indeed, the right to govern Iraq with his tyrannical exercise of government," Johnson argues, "his crimes meant he could rightly be deposed and replaced."[13] The war was justified because of Hussein's tyranny and oppression as much as his violations of international law. Johnson notes that arguments in favor of regime change also necessarily must be arguments for regime-replacement and regime-construction; that is, if the United States set out to topple Hussein's government, it was also accepting moral responsibility for putting something else in place. Writing in 2005, he found fault with the Bush administration's inattention to these obligations.

Biggar also rightly argues that the coalition had a reasonable (not optimal) case for its authority to wage war. If anything, Biggar understates the case because, in the course of the war, two more just causes came about which enhanced the coalition's authority. After the invasion, al-Qaida (or jihadist copycats taking al-Qaida's brand name) chose to make Iraq a central battlefield in their war against the United States, turning the Iraq War into another front in the (justified) war against them. And Iran did much the same thing, treating Iraqi Shia militias as proxy forces for pursuing hegemony in the region. Combating both Iran and al-Qaida were additional just causes Biggar and most other scholars overlook, but they are key to the justice of the war in Iraq and the coalition's authority to wage it after the initial invasion.

But a war may have just premises, a just cause, or a just initiation and still not be a fully just war – or even a prudent war. From the foregoing arguments, I concur with Biggar that it was morally permissible to invade Iraq, but I would argue that there is a subsequent argument about whether it was prudent for the United States and its allies to act on that permission. There is good reason to doubt that it was, and not just because of our hindsight knowledge of what actually happened. During the early years of the Iraq War, for example, I witnessed firsthand one of its unintended but foreseeable effects in how it distracted attention and resources from the war in Afghanistan, a cost not easily justified or outweighed by any of the arguments in its favor. This highlights the

[12] Johnson, *War to Oust Saddam Hussein*, 55.
[13] Johnson, *War to Oust Saddam Hussein*, 63.

need to embed just war arguments into a broader conversation about *just grand strategy* or *just strategic thinking*. I hope my previous book, *American Power and Liberal Order*, is a helpful exercise in that regard.

Jus Post Bellum

More importantly, I differ with Biggar in his judgment about a range of issues that he collects under right intention and proportionality but which are better situated as matters of *jus post bellum* – and Biggar's categorization is part of the problem. Early in his book, he denies that *jus post bellum* is a useful addition to just war inquiry because, he says, these issues "are already implicit in the *ad bellum* requirements of right intention."[14] I agree that *jus post bellum* could, in principle, collapse into right intention, but not in the way Biggar does in his analysis of Iraq. In his argument about policymakers' intentions in going to war in Iraq, Biggar focuses exclusively on prewar inner motivations and declarative policy statements by senior policymakers, which excludes any consideration of *jus post bellum* reconstruction or peace building. If we collapse *jus post bellum* into right intention, then we need to examine combatants' *post bellum* behavior, not merely their prewar statements, as evidence of their intentions.

Biggar treats *jus post bellum* issues, somewhat confusingly, under the heading of proportionality. Here Biggar concedes that the coalition went to war with disproportionate means; that is, the United States and its allies did not marshal means commensurate with the end of building peace and justice in Iraq. This, I think, is *the dispositive fact* about the Iraq War's justice. War is fought for the sake of a better peace. If policymakers deliberately disrupt order and unleash the evils of war, they had better do so fully prepared to work for an outcome that reflects a better order and a better justice. That obviously never happened in Iraq. Biggar seems to acknowledge, yet downplay, the importance of this fact. "The United States and the United Kingdom did make plans to secure the peace after a successful invasion. They were serious in intending regime-change and not merely regime-toppling," he argues, conceding that "Their plans were vitiated, however, by naïve optimism, impatience with human frailty and inconvenient counsel, unwise disdain for regional and local expertise, and consequent imprudence." He believes this mark against the war is morally surmountable: "Right and sincere intention to exchange the regime of Saddam Hussein for something significantly better was not lacking at the beginning, and over time that intention proved itself serious."[15]

---

[14] Biggar, *In Defence of War*, 3.   [15] Biggar, *In Defence of War*, 305.

Biggar's conclusion misreads the evidence on the basis of a flawed premise. The flawed premise is his belief that the intentions that matter are those held by top policymakers at the start of the war. But those are not the only, and perhaps not the most important, motives that regulate a war's conduct. There are hundreds of key decision-makers throughout the military chain of command and the civilian agencies involved in a complex undertaking like the Iraq War, and those motivations exercise daily pressure on how the war is conducted; for Iraq this lasted eight long years. We need to examine the intention of the United States government as a corporate entity.

We cannot, of course, hunt out the motivations of every actor, every day, for eight years. How can we judge the motivation of the United States government as a whole over the entire duration of the war? We can look at the United States' long-term pattern of behavior over the course of the war, not merely at the moment of the war's initiation. That is, we can look at the United States' "revealed preference." A "revealed preference" is the preference or intention an actor shows through his or her actions, choices, and behavior, regardless of that actor's statements. To discern a revealed preference, we look at an actor's actual behavior, rather than his or her statements, and infer the preferences and intentions that are consistent with that behavior. Instead of looking at one or two top policymakers at single point in time – Bush and Blair in late 2002, early 2003 – we should look at the behavior of the coalition as a whole over the course of the entire war.

Consider the record of postwar planning. According to most accounts, what planning there was for a postwar Iraq was rushed, shallow, and inadequate. Central Command, the military's headquarters in the Middle East, produced planning so poor that senior US officials ignored it. The president created the Office of Reconstruction and Humanitarian Assistance in January 2003, just two months prior to the invasion. Jay Garner, the director of the new organization, convened a conference of experts from across the government in February to review the reconstruction of Iraq, just weeks before the war started. One of the conference's main conclusions was that there had been inadequate planning for postwar operations. The Defense Department initially planned to withdraw most US troops within six months of the fall of the Ba'athist regime. American soldiers who were in Baghdad shortly after the Ba'athist regime fell from power literally did not have orders about what to do next.[16]

---

[16] See Ricks, *Fiasco* and Woodward, *Plan of Attack* for a narrative of the lead-up to the Iraq War.

"It wasn't that there was no planning," writes Tom Ricks, a journalist who covers military issues and who did extensive research on the issue. "To the contrary, there was a lot, with at least three groups inside the military and one at the State Department working on postwar issues and producing thousands of pages of documents. But much of that planning was shoddy, there was no one really in charge of it, and there was little coordination between the various groups."[17] This view showed almost no concern at all for Iraqis, excused sometimes by a naive belief that the Iraqis would be able to care for their own needs as soon as they were liberated from Ba'ath tyranny. The absence of serious planning for post-war Iraq suggests a lack of concern for peace or justice in Iraq among US war planners.

Consider as well the military's initial choices and actions after the fall of Baghdad. The US Army's initial response to the insurgency – heavy-handed and careless – was another of the United States' major mistakes of the war. In fairness, counterinsurgency is one of the most challenging of all military operations because it requires militaries to use force mixed with other tools of national power, such as reconstruction and development assistance. However, also in fairness, the United States has fought counterinsurgencies before, including a fourteen-year campaign in the Philippines (1899–1913) and, of course, in Vietnam. The problem was that the US Army learned the wrong lesson from Vietnam: "After it came home from Vietnam, the Army threw away virtually everything it had learned there, slowly and painfully about how to wage a counterinsurgency campaign," according to Ricks, who argues that the army "took away from the Vietnam war only the lesson that it shouldn't get involved in messy counterinsurgencies."[18] Similarly, the US government as a whole has for decades undervalued and under-resourced the tools of reconstruction, stabilization, and peace building.

As a result, the US military in Iraq in 2003 was untrained and unready to assume the responsibilities of administering postwar Iraq, to interact with Iraqi civilians, or to respond in an effective, proportional, calibrated way to the small acts of violence that cumulatively make up an insurgency. The US Army had prepared for decades for large-scale conventional war. In the early years in Iraq the army resorted to massive sweeps by large conventional forces to round up all military-aged males in a region; soldiers burst into houses, breaking furniture and housewares, to arrest men in front of their families; convoys tore up Iraqi streets; and doctrine called for artillery and airstrikes against insurgents that also destroyed buildings and infrastructure. These kinds of tactics make sense if your

[17] Ricks, *Fiasco*, 79.   [18] Ricks, *Fiasco*, 133, 264.

main goal is to kill enemies. They are counterproductive if your goal is to stabilize a country.

A crucial part of counterinsurgency is upholding order and supporting a legitimate government – that is, working for peace. One anecdote in Bob Woodward's book *State of Denial* captures the military's early disregard for these goals well. According to Woodward, a subordinate told General David McKiernan, the commander of US ground forces in Iraq in 2003, that US forces needed to stop the looting that had erupted after the fall of the Ba'athist government.

"Our mission is to reestablish the government, and we can't do it if everything's being destroyed," the subordinate said.

"I don't ever want to hear that from your lips again," McKiernan replied, "That is not my job."[19]

McKiernan reportedly believed that it was not his job to restore order to a country he had just invaded and occupied. If just war aims at peace, McKiernan's response was morally incompetent. When US forces did not stop the looting, "The message sent to Iraqis ... was that the US government didn't care," according to Ricks. In the face of these realities on the ground, the question of Bush's motives in 2002 or 2003 is beside the point. The United States government, as a corporate entity, manifestly did not have right intention on a day-to-day basis on the ground from 2003 through 2006.

The collective result of inadequate planning plus the army's initial rejection of counterinsurgency warfare led to catastrophe. The litany of American follies is long and famous: American forces permitted law and order in Iraq to collapse after the fall of the Ba'athist regime, a clear and inexcusable sin of omission. The Coalition Provisional Authority disbanded the Iraqi Army, immediately turning it into a pool of tens of thousands of young, armed, unemployed, and angry Iraqi men. Many US generals continued to use a heavy-handed conventional-war approach for years after the emergence of the Iraqi insurgency even when it became abundantly clear that such tactics were counterproductive. Billions of dollars meant to help reconstruct Iraq were lost to waste, fraud, and abuse. And some US soldiers mistreated, abused, and humiliated Iraqi prisoners. The US military is all the more culpable for its failings because most of those failings also went against the army's official counterinsurgency doctrine. The 2006 field manual on counterinsurgency generally counseled restraint and prescribed efforts to win hearts and minds, and even included a section on discrimination and proportionality in the use of

---

[19] Woodward, *State of Denial*, 179.

force.[20] The military cannot, then, plead ignorance for how it bungled its occupation of Iraq.

The United States' failings were the natural consequence of waging war without thought for the peace at which war is supposed to aim. If, instead, the idealistic intentions of stabilization and democratization had been backed up by the programs, policies, and budgets necessary to become a reality; embraced with enthusiasm by the Departments of State and Defense, from the senior leadership to the desk officer and the foot soldier; articulated, defended, and implemented with clarity, competence, and humility by the president and the Congress, the American intervention in Iraq might well have made the world a more just and peaceful place.

With that in mind, Biggar's emphasis on Bush and Blair's intentions in 2003 is only a snapshot in time and does not capture the revealed preference of the coalition from 2003–11. When we look at the record of the coalition as a whole over the course of eight years, it is extraordinarily difficult to argue that it truly fought for the goal of peace and justice in Iraq.[21] Bush and Blair almost certainly did intend that goal, but Biggar himself notes that Secretary of Defense Donald Rumsfeld did not, nor did military commanders at lower levels who relied on inappropriate and excessively brutal tactics from 2004–6. Again, Biggar notes that the coalition marshalled disproportionate means: it did not bring to the fight the manpower, strategy, or financial means necessary to achieve order and justice in Iraq. Simply looking at the United States' budgetary and deployment decisions should be enough to persuade us that, as a whole, the US government did not organize itself for the purpose of peace and justice in Iraq. Biggar argues that the coalition gradually improved, demonstrating that it really intended to do the right thing all along. This, I think, misreads the evidence. The coalition improved its military approach through the adoption of a counterinsurgency strategy and the surge of troops in 2007–8, which speaks well of Bush's right intent (and General David Petreaus'). But the surge never improved the United States' political or economic approach, which is paramount in an effective counterinsurgency operation.

The final proof is that the United States simply ended its operations and withdrew its troops in 2011, allowing an authoritarian Shia government to take root, a vacuum of power to emerge in the provinces, and the return of jihadist groups a few short years later. Critics of President Barack Obama's withdrawal plans correctly argued that it would lead to

---

[20] Department of the Army, *Counterinsurgency*.
[21] See Nardin, "Humanitarian Imperialism," 24, for a similar argument.

the unraveling of security in Iraq and the loss of progress made since the 2007–8 surge. The surge had created an opportunity for Iraq to approach conditions of peace and justice, which would have changed the entire moral character of the war, mistakes and all. The 2011 withdrawal vitiated that opportunity. The withdrawal was a shocking abdication of responsibility for the moral outcome of the war. Obama's argument in favor of withdrawal seems to bear some resemblance to Ramsey's ultimate verdict on Vietnam: it was not worth the cost, and so failed the test of proportionality. The argument works much better for Vietnam, which was a much larger, longer, bloodier war, victory in which was far more questionable than it was in Iraq in 2008. Obama's calculation about the costs and proportion of the Iraq War look, on retrospect, culpably hasty, politically self-serving, and naive. The best that can be said is that Obama enacted the policies of the voters who elected him on a platform of ending the war in Iraq, in which case the ultimate fault for the war's unjust ending lies with the American people.

On the most charitable reading, we can conclude that the United States and its allies probably had right intention in 2002–3, rediscovered it in 2007–8, and deliberately turned their back on it in 2011. We can even recognize other pockets of success, such as in Mosul in 2003 and Tal Afar in 2006, where commanders bucked prevailing trends and implemented early versions of the 2007 counterinsurgency strategy. But that narrative is insufficient to establish the justice of the war. We must carry the story to the end and recognize that the circumstances of the war's conclusion are also relevant to our judgment about its overall justice. If Patterson is right to stress the "morality of victory," the United States' abandonment of any opportunity to achieve victory in 2011 was profoundly immoral. Biggar alludes to this way of assessing the war when he writes, "When do instances of negligence or malice so vitiate the whole of a collective action so as to make it basically unjust and oblige that it cease? Answer: when the instances are symptoms of a basic flaw."[22] Biggar thinks there was no basic flaw in the Iraq War; I think the evidence says otherwise, especially the evidence of the war's ending. In the previous chapter I analogized to Good Samaritan laws and argued that intervening states should enjoy immunity from liability except in cases of gross negligence. Unfortunately, the United States in Iraq was grossly negligent for most of its time there, nowhere more so than in its 2011 withdrawal, which was clearly an example of leaving before the patient was stabilized.

Biggar published his argument in 2013, just months before the Islamic State of Iraq and Syria (ISIS) made its dramatic appearance on the scene.

[22] Biggar, *In Defence of War*, 314.

The rise of ISIS and the resumption of US military operations in Iraq later in 2014 is, I think, conclusive proof that the 2003–11 war did not achieve the peace and justice for which it was supposed to have been fought. Given how events turned out, how can we say that the war was rightly motivated? Or that it met the criteria of *jus post bellum*? Johnson rightly notes that having right intention "is an important first step, but to aim at peace does not mean only having an intention; it means taking the responsibility to achieve that peace," and that in Iraq, "there were important failures in actuality."[23] Despite my earlier criticisms of Walzer's analysis of Iraq, his conclusion on *jus post bellum* is correct: "Surely occupying powers are morally bound to think seriously about what they are going to do in someone else's country. That moral test we have obviously failed to meet."[24]

Afghanistan

The first dispiriting thing about the debate over the war in Afghanistan is that there hardly is one, and the one that happened was mostly beside the point. The unnecessary debate was about whether the United States and the international community had just cause to go to war. To my mind, the justice of the American and allied operations against al-Qaida and the Taliban in response to the terrorist attacks of 2001 is so obvious as to hardly merit explication or defense, yet a few voices raised dissents anyway, giving validity to the accusation that some critics are functionally pacifists without admitting it. One scholar was scandalized that moral arguments were "smoothly deployed to justify military action against Afghanistan," as if they should not have been – when military action was, in fact, easily justified. He concludes that "moral discourses are part of the warrior's political armoury ... moral rules about war's justification, process and restraint may function not so much as limitations on war as tools for its liberation," reflecting the view that just war should contain a presumption against force, even after one actor has been attacked by another. He bemoans "the subversion of effective peacekeeping in post-Taliban Afghanistan by US priorities," as if US counterterrorism operations in Afghanistan were immaterial to building peace there.[25]

---

[23] Johnson, *War to Oust Saddam Hussein*, 142.   [24] Walzer, *Arguing about War*, 165.
[25] Burke, "Just War or Ethical Peace?" 330, 350. For other examples of dissent, see Vorobej, "Just War Theory"; Rigstad, "*Jus Ad Bellum* after 9/11"; (parts of) Crawford, "Just War Theory." See also Blumenwitz, "Future of World Order," in De Paulo et al., *Augustinian Just War Theory*. Even a highly critical account such as Dorn, "Just War Index" concedes that the United States had just cause in Afghanistan.

Several scholars seem to be under the misapprehension that the United States went to war against the Taliban without having first tried to secure their cooperation against al-Qaida, despite President Bush's very public demand for exactly that on September 20, 2001. Moreover, some critics put the burden on the United States to concede to the Taliban on terms of cooperation rather than the other way around. But their logic is backwards. Because of the Taliban's prior history with and active support for al-Qaida from 1996 onwards, the United States' right of war against al-Qaida was presumptively applicable to the Taliban absent any countervailing proof, which the Taliban did not even try to provide despite US demands. The Taliban's support for al-Qaida has been one of their most consistent policies in almost thirty years of their existence.[26] Most observers rightly noted that the United States had just cause to go to war against al-Qaida in self-defense and against the Taliban because of their mutual interdependence with the terrorist group, but they then quickly moved on without deeper reflection on what the war should seek to achieve.

As I discussed in this book's opening pages, I always felt there was more to be said: simply pronouncing on the matter of just cause does not get at the heart of what it means to do justice in and through the war in Afghanistan or the war against al-Qaida and its affiliates. Complicating the issue is that the American and international response to 9/11 involved two separate but related operations: a campaign in Afghanistan that involved regime change and state building, and a global counterterrorism campaign that was broader in geographical scope but involved a smaller, more surgical use of force. They are related and the just war issues at stake partially overlap but also partially diverge. I consider both campaigns in turn.

Afghanistan and Peace Building

The war in Afghanistan is an excellent case for exploring who the "self" of self-defense is and what *jus post bellum* requires. The Afghan people had

---

[26] Vorobej, Rigstad, and Crawford all make this error, at least partly by accepting at face value that the Taliban were acting in good faith when they offered to hand bin Laden over to a "neutral" third party and asserting that the United States should have taken them up on the offer. The offer was transparently a stalling tactic; the Taliban did not denounce al-Qaida or sever ties with them (and still have not, as of this writing, almost twenty years later, not even after the February 2020 withdrawal agreement), nor did they accept the United States' other demands as laid out in Bush's September 20 speech. Scholarship that cannot be bothered to take stock of basic facts, speak directly and clearly, or recognize the responsibility of intellectuals to the public square only serves to reinforce the perception that academia is sometimes irrelevant, if not actively hostile to the society that promotes and protects their own academic freedom. Against such critics Elshtain's book-length riposte in *Just War against Terror* is definitive.

just cause to rebel against the totalitarian Taliban theocracy when it seized power in 1996 – especially Afghan Shia and Hazara, against whom the Taliban waged a campaign tantamount to ethnic cleansing – and they had a right to seek international partners in their causes. The Northern Alliance attempted to do so for five long years, fruitlessly because no international partners saw a national security interest at stake in Afghanistan's civil war, despite the fact that intervention before 2001 would have been permissible simply on humanitarian grounds.

The United States, of course, had ample just cause after the 2001 terrorist attacks in New York and Washington, DC to defend itself, punish al-Qaida and its Taliban allies, and deter future attacks. (As did most of the international community. Excluding the hijackers, citizens of seventy-seven nations died in the attack, with non-Americans amounting to more than 10 percent of the fatalities.) But if that were the sum total of what justice allowed and required in Afghanistan, coalition forces might have left in March 2002, after ejecting al-Qaida from the country, or in May 2011, after executing Osama bin Laden, and they might have left off the hard and messy work of state building and reconstruction that has in fact occupied much of the international community's attention since 2001.

There are at least four grounds on which to justify an enduring American and international obligation to Afghanistan. First, the United States and its allies have a moral obligation to their own citizens to provide for their security by winning the war against the Taliban and al-Qaida – which, in this context, means waging an effective counterinsurgency campaign. There is every reason to believe that al-Qaida or its fellow travelers, such as ISIS, will simply return to Afghanistan upon the United States' departure unless and until it is able to build a stable government and an indigenous security force capable of denying safe haven to jihadists with minimal international assistance. I recall again Patterson's insistence about the "morality of victory" and the moral imperative of order. If the war was just to begin with, it is just to win. The United States and the Taliban signed a deal in early 2020, as I was finishing this manuscript, obligating the United States to withdraw its troops within fourteen months. It is too early to say with certainty, but my initial judgment is that the deal serves the Taliban's interests more than the United States' because it does not require the Taliban to break with al-Qaida publicly, verifiably, and irreversibly. If the United States completes its withdrawal, it is likely to hand over much of the country to Taliban control and thus allow al-Qaida to regain safe haven. Like the 2011 withdrawal from Iraq, the deal seems to abandon any possibility of achieving a moral victory in Afghanistan.

Winning this kind of war includes state building. Building governance is an essential part of the counterinsurgency campaign against the Taliban. The Taliban were able to recoup and launch their insurgency in 2005 because the Afghan government remained weak and efforts to rebuild had been paltry. Seth Jones of the Center for Strategic and International Studies, the foremost American expert on the Taliban insurgency, argues that "Weak governance is a common precondition of insurgencies. The Afghan government was unable to provide basic services to the population; its security forces were too weak to establish law and order; and too few international forces were available to fill the gap. Afghan insurgent groups took advantage of this anarchic situation."[27] Countering an insurgency therefore critically depends on reconstruction and governance reform, on the effort to "foster the development of effective governance by a legitimate government," according to the US Army's counterinsurgency field manual.[28] Reconstruction and stabilization – the requirements of *jus post bellum* – are themselves weapons of war in a counterinsurgency. The United States' obligation to rebuild Afghanistan and its obligation to defeat the Taliban and al-Qaida are the same.

Second, the United States and its international partners have significant *jus post bellum* obligations in Afghanistan. This may seem odd because the war is not over and it is not really a *post bellum* situation yet. But those categories were formulated to structure theological and legal debate and do not always easily map onto messy cases of real-life conflict, especially unconventional conflicts. The United States and its partners overthrew the Afghan government, thereby taking on the steepest of *post bellum* obligations. The United States has to establish order, justice, and take steps towards conciliation, none of which have been accomplished yet. If the United States withdraws from Afghanistan precipitously, without ensuring the establishment of a stable government capable of upholding order, civil war will almost certainly erupt. The warlords who fought the civil wars of the 1990s can reestablish their brutal fiefdoms. The Taliban will take power over part or all of Afghanistan, and reprisal murders against supporters of the Kabul government will be widespread and swift – especially against women, Hazara, Shia, Tajiks, and other religious minorities. Al-Qaida, ISIS, or other copycats would reestablish their safe haven. The patient has not been stabilized, and the United States has an obligation to remain on the scene.

---

[27] Jones, "Rise of Afghanistan's Insurgency," 8.
[28] Department of the Army, *Counterinsurgency*, 1–16.

Third, states have a positive "duty to assist" those with whom they have a special relationship, including allies and those to whom they have explicitly promised aid. The United States has a special relationship with Afghanistan. That relationship dates back to 1979, when the United States used Afghanistan as a proxy against the Soviet Union in a highly destructive but ultimately successful war. That war imposed on the United States (and Saudi Arabia and Pakistan) some obligation to help Afghanistan recover from the war damage, a responsibility the United States shirked to its own detriment. The special relationship has been strengthened since 2001 by the United States' repeated, explicit promises to help Afghanistan. In 2005 President George W. Bush signed the US–Afghanistan Strategic Partnership Agreement, which expressed "a commitment to an Afghanistan that is democratic, free, and able to provide for its own security," and pledged to "help ensure Afghanistan's long-term security, democracy, and prosperity." Bush had promised in April 2002, "We know that true peace will only be achieved when we give the Afghan people the means to achieve their own aspirations."

President Obama similarly said in March 2009:

We are in Afghanistan to confront a common enemy that threatens the United States, our friends and our allies, and the people of Afghanistan and Pakistan . . . . That is a cause that could not be more just . . . . We have a shared responsibility to act – not because we seek to project power for its own sake, but because our own peace and security depends on it.[29]

To that end, Obama signed another strategic partnership agreement, this one in 2012, which pledged American help, "so that Afghanistan can independently secure and defend itself against internal and external threats, and help ensure that terrorists never again encroach on Afghan soil and threaten Afghanistan, the region, and the world." That same year he designated Afghanistan a major non-NATO ally, and in 2013 the two countries signed a bilateral security agreement with expansive ambitions. The agreement pledged the two countries to work together "to strengthen security and stability in Afghanistan, counter terrorism, contribute to regional and international peace and stability, and enhance the ability of Afghanistan to deter internal and external threats against its sovereignty, security, territorial integrity, national unity, and its constitutional order." These bipartisan, consistent, explicit, and repeated words of promise to the Afghans establish a strong and unique moral obligation to stay and rebuild.

Fourth, the war in Afghanistan is a justified war to defend the liberal international order. One way of clarifying these responsibilities is simply

[29] Obama, *Remarks by the President on a New Strategy.*

to ask who the "self" of self-defense is. As I argued in the previous chapter, the Augustinian and Liberal traditions of just war thinking understand the self differently than the Westphalian tradition. They understand that the thing needing defense is not a territorial unit but the common good, the common weal, the tranquility of order, the ideals of justice, or (in the Liberal tradition) human rights – and, crucially, we should defend the ideals of justice, order, and human rights *for our enemies and neighbors* as much as for ourselves. Some just war thinkers did not shrink from describing the "self" in global terms, as the unity of all humanity.

This broader way of understanding justice in war – to defend our allies and the ideals of ordered liberty among nations, not just our territory – points to a more expansive way in which the war against the Taliban can be justified: it is a war to vindicate and defend the ideals of the liberal international order and the principles of ordered liberty among nations, ideals which al-Qaida and their Taliban supporters violently attacked. Vindicating ordered liberty means that our war in Afghanistan should culminate with the construction of peace in Afghanistan, not simply the eradication of threats to us. Ramsey might say that if we love the Afghans as neighbors, *including the Taliban as our enemy neighbor*, our war in their country will aim at their good, not only our security.

The United States does not have a moral duty to intervene everywhere there is injustice: that would entail a global crusade of never-ending conflict worse than the disease it aimed to cure. Women, minorities, and political dissidents are oppressed around the world every day, and most of the time the United States is obligated to do exactly nothing. But the United States and its allies and partners have a special obligation in Afghanistan. Intervening states have an obligation to stay on the scene until the patient is stabilized, by which standard the United States and the international community have not yet discharged their duty to Afghanistan. That the United States' earlier mistakes have only pro-longed the crisis does not excuse its enduring responsibility; if anything, it increases it. In light of these considerations, the 2020 withdrawal deal between the United States and the Taliban is little more than abandon-ment, a dereliction of duty by the United States towards its Afghan partners. There is a very small chance that the Taliban and the Afghan government will successfully conclude negotiations to end the war and protect US security interests. I am deeply skeptical such an outcome is possible – and even in that highly unlikely scenario I argue the United States still has unfulfilled *post bellum* obligations to Afghanistan.

Arguing that we have a special obligation to help Afghanistan does not establish a universal precedent to intervene everywhere. It does not create an endless obligation to help Afghanistan forever. Nor does it give the

United States a writ to establish a liberal empire. The American obligation to Afghanistan is unique: it was established when the United States used them to fight a proxy war against the Soviet Union. It deepened when the United States overthrew the Afghan government, obliging the United States to help put something in its place. It deepened further when the United States, by its own actions, furthered the Afghans' misery through negligence and strategic errors that enabled the rise of the Taliban insurgency and prolonged the war. It deepened still further when the United States made repeated and explicit promises to help through several formal international agreements. The American obligation was formalized when it designated Afghanistan an ally of the United States. Afghanistan meets every possible criteria of moral obligation; it is hard to imagine a scenario which would generate stronger ties of moral obligation between two countries. If the United States has no moral duty to Afghanistan, there is no morality among nations and just war inquiry is empty of meaning.

Is the War in Afghanistan Proportional?

Let me respond to two objections. First, what does victory look like? Some critics claim that the kind of "victory" I am talking about – the reestablishment of order and justice – is too vague and aspirational. Some critics argue that because this kind of victory cannot be quantified and measured, it can never be definitively achieved. Defining the mission this way guarantees we will never win and never leave. I respond, first, with Aristotle: "Our discussion will be adequate if it has as much clearness as the subject-matter admits of, for precision is not to be sought for alike in all discussions . . .. It is the mark of an educated man to look for precision in each class of things just so far as the nature of the subject admits."[30] Defining victory in counterinsurgency war does not admit of a high degree of precision and it is counterproductive to push too hard for it. I do not think it is useful to talk about "exit strategies" in war or to insist that our war planners present, before the beginning of hostilities, a detailed blueprint for how they will end. The expectation we put on war planners to tell us what things will look like at the end of war and to define victory in precise and measurable terms, especially for a counterinsurgency war, puts an unrealistic expectation on human knowledge and human capabilities. We are not omniscient and we cannot orchestrate a precise chain of political and military events with complete control. To some degree,

---

[30] Aristotle, *Ethics*, book I, chapter 3.

victory in war is among those class of things for which "you know it when you see it."

To the extent we can define victory, the principles of *jus post bellum* are a good framework: order, justice, and conciliation; or, as I reformulated it, making right the wrongs that started the war, making right the wrongs of war, and preventing the recurrence of those wrongs. Order is easiest to define and measure, and, even by that minimal standard, the United States has not yet discharged its obligation because there is an ongoing insurgency and the Afghan government's army and police force cannot yet establish or enforce public order unaided. Together with the Afghans, we have taken meaningful steps towards a more just government in Afghanistan that the Afghans themselves accept – through its new constitution and repeated rounds of elections – and ongoing negotiations with the Taliban may set the Afghans on the road towards some kind of conciliation, but both efforts are a long way from a positive self-sustaining trajectory. Or if we use my reformulation of *jus post bellum*, the United States has arguably made right the wrong that started the war by overthrowing the Taliban and severely damaging al-Qaida, and has made some good faith efforts at making right the wrongs of war through reconstruction assistance (wasteful and ineffective though much of it has been). But with the insurgency still ongoing, it has clearly not established conditions to prevent the recurrence of the wrongs or set the country on a sustainable course. Whatever else victory may involve, it certainly involves an end to the Taliban insurgency as a necessary precondition to anything else.

My interpretation of the Afghan case shares some similarities, but more differences, with Patterson, one of the few scholars to give attention to just war in Afghanistan. Patterson argues that a major problem in Afghanistan is that we did not claim the mantle of victory and truly end the war. That we did not defeat the Taliban is, of course, a significant problem, though this is a bit more complicated than simply announcing victory. Patterson rightly criticizes the injustices and corruption of the Afghan government as a major source of ongoing difficulties. But he also complains that the West "implemented the sort of post-conflict cookie-cutter 'packages' envisaged by the R2P document," and accuses the United States of adopting a "development first" framework.[31] Reconstruction efforts have certainly been problematic, but I think the main problem has been inattention and underfunding rather than the shape of the "package" used, and the overall effort has been too incoherent to characterize it as prioritizing development over governance or security. Patterson

---

[31] Patterson, *Ending Wars Well*, 174.

complains that the US mission turned from defeating terrorists to nation building; as I've argued, I think the one entails the other. We cannot claim the mantle of victory without some attention to stabilization and reconstruction. He warns against "the hubris which inspires ever-inflating war aims" and against turning post-conflict stabilization operations into a "crusade" or a "revolution."[32] Again, I see little merit to the accusation of "hubris." The main problem has been that the United States has done too little, not too much, and that its ambitions are too small, not overweening or arrogant. Finally, Patterson criticizes the new government in Kabul for trying to govern according to a Western blueprint in an Afghan context. This, I think, is baseless because there is nothing uniquely "Western" about the rule of law, bureaucratic efficiency, standards of transparency and honesty, nor even majoritarian rule and representative institutions. Human rights, religious freedom, and women's rights are the closest things to "Western" norms implemented in Afghanistan today, but they are hardly the root cause of Afghanistan's ongoing difficulties.[33]

The other objection I want to respond to is, after nearly twenty years, have we not discharged our duty? When is our obligation over? Some critics of the war claim that we have tried and failed to rebuild Afghanistan; therefore, they say, the war does not have a reasonable chance of success and its costs outweigh its potential benefits. This is essentially the argument that ultimately turned Ramsey against the Vietnam War. But the argument does not work well for Afghanistan. These critics are wrong because they misunderstand what the United States and the international community have actually done in Afghanistan. My response is thus empirical, not theoretical: we have to understand what has actually happened in the international project in Afghanistan to understand whether or not we have succeeded or failed, what the relative costs and benefits are, and thus whether the war can be counted as properly proportional.

The United States has done, spent, and fought in Afghanistan far less than is widely understood. Between 2001 and 2005, and again from 2012 to 2020, in particular, the United States devoted almost no resources to reconstruction, stabilization, counterinsurgency, or state building but was focused almost solely on counterterrorism and on training the Afghan military. We cannot conclude that the war was disproportional, that it was too costly, or that the United States proved the futility of peace

---

[32] Patterson, *Ending Wars Well*, 173–174.

[33] I've emphasized my differences with Patterson here, but our views ultimately overlap more than they differ. See also Patterson, "Ethics and US Af-Pak Policy" and "Bury the Bloody Hatchet," for the further development of his views on Afghanistan.

building in Afghanistan through its failure because the United States never fully tried.

The confusion stems from the fact that there has been a sharp disconnect between the United States' declarative policy and its actual policy choices. There has been a persistent gap between the United States' publicly declared goals, which have often been far-reaching and ambitious, and the revealed preference of its policymakers to do only what is minimally required to stave off immediate or catastrophic defeat. The result is a constant sense of failure and a belief that the United States has been trying, and failing, to achieve lofty goals for nearly two decades.

President George W. Bush spoke grandly about his desire to spread democracy and rebuild nations, but in practice he adopted a "light footprint" approach and tried to outsource state building efforts to the United Nations. After the emergence of the Taliban insurgency in late 2005 and early 2006, Bush began to shift towards a counterinsurgency strategy, but his simultaneous move in Iraq starved the Afghan mission of needed resources. President Obama initially embraced and dramatically expanded the counterinsurgency strategy and shrunk the gap between rhetoric and policy – but undercut himself by announcing a withdrawal deadline in advance and (a widely underreported part of Obama's failure) never following through with adequate funds for civilian reconstruction. I tried, and failed, to persuade both presidents to change course while working in the White House for their administrations.

Another way of putting it is that the United States has pursued two different goals across two different time frames and with two different sets of tools. The United States' long-term goal is, ostensibly, a secure, stable, democratic Afghanistan capable of defending itself and its borders and denying terrorists safe haven with its own security forces, which is consistent with the demands of just war. At the same time, the United States' actual policy choices as reflected in its budgetary and deployment decisions – its de facto strategy or revealed preference – show a different set of goals and priorities. American policymakers consistently implemented a different strategy than they have claimed. The implemented strategy has prioritized killing and capturing jihadist militants while investing just enough in counterinsurgency and stability operations to preserve operational freedom for American counterterrorism forces. The Trump administration continued the same short-term strategy without the pretense of pursuing the longer-term goals, and then signaled its intent to give up on even the short-term goals with its 2020 withdrawal agreement.

Policymakers' persistent prioritization of short-term goals has a self-defeating quality: the United States has perfected the art of killing and capturing jihadist militants while enjoying less success in preventing their radicalization in the first place, ensuring the war will never end. That is why, under the current strategy, the net effect of all of America's efforts in Afghanistan will never result in justice or peace in Afghanistan. Two scholars wrote of the intervention:

> The tensions between the real grounds for the intervention and the alternative justifications for it have come to haunt the stabilization and state-building process in Afghanistan. The intervention was conducted not to promote security or stability in Afghanistan, but to ensure that Afghanistan could no longer be a source of insecurity for the United States and its allies. This has resulted in a state-building process hampered by competing and largely incompatible agendas.[34]

The worst aspects of President Donald Trump's approach to the war, until the withdrawal agreement, was his declared intent to avoid "nation building" and his rejection of any plans to reinvest in reconstruction or stabilization operations. Trump was doubling down on the strategy of killing bad guys while ignoring the broader conditions that make Afghanistan ripe for jihadist violence and a terrorist safe haven, an approach that created the ideal conditions for Taliban insurgency when Bush tried it from 2002 to 2005. This strategy cannot succeed at defeating the Taliban, winning the war, rebuilding Afghanistan, or establishing conditions for long-term stability – because it was not trying to accomplish those goals.

Giving up on aspirations to win the war meant the American soldier was trapped waging a never-ending frontier conflict on the furthest edges of the international system, the proverbial "endless war" that Trump and others rightly criticized. But "endless war" is not a sign of policy failure: it is what US policymakers, including Trump, have deliberately chosen because they will neither accept defeat nor pay the price of a more ambitious campaign to win. It is a feature, not a bug, of American strategy. Until the 2020 withdrawal agreement, American strategy aimed to sustain an indefinite counterterrorism presence in South Asia to kill or capture militant leaders while avoiding a Taliban takeover in Afghanistan. By that standard, the policy was a complete success, was indefinitely sustainable, and was morally indefensible. It is fundamentally unjust to deliberately prolong the conditions of war out of convenience, to fight because it is easier than investing in conditions of lasting peace.

That also means critics have no grounds to declare that the course of the war proves that the strategy I recommend is too costly, disproportional, or doomed to failure. At no point in the nineteen years since the initial

---

[34] Ayub and Kuovo, "Righting the Course," 647–648.

intervention has the United States implemented the kind of strategy I recommend, the kind of strategy designed to achieve lasting peace and justice in Afghanistan. Instead, the US government and its international partners have consistently sought to minimize their costs and investment and their liability for the course of events in Afghanistan. Even during the high point of US involvement, President Obama starved it of the one resource it most needed: time. Critics are right to highlight the consistent record of failure and underperformance in the war – but that failure is because the United States long ago stopped trying to achieve peace and justice in Afghanistan, not because it spent too much, tried too hard, or fought too long to achieve it.

Forever War: The War on Terror

My critique of the war in Afghanistan is by and large the same critique I want to level against the global counterterrorism operations against al-Qaida and other jihadist groups as a whole. The way these operations are being waged bespeaks no intention to end the war or usher in justice or peace, anywhere, even under the far lower standard of *jus post bellum* it should meet given the more narrowly targeted use of force in these operations. The United States has just cause for war against jihadist groups, but it is abusing that authority, holding onto it like a permission slip with no expiration date, to sustain an indefinite, never-ending assassination campaign against anyone it unilaterally deems to be a terrorist, anywhere in the world, forever. To be clear, I do not believe the United States has misused this authority or deliberately attacked anyone without just cause, but the unaccountable, unchecked, open-ended nature of the authority the US government has arrogated to itself is appalling and indefensible.

One of the best critiques of the United States' war against jihadists was, ironically, by President Obama, who did very little to effect the change he called for in his 2013 speech about the war at the National Defense University. Of the war against al-Qaida, Obama rightly said, "this war, like all wars, must end." He described victory the right way, as the return of conditions of justice and peace. "Victory will be measured in parents taking their kids to school; immigrants coming to our shores; fans taking in a ballgame; a veteran starting a business; a bustling city street; a citizen shouting her concerns at a President." This kind of victory must obtain abroad as well as at home: "This means patiently supporting transitions to democracy .... And we must help countries modernize economies, upgrade education, and encourage entrepreneurship."[35]

---

[35] Obama, "Remarks by the President."

Obama was right that the war against al-Qaida must end; that the United States must aim for some kind of victory; that victory means justice, peace, and democracy at home and abroad. Obviously, this is not and cannot be an open-ended obligation to coercively democratize the world. No serious scholar or policymaker advocates such a course (that is certainly not what I am arguing in this book), and critics who argue against it are arguing against a straw man. And our obligations are limited by other considerations. Elshtain rightly argues that our responsibility to rebuild is commensurate with the degree of our involvement, which suggests a lower level of responsibility for surgical counterterrorism operations than for the large-scale and invasive operations in Iraq and Afghanistan.

How do we judge our responsibility to other countries in wartime and afterwards? I argued in Chapter 7 that our responsibilities for post-conflict peace are deeper if we have special ties to the state in question, if we have made explicit promises to them, if we bear any responsibility for the conditions that led to their emergency, and so forth. Under those criteria, the United States has the greatest responsibility for Iraq and Afghanistan, which I have already discussed at length. Regarding the wide region of the world in which the United States is engaged in its war against al-Qaida and other jihadist groups, the United States has comparatively smaller obligations – but there are obligations nonetheless. If we are going to drop bombs on terrorists in Yemen and Pakistan, train security forces in Ethiopia or Saudi Arabia, and fund other states' military operations against our common enemies, we have some obligation to see that our influence is a net positive in the region, that we nudge states and nations towards, and not away from, ordered liberty.

Even by that minimal standard, the United States is failing. But the United States' sin is not that it tried and failed; rather, it simply has not tried. The Obama administration, for example, did little to discourage coups against democratically elected governments in Mali in 2012 or Egypt in 2013 or to address the slow erosion of democracy in Turkey. When Iranians took to the streets in their Green Revolution in 2009 and when the Arab Spring broke out in 2011, his administration largely stood by and watched events and spoke out haltingly and late. US foreign assistance – a crucial tool for shaping events, supporting democratic movements and investing in allies around the world – declined from $47.6 billion in 2011 to $36.6 billion in 2016. The decline was not wholly due to the drawdown in military assistance to Iraq and Afghanistan: democracy assistance declined globally from $3.5 billion in 2010 to a low of $1.2 billion in 2016. And, of course, Obama withdrew from Iraq and (after a brief surge) mostly from Afghanistan as well, leaving both worse off than when he took office. While superficially appealing for its apparent realism and humility, the net effect of Obama's counter-terrorism strategy was to abandon any effort to achieve lasting peace and to consign the Middle East and South Asia to a state of endless war.

Instead of investing in ordered liberty, Obama's policies – and, to be fair, those of his predecessor and successor – prolonged the war against al-Qaida and other jihadist groups by avoiding the commitments necessary to win it. Bush and Obama at least got the rhetoric right by talking about the importance of democracy and accountable governance as long-term solutions to the challenge of jihadism, which Trump has abandoned. But in practice, instead of investing in human development, civil society, and liberal reform across the region that is affected by jihadist violence, the United States has instead deployed an astonishingly efficient, highly discriminating, open-ended, and unaccountable assassination operation. The war against al-Qaida has set aside *jus post bellum* and instead become a never-ending whack-a-mole campaign in which jihadists are the mole and unmanned aerial vehicles, or drones, are the mallet.

This critique is likely to find favor with scholars who have made similar criticisms of US counterterrorism policy – but if so, they should recognize the implications of my argument. I am not calling for an end to the war but, effectively, its escalation. I do not mean the escalation of military operations necessarily (though that may be the case in, for example, Afghanistan) but the escalation of all other means of bringing about an ordered peace in areas threatened by jihadist violence. I recognize that this takes us beyond a narrow conversation about just war into a broader conversation about just grand strategy, but the nature of a global coun-terterrorism operation justifies this approach: the war cannot be won unless it is embedded in a coherent and just grand strategy that integrates all components of national power. Because we are warring against jihadist groups worldwide, we have a responsibility to seek a plausible end to that war. That means we must work towards the eventual defeat of jihadism as an ideology, as a social and cultural movement as much as a military force, and work for its replacement with something approximating ordered liberty. That effort requires tools of peace building as much as war making.

Critics are sure to argue that my call for "winning" the war against al-Qaida and investing in peace across the Middle East, North Africa, and South Asia is far too vast, undefined, and ambitious, and, therefore, it has no reasonable chance of success and cannot be pursued in a proportional way. I agree that there is no immediate prospect for turning the entire region into a model of liberal democracy, but that is not the standard of "victory" I have in mind. My point is that, by any minimal standard, the

United States has mostly failed to make an appreciable difference in favor of peace, justice, or liberty anywhere in the region, despite opportunities to do so.[36]

The United States has had opportunities to make real progress towards ordered liberty in the region. There are achievable milestones of progress at which the United States and local partners can and should aim. Both Iraq and Afghanistan, where the United States has been most intensively engaged, have held repeated rounds of national elections, liberalized press freedom, expanded women's rights, and more. Both countries have (precariously) sustained their new democratic constitutions, albeit with serious challenges from corruption, sectarianism, and ongoing violence. Outside Iraq and Afghanistan, the region has seen a few fleeting signs of progress. In 2018, Freedom House ranked Tunisia "free," based on its transition to democracy after the Arab Spring, and Morocco, Jordan, Kuwait, and Pakistan as "partly free." The Arab Spring itself (and the Green Revolution in Iran) was testament to the palpable desire for more accountable, responsive government across the region. Critics who argue that there is no reasonable chance of success for ordered liberty in the Middle East, North Africa, or South Asia are largely arguing against the wishes of the very people who live in those regions. Progress is possible: there is a reasonable chance of some kind of progress.

But those few examples only serve to highlight that, by and large, the United States has mostly failed to make use of those opportunities for progress. Take Patterson's criteria of *jus post bellum*. The first and most important criteria, without which we are unable to pursue any others, is the reestablishment of public order. Or take the first criterion I suggested: righting the wrongs that started the war in the first place. Even by those minimal standards, the United States has failed. There is no public order in Iraq, Afghanistan, Syria, Libya, or western Pakistan. In the case of Libya, the United States and its NATO allies were directly responsible for the breakdown of public order because they overthrew the government without following through to help with political reconstruction afterwards.

More importantly, jihadist groups are thriving across the region. Jones estimated in 2018 that there were up to 270 percent more jihadist fighters around the world than in 2001, organized into sixty-seven different groups – at or near an all-time high at least since 1980, when the dataset begins.[37] Jihadist groups are more popular, more widespread, and more powerful in 2020 than at any point since 2001. Whatever the United

---

[36] I tried to outline a grand strategy against jihadism in Miller, "How Does Jihadism End?"
[37] Jones, *Evolution of the Salafi-Jihadist Threat.*

States has done and however scholars characterize its strategy or define success, the net effect is the opposite of what it should be. There is less order and more wrong than before the war started.

Some critics are worried that an overly militarized response to terrorism would be counterproductive and unjust. I sympathize with this, but two points are important to keep in mind. First, there is a legitimate role for the use of force to combat armed militants and (probably more importantly) train local security forces to uphold public order. Perhaps the first and most important thing the United States could do is dramatically expand its security assistance programs in those countries willing to learn what accountable policing under law looks like. Second, in response to critics who want to cordon off the conversation about nonmilitary post-conflict operations that foster reform and liberalization from just war thinking to avoid polluting one with the other, I respond that it emphatically does belong in this discussion about *jus post bellum*. We cannot simply note that nonmilitary efforts are needed, and then move on as if other scholars in other fields will pick up the baton. They might, but not under the just war perspective and not with attention to the ethical obligations inherent in post-conflict operations. Leaving the discussion to others will do nothing to bridge the gap between civilians and the military, and between ethicists and practitioners, that has plagued this effort. We also cannot expect policymakers to pick up the baton because they palpably have not done so. We must stress and repeat the moral imperative of planning and budgeting for reconstruction, stabilization, and post-conflict operations *in and with* military planning for them to be effective. Military operations that do not plan for their termination and aftermath are unjust.[38]

The Ethics of Drone Warfare

This is the right context in which to consider the ethics of drone warfare. In his 2013 speech, President Obama publicly acknowledged that the United States used drones (technically, remotely piloted, unmanned aerial vehicles) for "lethal, targeted action against al Qaeda and its associated forces."[39] According to the New America Foundation, the United States used drones to bomb suspected terrorist targets in Pakistan, Yemen, and Somalia over 1,030 times from 2001 to mid-2020 (57 percent of them under the Obama administration), killing between 5,200 and 7,300 people.[40] By itself, there is not much novel to say about the

---

[38] Schadlow, *War and the Art of Governance.*   [39] Obama, "Remarks by the President."
[40] New America Foundation, "America's Counterterrorism Wars."

ethics of drones, other than that their use should abide by the same principles of discrimination and proportionality as all other tools of warfare (principles for which drones seem to be exceptionally well suited; according to the New America Foundation's high estimate, only 7.6 percent of casualties from drone strikes have been civilians).

But the strategic context in which they have been allegedly deployed since 2001 matters a great deal, as does the convenience with which policymakers can use drones as a tool instead of other, costlier courses of action. Once again, Obama himself offered this critique. "The same human progress that gives us the technology to strike half a world away also demands the discipline to constrain that power – or risk abusing it," he said in the same 2013 speech. "The very precision of drone strikes and the necessary secrecy often involved in such actions ... can also lead a President and his team to view drone strikes as a cure-all for terrorism."[41] That is exactly what Obama did throughout his presidency and what Trump seems on course to do as well.

Scholars have generally agreed with Obama's caution, even before he voiced it. Some made a similar point in response to the Bush administration's military operations, arguing they were overly militarized responses to the challenge of jihadist terrorism. "It is relevant to both the conditions of last resort and prospect of success that we need to avoid an obsession with purely military means for combating terrorism. The use of military force is very rarely sufficient to solve terrorist problems," Tony Coady wrote in 2005. "Massive aerial bombardments to aid the military overthrow of ugly regimes or outright wars against those regimes are likely to be politically and morally inadequate as responses to terrorism."[42] Crawford, similarly, has argued that "The *jus ad bellum* criterion of undertaking war only if there is a likelihood of success and if war is proportionate to the stakes involved is not clearly met by a counterterror policy that emphasizes military action." The same point applies to drones: just because they are smaller and less destructive does not mean they are any more morally or politically sufficient as a response to terrorism. They are a perfect example of relying on a purely military approach. Crawford rightly calls for the "prevention [of terrorism] by long-term diminution of the attractiveness of terrorism as an option."[43]

In fact, because drones are small, less expensive, less risky, less invasive, and more discriminating, their use is less politically costly at home and abroad, which means it is even more tempting for policymakers to rely on

---

[41] Obama, "Remarks by the President."
[42] Coady, "Terrorism, Just War, and Right Response," 147, 146.
[43] Crawford, "Just War Theory," 16–17, 20. See also Bellamy, "Is the War on Terror Just?" for another critical perspective on the war against al-Qaida.

them and thus rely on a purely military approach. Daniel Brunstetter and Megan Braun, the former an ex-drone pilot, have given the best exposition of this danger:

> To the extent they are successful, drones arguably raise the threshold of last resort of large-scale military deployment by providing a way to avoid deploying troops or conducting an intensive bombing campaign while still counteracting perceived threats. Paradoxically, however, the increased use of drones suggests that they may encourage countries to act on just cause with an ease that is potentially worrisome.[44]

To be clear, Brunstetter and Braun rightly emphasize the positive elements of drone technology: "Drones arguably provide a government the means to act on just cause more proportionately in responding to such a threat because they require minimal on-the-ground logistics, are less expensive and less invasive than ground troops, and can more specifically target the threat itself – that is, individual terrorists." Drone technology "arguably provides leaders with a minimally violent means of addressing a perceived threat . . . a potentially effective way of avoiding broad military deployment while still confronting a perceived threat."[45] We should recognize that advanced technology makes it ever easier to abide by the principles of *jus in bello*.

However, these very virtues have a downside. Drones lower the cost of warfare and therefore are highly likely to increase the frequency of it. Policymakers can be lured into believing that "the last resort criterion does not apply to drone strikes themselves because the targeted killing of (alleged) terrorists becomes the default tactic." Brunstetter and Braun call this the "drone myth," which they define as the "belief that technologically advanced drones increase the probability of success while decreasing the risk to our soldiers and of collateral damage." The drone myth is pernicious not only because it relaxes the criteria of last resort, but because it can even distort our understanding of just cause. The drone myth "may lead to more frequent and less stringent interpretations of just cause that actually reduce the long-term probability of success in diminishing the external threat."[46]

This is also my main concern regarding one-off punitive strikes, whether by drone, manned aircraft, cruise missile, or special forces. There are surely times when a surgical, single strike is appropriate, such as the raid on Osama bin Ladan's compound in Abbottabad, Pakistan in 2011. (Such operations run a different risk, i.e., running afoul of right

[44] Brunstetter and Braun, "Implications of Drones," 339.
[45] Brunstetter and Braun, "Implications of Drones," 343–344.
[46] Brunstetter and Braun, "Implications of Drones," 346.

intention, veering into revenge and bloodlust. But punitive strikes could, in principle, be motivated by the rightful intention of removing an enemy of peace and justice, much as with an executioner carrying out a sentence.) But an ongoing and continuous campaign of punitive raids and strikes – which is essentially what the drone war is – amounts to waging war without accepting commensurate responsibility, a deliberate strategy to avoid the moral duties that going to war involves. The fault, to be clear, lies not with the drone pilots or their commanders but with the policymakers and decision-makers who chose to rely exclusively on drones.

Walzer argued in 2006 for a concept of *jus ad vim*, or the just use of force below the threshold of war, which would be "more permissive" than conventional *jus ad bellum*.[47] His understanding of *jus ad vim* might permit the use of drones in the fashion I have been criticizing because of their precision and lower risk. Walzer's notion of *jus ad vim* is useful, but in the opposite way than he intends: it is helpful precisely insofar as it forces us to recognize that there are a range of lethal acts that are not "war" in the conventional sense but that nonetheless should be held up to the same moral standard of war – including the standards of proportionality and last resort – because of their potential to take human life. The calculation of proportionality will naturally look different given the lower costs of surgical strikes, which is the one sense in which the moral framework for this kind of military action is indeed "more permissive." Otherwise, I am inclined to agree with those who deny that we enter into a special zone of moral consideration in wartime, as if some rules apply in war that do not apply elsewhere.[48] Killing is killing, and we should have a unified body of political ethics to explain why it is almost always wrong as well as occasionally right to kill. *Jus ad vim* should raise the moral requirements of sub-conventional violence, not lower the barriers to its easy and frequent use. Brunstetter and Braun rightly argue that military options below the threshold of war should not be seen as steps to take in the lead-up to war or measures to perform before satisfying the last resort criterion but alternative strategic options once the last resort criterion has been met. Drone-bombing is not a lesser step to take before conventional war but an alternative to conventional war that is permissible if and only if the criteria of last resort action has already been met before any military action, including drone strikes, is undertaken. Similarly, Brunstetter and Braun argue that we should have to justify the maximum possible level of force we intend to use, not the minimal level from which we might later have to

---

[47] Walzer, *Just and Unjust Wars*, 4th edition, xv–xviii.
[48] Frowe, "On the Redundancy of *Jus Ad Vim*."

escalate, again highlighting that *jus ad vim* should raise, not lower, the moral requirements that policymakers face.[49]

I would go further: drones excuse policymakers from having to think about right intent or *jus post bellum*. When policymakers act as if drones do not count as real warfare, they excuse themselves from responsibility for thinking about how to end the war or invest in peace building. Put another way, when drones become not just one tool among many but a strategy, an entire way of warfare, the sole or predominant way of prosecuting a war, then that war has become entirely about killing rather than about building a better peace. Brunstetter and Braun warn that "drones may therefore lead to the promotion of insecurity short of war," a state of insecurity that benefits the United States at the expense of entire societies consigned to disorder.[50] Such a war violates the fundamental purpose of a just war: we fight it for the sake of peace. With drones as a kind of "virtuous war," there is "a high risk that one learns how to kill but not to take responsibility for it," as James Der Derian cautions.[51] In Boyle's assessment of just war against terrorism, he rightly warns that "a just cause must serve peace and not simply protect an unjust status quo."[52] The US counterterrorism strategy since 2001 has, by and large, been content to allow an unjust status quo to prevail across the region so long as it does not interfere with the United States' operational freedom to kill terrorists. Once again, Obama himself had the right words, with seemingly no awareness for how his policies contradicted his words: "We cannot use force everywhere that a radical ideology takes root; and in the absence of a strategy that reduces the wellspring of extremism, a perpetual war – through drones or Special Forces or troop deployments – will prove self-defeating, and alter our country in troubling ways."

Syria and Humanitarian Intervention

The Syrian Civil War is one of the largest and bloodiest wars of the twenty-first century. It started against the backdrop of the Arab Spring, a wave of peaceful protests against corruption, inequality, and oppression that started in Tunisia in December 2010 and swept across the Arab world. The backdrop is important because it shows that the Syrian government was a clear aggressor and it could have acted differently, as several neighboring governments did. In the face of similar protests, governments in Tunisia, Jordan, and Morocco made concessions,

[49] Brunstetter and Braun, "From *Jus Ad Bellum* to *Jus Ad Vim*."
[50] Brunstetter and Braun, "From *Jus Ad Bellum* to *Jus Ad Vim*," 99.
[51] Der Derian, *Virtuous War*, xvi.   [52] Boyle, "Just War Doctrine," 170.

undertook peaceful reform, or even allowed a change of regime. In Syria
(and Libya), the government responded with violent force, sparking an
armed uprising in response. While scholars and policymakers have
debated the merits of an international humanitarian intervention since
2011, the international community has so far limited itself to counterterrorism operations against ISIS.

On the moral case for humanitarian intervention, the argument has
been muddled. Most of the moral criticism of the Syrian government
has focused on its use of chemical weapons. This seems to me entirely
beside the point. It is certainly wicked that President Bashar al-Assad
murdered civilians with chemical weapons, but it is not worse than his
murder of a far larger number of civilians with bombs and bullets in
preceding years. If the use of weapons of mass destruction is the
standard of humanitarian crime against which the international community must intervene, then the Interahamwe's use of machetes in their
1994 genocide of Rwandan Tutsi and dissident Hutu was morally
inconsequential. That standard is, of course, ridiculous. President
Obama's infamous "red line" against the use of chemical weapons in
2012 was morally arbitrary and President Trump's enforcement of it
with air strikes in 2017 and 2018 equally so. It communicated to the
world's tyrants that they may murder and kill with impunity so long as
they do so as gentlemen, with regular weapons, as if there were such
a thing as humane murder.

If there is a case for humanitarian intervention against the Assad
regime, it is this: the regime declared war on its own people, giving
them just cause to rebel and a right to request international assistance.
Both Biggar and Niamh O'Sullivan argue that there is adequate just cause
for an intervention in Syria on humanitarian grounds.[53] Given the evidence of the uprising in 2011 and the regime's response, I think this is
persuasive but not conclusive. Other considerations weigh against an
intervention.

O'Sullivan too readily grants that the combatants in an intervention
would have right intention. It may be true that any international intervention would fight for peace and justice in Syria; it is unclear if the Syrian
rebels are doing the same. One of the major problems in Syria is the
absence of "good guys" strong enough to control the outcome of the war.
A rebel victory is more likely to hand power to jihadist factions, including
ISIS. In other words, though the Syrian people had just cause to rebel
against Assad, and thus a right to request international intervention, the

---

[53] O'Sullivan, "Moral Enigma."

strongest rebel factions lacked right intention. They had justice on their side but were not fighting for it; they were fighting for their own version of injustice.

Biggar rightly raises a similar concern in his treatment of the Syrian case, warning that the rebels could not claim to represent the Syrian people nor "to offer a coherent alternative to the Assad regime and Baathist state, since the opposition movement is riven with political, if not military, disagreement." Oddly, then, Biggar does not discount the justice of the rebellion and even suggests international intervention should be considered in order to help the rebellion gain coherence and persuade the Assad regime to compromise.[54] History does not support Biggar's optimism about what intervention can achieve. It is more likely that rebel factions would seek to use international resources to pursue their own ends, not change those ends to align with international preferences. In my view, the character of the rebellion argues strongly against any intervention because it makes the achievement of a just peace highly unlikely.

O'Sullivan also argued (in late 2012) that an intervention would not truly be a last resort because the Free Syrian Army was still in existence. According to J. S. Mill's standard, the international community ought to stand back and allow local rebels to prove themselves worthy of success by their own efforts or fail by the same standard. As I argued in my engagement with Walzer (Chapter 5), this is a nonsensical standard that ensures rebels with just cause but insufficient military power would be slaughtered – only then triggering an international intervention over the humanitarian catastrophe of the rebels' defeat, an intervention that would be even less likely to succeed because of the loss of local partners. If that is what just war reasoning recommends, better to throw it out altogether. If there were or are coherent rebel forces truly fighting for a just cause and right intention, the international community should not stand back and let them fight it out. It should help them consolidate their strength and fight more effectively.

Finally, O'Sullivan concludes against the justice of an intervention because, she argues, it would fail to meet the test of proportionality – using the category somewhat as Biggar did with Iraq, subsuming into it *jus post bellum* as well as the requirement that an intervention have a reasonable chance of success. Regardless of how she has categorized it, I think she is largely correct. The chance that an international intervention would lead to peace and justice in Syria – that the international community could possibly meet the requirements of *jus post bellum* – seems very low. That judgment is based partly on the conditions on the ground in Syria and the lack of

---

[54] Biggar, "Christian Just War Reasoning," 398.

credible Syrian partners but also on the political will and capabilities of the international community in the post-Iraq era. It seems extraordinarily unlikely that any international institution or coalition, much less the United States by itself, could muster the resources and effort required to impose a solution on Syria. (O'Sullivan also argues that an intervention would lack right authority because of the absence of an international consensus, let alone UN authorization. As I argued regarding Iraq, I am not so hung up on international consensus, international law, or UN authorization, again echoing Ramsey's counsel not to conflate what is legal with what is just.)

Against that, we do have to weigh the costs of not intervening, which are high. They include several hundred thousand dead, the likely restoration of the Assad dictatorship, and the expansion of Russian and Iranian influence; or, alternatively, a stalemate in the war along with continued safe haven for ISIS. If the alternative were an intervention followed by stable democracy in Syria that would obviously be a more just outcome. Sadly, it seems, the alternative would look much more like Libya: intervention followed by state collapse, civil war, jihadist safe haven, the decline of human development among millions of Syrians, and possibly the resurrection of some other form of authoritarianism at the far end of a long and miserable process. There seems to be no just intervention possible in Syria for the foreseeable future.

North Korea, Nuclear Deterrence, and Preemptive War

The recovery of the just war framework in the mid-twentieth century was motivated in large part by the advent of nuclear weapons and the devastation of World War II. Given the realities of nuclear weapons and war in the twentieth century, could war be fought justly? That was the question that launched Ramsey's inquiries and, with him, much of twentieth-century just war thinking. The question is still with us, today most especially on the Korean Peninsula. Oddly, there is almost no recent just war reflections on the possibility of war with North Korea. This seems to reflect a weakness in just war scholarship: it is often reactive, commenting on wars after they have happened or only when they are so imminent as to be nearly unavoidable. The gravity of a possible war with North Korea is so immense that we cannot afford to wait until it is upon us.

The United Nations and North Korea have remained in a legal state of war since North Korea's invasion of South Korea and the UN Security Council's subsequent authorization of the multinational United Nations Command in 1950. In the decades since, North Korea has accumulated an impressive record as one of the worst governments in history, guilty of enslaving and starving its own population while brainwashing them with a repugnant ideology, sponsoring terrorism, and becoming one of the foremost currency counterfeiters in the world. Most recently, after decades of international negotiations to prevent its acquisition of nuclear weapons, North Korea flouted the international community, withdrew from the Nuclear Non-Proliferation Treaty, violated its obligations under several other agreements, and publicly tested its first nuclear weapon in 2006. It also tested several delivery systems, including intercontinental ballistic missiles capable of reaching the United States, in 2017 and 2018.

The issues at stake are remarkably similar to those surrounding the Iraq War, with the exception that North Korea actually has nuclear weapons and delivery systems. The United Nations Security Council has repeatedly called on North Korea to cease its weapons development and rejoin the Non-Proliferation Treaty, akin to its demand that Iraq disarm itself of all weapons of mass destruction. North Korea's human rights record is on par with Iraq's (or worse) for its atrocity and barbarism. Its record of international aggression is similar to Iraq's, having invaded South Korea and undertaken regular and deliberate provocations ever since. Does the international community have just cause to preemptively invade, disarm, and change the regime of North Korea?

There are two major reasons to pause before that conclusion. First, North Korea's possession of nuclear weapons should change our calculation about the proportionality of the war and our reasonable chance of success. The costs of a war with North Korea would undoubtedly be dramatically higher than the war in Iraq (or any war since World War II). For the same reason, the chance of success – and I mean not success at disarming North Korea but success at building a just and lasting peace within North Korea and between North Korea and the world – seems low. For a war with North Korea to be proportionate – for the end result to be worth the evils likely to result from the war – and for success to be achievable, the United Nations and its member states must be capable of an ambitious undertaking. They must be able to reliably find and destroy or sabotage North Korea's nuclear weapons at the start of the war, with virtually no room for error. They must subsequently be capable of defeating North Korea in a conventional war (which is highly likely) *and* mounting a competent and successful postwar occupation to rebuild the country (which is not) – while simultaneously preventing the war from escalating into a conflict with China (as the first Korean War did). If, as seems probable, the United Nations is unable to do this, then it seems unlikely that a war with North Korea could serve the ends of peace and justice.

If this seems to be a definitive argument against war with North Korea, we have to keep in mind the second major way our calculations should change. The fact that North Korea possesses nuclear weapons does not only change what a hypothetical war would look like. It also changes what the alternatives look like – namely, the alternative of containment. Containing Saddam Hussein required no-fly zones, sanctions, diplomatic pressure, and the threat of war, which Biggar rightly argued was unsustainable. Containing North Korea requires nuclear deterrence, some versions of which Ramsey rightly argues are immoral.

Ramsey's extensive work on deterrence is suddenly more relevant than it has been in decades. He famously argued that if it is immoral to do a thing, it is immoral to threaten the same thing. For that reason, counter-city or counter-population deterrence was, for him, unacceptable because it involves indiscriminate targeting of civilian populations. While I have not dwelt on this issue in this book, I broadly agree with Ramsey's views (though not necessarily with his exploiting the ambiguity of nuclear weapons and their capacity for massive retaliation as a foreseen but unintended effect of deterrence). Insofar as large-yield nuclear weapons cannot be used with discrimination or proportionality, they are immoral weapons that cannot be used in any morally defensible way – which also means the threat of their use as a deterrent is immoral.

However, this argument applies most strongly to the nuclear technology and doctrine prevalent in Ramsey's day – nuclear bombs whose yield is measured in megatons, "city busters" so big they cannot meet the requirements of discrimination, proportionality, or strict military necessity. There are now much smaller nuclear bombs matched with precision-guided delivery systems that can arguably be used with something approaching proper discrimination and proportionality. For example, the United States started developing the W76 and W87 nuclear warheads in the late 1970s and 1980s. They have yields in the 100–300 kiloton range; the B41 and B53, developed in the 1960s, had yields between 9 and 25 *mega*tons. Some scholars and military planners have called for the development of even smaller weapons. Ramsey was right to draw a distinction between types and kinds of nuclear weapons, even before the technology had fully matured, in his effort to craft a morally defensible doctrine of nuclear deterrence and nuclear war.[55]

Critics will dislike the effort to normalize and accept any nuclear weapons. The US National Conference of Catholic Bishops argue in their 1983 letter that nuclear weapons cannot be justly used because

---

[55] For an overview and critique of Ramsey's views on nuclear deterrence, see Miller, "Love, Intention, and Proportion."

they are inherently indiscriminate and disproportional.[56] They further argue (like Ramsey, whose work they cite) that if nuclear weapons cannot be used in war, they also cannot be used for deterrence: "it is not morally acceptable to intend to kill the innocent as part of a strategy of deterring nuclear war."[57] But unlike Ramsey, the bishops dismiss any distinction among types or sizes of nuclear weapons in their condemnation of them, claiming that "the possibilities for placing political and moral limits on nuclear war are so minimal that the moral task, like the medical, is prevention: as a people, we must refuse to legitimate the idea of nuclear war," highlighting what they viewed as the inevitability of escalation and the problems of radiation.[58]

Even if the bishops were correct about the likelihood of escalation in the context of the Cold War rivalry and the indiscriminate nature of the weapons prevalent then, geopolitics and technology have changed. The bishops' guidance cannot be a universal template for interpreting all possible conflicts involving nuclear weapons. And there is good reason to hope the bishops were wrong. It is precisely our ability to place limits and draw distinctions between types of nuclear weapons that allows us to construct a morally defensible regime of deterrence against North Korea and thus avoid war. If we abandon nuclear deterrence as a viable option, conventional war with North Korea becomes far more likely. Some will feel uneasy with the implication that the United States should abandon the "nuclear taboo" that has prevented their use since 1945. But the nuclear taboo is morally empty; in fact, it may be immoral if it prevents the use of the best weapons available to fight and win just wars.

A regime of counterforce nuclear and nonnuclear deterrence – as opposed to counter-city or counter-population deterrence – would identify North Korean military targets at a distance from civilian centers, such as its large concentrations of artillery and armor deployed along the demilitarized zone, missile silos, nuclear research and development sites, air fields, naval port facilities, underground command and control facilities, and the like, as targets for nuclear reprisal in the event of North Korean provocation. Assuming such targets can be found (and I am not competent to say if they can be) and nuclear weapons and conventional bombs are small enough, this form of deterrence is suited to the case

---

[56] US National Conference of Catholic Bishops, *Challenge of Peace*. See Johnson, "Just War Idea" and Sharma, "Legacy of *Jus Contra Bellum*" for examples of the debate surrounding the bishops' letter.
[57] US National Conference of Catholic Bishops, *Challenge of Peace*, paragraph 178.
[58] US National Conference of Catholic Bishops, *Challenge of Peace*, paragraph 131; see also paragraphs 142–161, in which the bishops make clear their disbelief in the possibility of any limits in nuclear war.

because it would be both discriminate and proportionate and, for that reason, it is a more credible threat that is likely to result in stable deterrence. The United States should feel no moral qualm about using small nuclear weapons and large conventional weapons in combat if those weapons are the most effective for the requirements of the military mission and if they can be used discriminately, away from population centers. The goal of defeating the North Korean military – one of the largest in the world – at the least expense of human life and greatest chance of victory would surely be served if nuclear weapons were able to destroy or damage a large portion of that military's heavy equipment, air and port facilities, and command and control capabilities, at least those not in close proximity to civilian population centers. Such an approach would surely make any war much quicker than otherwise and save an untold number of lives, North Korean civilians not least among them.

What I want to stress is that, in order to come to a judgment about the North Korean case, it is not enough to weigh the case for or against war. We have to do that, but we also have to weigh the case for and against the alternative (containment) – and then we have to weigh the net balance of each option against one another. A final point: the standard of judgment is not military victory, or disarmament, or body count, or the preservation or abrogation of the nuclear taboo, or anything else. These issues matter for a calculation of costs and benefits, but they cannot be dispositive by themselves. The key question is: how likely is it that this option, as opposed to the other option, will build a just and lasting peace? While some options, such as counter-population deterrence, are morally disallowed on their face because they do not create a true or just peace at all, weighing the balance of permissible options is largely a prudential call and requires far more detailed knowledge of the case than I have outlined here. From my limited perspective, I doubt the ability of the international community to launch a preemptive war and carry it to a successful conclusion, according to the standards of success I have laid out here. Containment via deterrence with low-yield, precision-guided nuclear weapons augmented by conventional weapons is likely the better option – but it must rest on a real and credible threat of proportional and discriminate nuclear war to be effective.

Cyberattacks: Stuxnet and Anonymous

The literature on just war and cyber capabilities is growing rapidly.[59] Some of it simply applies the conventional just war framework and

---

[59] Barrett, "Warfare in a New Domain"; Cook, "'Cyberation' and Just War Doctrine'"; Dipert, "Ethics of Cyberwarfare"; Eberle, "Just War and Cyberwar"; Finlay, "Just War,

categories to cyber capabilities. As with drones, I am not convinced there is much to be said in isolation about a single new tool or weapon: we can reiterate that cyber capabilities should be used with proportionality and note how difficult they are to use with discrimination. If we believe the direst scenarios, cyberattacks could be used to shut down a nation's critical infrastructure, causing widespread damage and loss of life by cutting off electricity to hospitals or air-traffic control towers. Ramsey's critique against large-yield nuclear weapons seems relevant here: widespread, indiscriminate attacks on civilians is indefensible and would justify a conventional military response. (Attacks on dual-use infrastructure are more defensible, but keeping control of cyber-weapons once used, and preventing their release into the broader civilian infrastructure, could be challenging.) Some scholars have analogized cyberattacks on infrastructure to biological warfare on food sources because of the indiscriminate nature of both attacks.[60]

But barring that scenario, it is more useful to begin with an observation about how cyber capabilities are used in the contemporary security environment. The overwhelming majority of malicious cyber activity is private-sector theft of sensitive information, and as such falls outside the scope of this book. Even cyberattacks in military contexts have not yet been used to kill people, at least not publicly or in any acknowledged attack, though it is still a form of force insofar as it is an exercise of power to cause real harm to other actors.[61] In wartime, cyberattacks can be a useful tool in support of conventional warfare – for example, by disrupting the adversary's command, control, and communications networks. Russia appears to have used cyberattacks in this fashion during its (unjust) wars in Georgia and Ukraine. Like drones, the ethics of cyber capabilities in this setting is relatively straightforward: their use should follow the same rules as other weapons. The fact that the weapon employs the movement of electrons rather than bullets, that it targets data instead of matter, is immaterial to the moral quality of its use.

The more interesting case is the targeted, political use of cyber capabilities in peacetime. By their nature, and unlike conventional weapons, the use of cyber capabilities does not automatically trigger a transition to war. Estonia sought to invoke NATO's mutual defense obligation after a Russian cyberattack in 2007 that temporarily disrupted government and financial websites but caused no loss of life and no permanent damage. The other members of NATO rightly declined to declare the

---

Cyber War"; Liaropoulos, "War and Ethics in Cyberspace"; Rowe, "Ethics of Cyberweapons in Warfare"; Taddeo, "Analysis for a Just Cyber War."
[60] Rowe, "Ethics of Cyberweapons in Warfare," 23.   [61] Finlay, "Just War, Cyber War."

cyberattack an act of war but left unresolved the question of how to respond, short of war, to a clearly unjust act of nonlethal aggression. Indeed, whether a cyberattack could justify a conventional military response is a contested question.[62] Cyberweapons are "expanding the range of possible harm and outcomes between the concepts of war and peace," according to one of the best scholarly treatments of the subject.[63] Their use thus falls into a moral, political, and ethical gray area. (Though sometimes it does not: North Korea's cyberattack and blackmail against Sony Pictures in retaliation for a movie satirizing Kim Jong-un in 2014 was plainly unjust, not because of the use of cyber tools but because of the North Koreans' unjust cause.)

Actors can use cyber capabilities to cause intentional, nonlethal harm to others that is neither crime nor war. What kind of harm? Most politically motivated peacetime cyberattacks generally fall into one of two types: sabotage or espionage. Cyber capabilities are new tools for an old mission: stealing information and wrecking stuff. The ethics of cyberattacks turn out to be the ethics of sabotage, espionage, and covert action. The case of the Stuxnet worm illustrates many of the issues involved.

Stuxnet

In 2010, news outlets reported that a computer worm called Stuxnet had been discovered on computer systems worldwide, mostly concentrated in Iran. Stuxnet was designed to interfere with the control of certain industrial processes. It caused no damage outside Iran but, inside, took control of parts of Iran's nuclear programs and altered parameters "that control the speed of a motor by regulating how much power is fed to it," damaging centrifuges used in uranium enrichment. News outlets reported that Stuxnet had been engineered by the US government, possibly with British or Israeli assistance.[64] Stuxnet appears to be a case of state-sponsored cyber-sabotage against another state in peacetime. Stuxnet seems to have been discriminate: it was targeted to cause damage only to specific industrial processes, only in Iran; it did not harm any human beings; and it was programed to delete itself after a certain date, all relatively rare features of cyberattacks. But if we want to know if it was a just use of cyber capabilities, there are more important questions to answer: why was it done and in response to what perceived injury?

[62] Cook, "'Cyberation' and Just War Doctrine'"; Dipert, "Ethics of Cyberwarfare"; Eberle, "Just War and Cyberwar."
[63] Kello, "Meaning of the Cyber Revolution," 8.
[64] Farwell and Rohozinski, "Stuxnet and the Future of Cyber War."

Here is where the nature of cyberattacks makes the ethical question difficult. In most cyberattacks, attributing it to a specific attacker can be technologically difficult.[65] If we do not know who launched the attack, we can only speculate about why it was launched, which retards our ability to judge just cause and right intention. In principle, the attribution problem could be a serious barrier for just cyberwar. Just war thinkers used to insist that war be publicly declared and its reasons proclaimed to give the enemy a chance to respond and either redress known grievances or air its side of the story; similarly, some thinkers condemned certain kinds of perfidy, deceit, and ruses, which would seem to leave little room for unattributed, anonymous acts of sabotage (or even for any kind of covert action).

The advantages of anonymity are an incentive for attackers to develop unattributable cyber tools. States wronged by a cyberattack might respond in kind, also covertly, against whomever they suspect was behind the attack, leading to a perpetual cycle of tit-for-tat cyberattacks, some of which may not even be targeted against culpable parties. I thus do not agree that most forms of cyberattacks are "morally on a par with ordinary economic conflict," as Eberle argues, or that "cyber-conflict is far easier to justify than waging war."[66] Ordinary, legal economic conflict is open, transparent, and nondestructive, and takes places within a framework of ordered liberty under law. A covert, anonymous cyberattack, even when it does not kill anybody, involves trespassing, fraud, vandalism, theft, and sabotage. An endless cycle of covert, anonymous acts of sabotage and reprisal is hardly consistent with ordered liberty or the norms of just war.

The question is: can covert acts of cyber sabotage evade this problem? I think the answer is yes. First, there is obviously a place for secrecy in warfare and I do not agree that cyberweapons must be accompanied by digital signatures of their owners or developers, as some scholars propose. I would extend that liberty to some peacetime conditions: conditions of near-war, cold war, or intense conflict between rivals and enemies. In other words, I want to extend the just war framework beyond conventional war to cover the conditions of suspicion and competition that are often prevalent in relations between enemies and rivals. Doing so also extends the just war framework to encompass the tools of statecraft used in such scenarios, including coercive diplomacy, espionage, covert action, and cyberattacks. With that in mind, I argue that cyberweapons, like drones, can be legitimate but must not be mistaken for a strategy disconnected from other instruments of statecraft

---

[65] Rid and Buchanan, "Attributing Cyber Attacks."
[66] Eberle, "Just War and Cyber War," 59.

designed to resolve whatever underlying political and security issue motivated their use in the first place.

In practice, attribution is not insurmountable because attacks do not occur in a vacuum. We can judge the case based on the broader political context and circumstantial evidence. In the case of Stuxnet especially, we can feel confident in our guesswork: it was aimed at sabotaging Iran's ability to enrich uranium and thus build nuclear weapons. The United States and Israel had been (and continue to be) vocal about their concerns over Iran's nuclear programs. And they were not alone: the United Nations Security Council had repeatedly instructed Iran to suspend uranium enrichment and sanctioned it for its refusal to comply. The IAEA had called repeatedly for Iran to be more transparent about its nuclear programs, discovered unauthorized highly enriched uranium at Iranian facilities, and found other evidence of Iranian deceit. Stuxnet, then, seems to have been a covert, extrajudicial attempt to enforce the international community's demands on Iran (extrajudicial insofar as it was probably outside the bounds of international law, though international law is underdeveloped in this area).

As with the US invasion of Iraq, I am less bothered by unilateralism than other scholars. In Iraq, it was clear that international efforts to enforce disarmament were collapsing; unilateral enforcement was the only alternative to no enforcement. The same case could be made in the Iranian case: perhaps unilateral enforcement was necessary. The Iranian case had not deteriorated as far as that in Iraq – the international community, through the UN, sustained sanctions on Iran from 2006 until the 2015 nuclear deal (the Joint Comprehensive Plan of Action), so there was a weaker case for unilateral action. But the Stuxnet sabotage was a lesser measure than invasion or military force, and in fact may have been the main alternative to it. In that sense, Stuxnet could be justified as a proportional response – a relatively small, targeted measure to supplement international pressure on Iran.

We need to make two comparisons to judge the ethical merits of Stuxnet. The first comparison is between Stuxnet and other enforcement alternatives. The main alternatives were sanctions and military action. (Containment would be an option were Iran to acquire nuclear weapons; I am concerned here with options for preventing that acquisition in the first place.) The international sanctions regime was clearly sustainable in 2010, though not effective. For example, in 2009 US, British, and French intelligence forced Iran to admit it had concealed the existence of a uranium enrichment facility in Qom, in addition to the previously disclosed facility in Natanz, proving that sanctions (which started in 2006) had not stopped Iran's uranium enrichment nor its practice of deception surrounding its nuclear activities.[67] The Stuxnet attackers were correct that sanctions alone were insufficient enforcement mechanisms. Cyber-sabotage could be seen as the next step up the ladder of coercive diplomacy.

But why not skip to the top rung? What about military action? Speculation was rife that Israel or the United States had been planning a military operation against Iran's nuclear facilities since Iran resumed constructing centrifuges in 2004, restarted uranium conversion in 2005, and ceased cooperation with the IAEA in 2006. In the midst of ongoing US operations in Iraq and Afghanistan (some of them against Iranian proxies) and Israel's war against Hezbollah in 2006 (a longtime Iranian ally), an extension of those conflicts to Iran itself seemed not only possible but a logical way of seeking to resolve many conflicts at once.

But war against Iran in 2010 (or before) would clearly not have been a last resort. This was proved by subsequent efforts: sanctions and diplomacy led to the 2015 nuclear deal, however flawed and incomplete it was. As importantly, the chances of a successful military strike leading to a sustainable, just peace in the aftermath were extremely low. A limited strike would almost certainly have only delayed, not destroyed, Iran's progress towards building nuclear weapons while hardening its resolve to do so and prompting it to upgrade its defenses. A large-scale war involving invasion and occupation, besides being logistically and practically almost impossible, would have been so costly and destructive as to outweigh the good achieved by disarming Iran.[68] If sanctions were ineffective and war impractical, cyber-sabotage was a reasonable middle course to ratchet up pressure on Iran with a lower risk of escalation.

But it still held some risk. The second comparison we have to make is between Stuxnet and the problem it was designed to solve: Iran's nuclear program. We cannot be blasé about the risk of normalizing cyber-sabotage as an instrument of statecraft.[69] The proper goal of statecraft is the preservation of ordered liberty within and among nations. Several features of cyber-sabotage, including in the case of Stuxnet, undercut that goal: its secrecy, anonymity, offensive nature, novelty, and the absence of any established normative or legal framework. Cyberattacks in this context could be highly destabilizing and set destructive precedents for the future. That does not mean cyberattacks and cyber-sabotage cannot be used justly but that their use must outweigh the unique harm they

---

[67] Sanger and Broad, "US and Allies Warn Iran."
[68] See Kroenig, "Time to Attack Iran" and Kahl, "Not Time to Attack Iran" for a discussion of military options.
[69] See, for example, Taddeo's discussion of the harm cyberattacks cause to the broader "Infosphere"; Taddeo, "Analysis for a Just Cyber Warfare."

necessarily do by their distinctive nature. The standard is not merely that cyberattacks have to show a net positive balance of good achieved against evil perpetuated. The standard is higher: the net balance of their use must be better than the net balance of the alternatives, including sanctions and war.

In this case, Stuxnet probably met that standard. Given the strong international consensus against Iran's nuclear activities, as reflected in multiple UN Security Council resolutions and years of IAEA inspections, I take it as given that preventing Iran from acquiring a nuclear weapon, enforcing greater transparency in its nuclear research, and halting its uranium enrichment were just aims for the international community. Iran's acquisition of nuclear weapons would be a grave and destabilizing threat to international peace, probably more so than North Korea's because of Iran's neighborhood, support for terrorism, access to oil wealth, and control over one of the world's most important maritime chokepoints (the Strait of Hormuz).[70] Sanctions alone were not effective and there was (and remains) no prospect of a reasonable military solution. Cyber-sabotage, while imperfect and risky, was a defensible alternative; Stuxnet, because of its discriminating design, seemed especially well-suited to the case. Finally, Stuxnet may have helped secure the 2015 deal because of Iran's awareness that such tools were in play and could be deployed in the future with greater effect.

Anonymous

Cyberattacks raise another question: right authority. Cyber tools, like conventional small arms, are widely available, relatively cheap, and already in the hands of nonstate actors and private individuals. In the case of conventional small arms, the state enjoys presumptive authority over their regulation and use because of its role upholding order. Circumstances favor the state's authority over small arms: private militias and terrorist groups have an extraordinarily hard time operating on a global scale. The reverse is true with cyber tools. The anonymity of cyberspace and the ease of copying or modifying digital code enables cyber actors to proliferate and operate with relative ease, and nonstate cyber actors operate across international borders on a routine basis. The state's claim to have the exclusive right authority for the use of force is under siege in cyberspace, with little parallel or precedent.

---

[70] A minority of scholars disagree, arguing that nuclear weapons contribute to stability and their proliferation is a good thing. See Waltz, "Why Iran Should Get the Bomb."

Probably the most active nonstate cyber actors today are the quasi-state Russian and Chinese hacker groups who act as proxies for their respective governments. I will set them aside because their proximity to state power makes them less interesting for our purposes. Instead, let us consider the case of Anonymous, a hacktivist collective that first formed around 2004. Apparently a loose collection of volunteer hackers with a roughly libertarian or anarchist agenda, Anonymous is not a state, quasi-state, or state-backed group. It cyberattacks targets for political purposes, not private gain. It employs a variety of tactics, ranging from cyber-pranks and vandalism to denial-of-service attacks, doxing, and more serious attacks

Its pattern of attacks suggests a strong antipathy to concentrations of power in favor of individualism, free speech, deregulation, and an open internet. Its targets have included the Church of Scientology, copyright associations, credit card companies, Israel, ISIS, child pornography websites, Stratfor (a private-sector geopolitical intelligence firm), legislation against digital piracy, and more. It has also undertaken efforts in favor of Iran's 2009 Green Revolution, the 2011 Arab Spring, WikiLeaks, Occupy Wallstreet, and similar protest movements.[71]

Perhaps some of Anonymous' agenda is consistent with liberty (at least some versions of it), but it is not consistent with order. Just war thinkers have always been skeptical, to say the least, of private violence. Cyber coercion should be subject to the same standard. Private individuals may use force for personal self-defense, other-defense, or in cases of justifiable revolution. Some of Anonymous' activity might be considered other-defense (its support for the Arab Spring, for example, or attacks on child pornography sites), but by and large it is not. Again, there are conditions under which private citizens may act with the state's authority, as with a citizen's arrest (and Anonymous' actions against child porn sites and other clearly criminal actors might be seen as a version of that). But for the most part, the hackers of Anonymous are cyber-vigilantes. Vigilantism is the arrogation by a private individual of the state's authority, not for the purpose of self-defense or for replacing the state in case of justifiable rebellion but for circumventing the state because one is dissatisfied with its policies or performance. A citizen's arrest does not threaten the state; it only reacts to an emergency; and it bolsters the state by temporarily filling in and stepping back when authorities are present. Vigilantism is proactive, seeking out and selecting its own targets, and it sidesteps the state rather than deferring to it.

Anonymous thus violates the principles of right authority – but it does seem to be responding to a legitimate need. Cyberspace is so poorly

[71] Coleman, *Anonymous in Context.*

governed that it resembles lawless regions, a failed state, or ungoverned space – *terra nullius* – in which malicious actors can operate and hide with impunity. Some of what Anonymous does, such as targeting child pornography sites, is essentially providing a governance service because governments are incompetent. There is precedent for bad actors exploiting poor governance to operate with impunity: pirates who abused the vastness of the high seas to terrorize, kidnap, thieve, and murder. Governments were unable to police the huge expanse of the planet's oceans, so they contracted out their responsibilities to private-sector actors: privateers, authorized with letters of marque to act with the state's commission against pirates for profit. Some scholars have called for cyber-privateers to be commissioned by legitimate governments with new letters of marque to attack hackers and other malicious cyber actors.[72] This raises the thorny issue of the use of mercenaries in warfare, but the idea at least merits further attention because it could help bring greater order to cyberspace. At the same time, it would force people who participate in groups like Anonymous to make a choice. If they are truly motivated by legitimate goals, they can accept the legitimating authorization of a government and thus act with right authority. Hackers who care more for their own autonomy or for the thrill of hacking than for the just cause at stake will, rightly, be seen as little more than vandals and criminals.

Autonomous Weapons

I conclude with brief reflections on what is sure to be a major issue in the next generation of just war thinking: autonomous weapons.[73] Some autonomous weapons, such as automatically triggered land mines, have been in use for decades. They have long been criticized for their lack of discrimination and a 1997 treaty sought to outlaw antipersonnel mines altogether. More recent autonomous defensive systems include the US Navy's Phalanx CIWS, essentially a gun controlled by a computer and guided by radar that identifies and fires on threats to ships, including missiles and aircraft. The Phalanx is not designed for antipersonnel or offensive operations, and the use of autonomous weapons for defensive purposes in ways that do not kill humans seems unproblematic, but it is easy to imagine how the technology and concept could be adapted.

Efforts to adapt technology for offensive operations are already underway, including the development of autonomous aerial, undersea, and

---

[72] Rosenzweig et al., "Next Steps for US Cybersecurity."
[73] Krishnan, *Killer Robots*; Roff, "Strategic Robot Problem"; Schulzke, "Autonomous Weapons and Distributed Responsibility"; Schulzke, "Robots as Weapons in Just Wars."

land machines capable of lethal action and guided by artificially intelligent systems. These are different from the kind of drones discussed above; those drones are remotely piloted by humans, while the new systems are entirely controlled and piloted by computers. The main issue with autonomous weapons is not whether they will make a mistake and kill civilians by accident. They surely will, but so do humans, possibly at higher rates. Any weapon system must be held to the same standard of discrimination and proportionality – that is as true of killer robots as anything else. Rather, the novel issue with autonomous weapons is whether or not they meet the standard of right authority. Just war has always insisted that the responsibility of waging war lies with the sovereign, not with private actors. In its original formulation, the criterion of right authority was meant to prevent criminals, lesser magistrates, feudal lords, mercenaries, or private citizens from waging war on their own authority. Do killer robots have right authority to kill humans? What insight should the principle of right authority give us on the issue of autonomous weapons?

The sovereign has always had the right to delegate some decisions to military commanders, and they in turn can delegate down the chain of command. The principle of right authority does not demand that the commander-in-chief personally make every decision in warfare. Delegating some decisions to machines does not seem problematic on its face. But note what is being delegated: prudential decisions about how and when best to implement the state's overall guidance once a decision has been made to go to war. The state can delegate tactical and operational considerations, not the initial decision about whether or not to go to war. The state alone – specifically, the humans who comprise the state – has the moral responsibility to decide when war is the just and appropriate response to a breach of ordered liberty. That would argue against turning over complete control of our nation's defenses to an AI.

Does that mean offensive autonomous weapons are allowable once war has been declared? Perhaps, though I think the requirement for strong human oversight of their use remains critical. The ethics of autonomous weapons seems different depending on the type of conflict involved. It would surely be easier to use autonomous machines ethically in a conventional interstate war with easily identifiable opponents on distinct battlefields away from population centers. In this scenario autonomous machines would simply speed up the process of targeting and will probably be necessary because of the inevitable arms race in autonomous weaponry. Once one state fields autonomous weapons, others will have to do the same to stay competitive, and conventional war might become a war largely between armies of killer robots. If so, the advent of autonomous machines might save human lives.

The use of autonomous machines would be more problematic in unconventional or counterinsurgency war in which human judgment plays a larger role. In unconventional conflicts, combatants and civilians mix, political considerations loom large, and warfare is often carried out in dense urban environments. The chances that an AI could outperform a human in correctly deciding when lethal violence was appropriate seems lower than in conventional war. In either case, I think it would be especially important to designate a human commander who bears responsibility for any wrongs done by a machine under his or her command. Human commanders should, at the very least, retain control over defining the battlespace – the physical boundaries within which the machine is allowed to operate, lest a machine wander outside the battlefield and wreak havoc where there is no war.

More broadly, sustaining human culpability for machine action would ensure commanders are vigilant about the design and use of such machines. Of course, a commander's responsibility for the actions of a machine under his or her command will look different than his or her responsibility for the actions of human subordinates. One scholar who has argued for a similar doctrine of human accountability states that, "This does not mean that commanders should be held responsible for a robot's unethical actions as though they were responsible for the actions themselves. Rather, the blame should be distributed according to how their actions influenced the actions of [autonomous weapons]."[74] Does that mean commanders should be held responsible if they do not understand how an autonomous weapon's programming caused it to take a certain action? Or if the programmers failed to anticipate a given scenario? Or if the dataset used to train a machine to distinguish between combatant and civilian had flaws? These seem extraordinarily complex, yet necessary, questions. Defining more precisely the nature and scope of human responsibility for machine action seems to be an urgent need in the ethics of autonomous weapons.

---

[74] Schulzke, "Autonomous Weapons and Distributed Responsibility," 215.

9   Conclusion

When is war just? What does justice require? The just war framework is an attempt to answer those questions. But there is no singular tradition and no consensus on the answers. Just war inquiry is best understood as three traditions: the Augustinian, the Westphalian, and the Liberal. Augustinians understood war to be a just response and an act of love to defend the tranquility of order when that order was violently disrupted, including exceptional cases of a disruption in other states. Justice required the restoration of a just peace. Westphalians reinterpreted sovereignty so that it was no longer understood as responsibility for the common good but as defense of international borders and the sanctity of national autonomy and independence. War was just when it was waged to defend the state from external attack and, sometimes, to preserve a balance of power and prevent any one state from amassing enough power to threaten others' independence. Justice required the maintenance of international order and stability. Liberals sought to amend the Westphalian settlement to make greater allowance for the protection of human rights. For them, war was just when it was waged to defend the state from external attack, but it could also be just when waged to vindicate human rights abroad, as in humanitarian interventions. Justice required expansive post-conflict obligations to rebuild peace and justice in the aftermath of conflict.

There are broad similarities between the Augustinian and Liberal traditions. They both envision a limited, conditional form of sovereignty. States are accountable to a standard of justice external to themselves – nature and nature's God, for the Augustinians; human rights, for the Liberals. They both argue that war is a just response to a failure of sovereignty. I use this similarity to argue for a reformulation of just war thinking. The standard of *just peace* should be understood as a standard of *ordered liberty*. That helps answer the questions animating this book. When is war just? War is just when it is a response to the violent disruption of ordered liberty. This speaks to the problem of intervention and

250

rebellion: when a state is incapable of providing ordered liberty through state failure, or deliberately flouts it through unusually cruel tyranny and oppression, the people may rebel and other states may intervene. What does justice require? Justice requires the restoration of ordered liberty. When states intervene, they incur an obligation. They must see it through to victory, understood not merely as the military defeat of enemies but as the reestablishment of justice and peace. If it is just to intervene, it is just to win.

My thinking on war has taken shape in the shadow of the wars in Iraq and, especially, Afghanistan, as well as the United States' global counter-terrorism operations. I find fault with quite a lot of how the United States has gone about those wars, even as I argue that it had just cause for all of them. And my critique is not the same as the functional pacifism of many critics of America's wars since 2001. The weight of my argument is that the United States has, on balance, done too little, not too much. The goal of a just war is the reestablishment of a just peace. There is no sign of just peace on the horizon for Iraq, Afghanistan, or the broader region, calling into question the justness of the United States' strategies in those wars – though much more fault lies with the terrorists, insurgents, and jihadists whose unjust cause and acts of aggression are the main reason the region has been consigned to decades of misery and violence. But abandoning the wars altogether will not accomplish more justice or peace, and (in Afghanistan at least) would amount to a dereliction of moral duty by the United States to provide for its own security. I do agree with critics who warn about an unhealthy reliance on the military tools of statecraft. Much of what the United States needs to do more of is peace building.

I want to conclude on a note about how we should reason together to be aware of our blind spots and avoid moral paralysis. Just war depends on good motives and good judgment. But the same body of political theology from which I have been drawing throughout this book also warns about the effect of sin on the soundness of our own motives and the reliability of our judgment. Augustine was admirably clear and consistent on this point, and he was entirely correct. The human person is imperfect. Our motives and our judgment are routinely compromised by self-interest. We fall prey to motivated reasoning and other cognitive biases too easily. How can we trust the judgments of ethicists or policymakers who profess their best motives and their best judgment in favor of war?

At the same time, we need to beware of a countervailing tendency. The lesson of self-critique has been taken to heart so well – perhaps too well – in some corners of the academy that some critics seem to have fallen prey to reflexive *ressentiment*. For them, there is no possible right intention in anything that the United States or its allies do and no possible scenario in which the criteria of just war can effectively be met in the real world. Elshtain catalogued the reality of this phenomenon in *Just War against Terror*. Its presence is a large reason much of the thinking public routinely ignores scholarship and expertise as untrustworthy, unpatriotic, obscurantist pedantry.

I have a unique perspective on this, having spent one decade in public service and a second in the academy. I am well acquainted with the reality of governmental incompetence, cynicism, and amorality, as I hope my case studies show. Yet, hard as it is to image, I think the academy routinely overstates the case. Too often scholarly assessments of the government and its military seem reflexive, dogmatic, and predictable rather than data-driven, curious, or insightful. If thinkers too close to power can be captured by it and become propogandists, thinkers too removed from it can be alienated from their community and become muckrakers. Cicero, Augustine, Gentili, and many of the thinkers in this volume achieved their insights through a precarious position of proximity to, and critical distance from, power: they could appreciate the necessity of government and recognize the painful dilemmas decision-makers face, yet still hold them to a high moral standard. That is the heritage of the best of the just war traditions.

How can we avoid the pitfalls and avoid moral paralysis despite an awareness of our own sin? The answer, I think, is to reason together in community – including in community with those who have gone before us. That means we should engage in spirited public dialogue with full awareness of how our forebears have reasoned together about war and peace. Just war thinking is not best practiced by writing isolated op-eds whenever the next military crisis occurs, by delivering a monologue in class or on camera, or by reciting on a television talk-show the checklist we learned in our undergraduate surveys of Western philosophy. Those seem to me too didactic, too one-sided, too prone to motivated reasoning and individual bias. Just war thinking is best practiced in community, under the accountability of other people to probe and push back on our arguments: in a seminar dialogue, not a monologue; in a roundtable debate, not a lecture; in schools and churches, not in front of the mirror; in discursive point–counterpoint essays, not stentorian, declarative op-eds.

It also means we practice this dialogue with the community of the dead, with our ancestors, inviting the accountability of the progenitors of the traditions in which we stand (while holding them to account for the ways they got it wrong). That, at least, has been the hope and burden of this book. This book dwelt on the history of just war thinking through my conviction that such dialogue was necessary before advancing an argument of my own. It is not an exercise of pedantry or vanity, I hope, but humility. It is only through dialogue with the traditions, by understanding the antecedent narrative to which we are heirs, that we can carry the story forward to its next chapter and discern the outlines of justice, however dimly, for our day.

Works Cited

Annan, Kofi. "Two Concepts of Sovereignty." Speech delivered to the United Nations General Assembly in New York, September 18, 1999.

Aquinas. *On Law, Morality, and Politics*. Ed. William P. Baumgarth and Richard J. Regan. Hackett, 1988.

Aquinas. *Political Writings*. Ed. R. W. Dyson. Cambridge University Press, 2002.

Aristotle. *Nicomachean Ethics*. Trans. Martin Ostwald. Library of Liberal Arts, 1962.

Aristotle. *Politics*. Trans. Ernest Barker. Oxford University Press, 1998.

Augustine. *The City of God against the Pagans*. Trans. R. W. Dyson. Cambridge University Press, 1998.

Augustine. *Political Writings*. Ed. E. M. Atkins and R. J. Dodaro. Cambridge University Press, 2001.

Ayub, Fatima, and Sari Kouvo. "Righting the Course? Humanitarian Intervention, the War on Terror and the Future of Afghanistan." *International Affairs* 84, no. 4 (2008): 641–657.

Bacevich, Andrew. "Limiting Moralism." *First Things*, February 2013.

Barrett, Edward T. "Warfare in a New Domain: The Ethics of Military Cyber-Operations." *Journal of Military Ethics* 12, no. 1 (2013): 4–17.

Begby, Endre, Gregory Reichberg, and Henrik Syse. "The Ethics of War, Part I: Historical Trends 1." *Philosophy Compass* 7, no. 5 (2012): 316–327.

Bell, Daniel M. *Just War as Christian Discipleship*. Wipf and Stock, 2005.

Bellamy, Alex J. *Fighting Terror: Ethical Dilemmas*. Zed Books, 2013.

Bellamy, Alex J. "Is the War on Terror Just?" *International Relations* 19, no. 3 (2005): 275–296.

Bellamy, Alex J. *Just Wars: From Cicero to Iraq*. Polity Press, 2006.

Bellamy, Alex J. "The Responsibilities of Victory: *Jus Post Bellum* and the Just War." *Review of International Studies* 34, no. 4 (2008): 601–625.

Bellamy, Alex J. *Responsibility to Protect*. Polity Press, 2009.

Biggar, Nigel. "Christian Just War Reasoning and Two Cases of Rebellion: Ireland 1916–1921 and Syria 2011–Present." *Ethics & International Affairs* 27, no. 4 (2013): 393–400.

Biggar, Nigel. *In Defence of War*. Oxford University Press, 2013.

Blair, Tony. "The Doctrine of the International Community." Speech delivered to the Chicago Economic Club, Chicago, IL, April 22, 1999. www .globalpolicy.org/component/content/article/154/26026.html

Boyer, Pascal. "The Stuff 'Traditions' Are Made Of: On the Implicit Ontology of an Ethnographic Category." *Philosophy of the Social Sciences* 17, no. 1 (1987): 49–65.

Boyle, Joseph. "Just War Doctrine and the Military Response to Terrorism." *Journal of Political Philosophy* 11, no. 2 (2003): 153–170.

Boyle, Joseph. "Traditional Just War Theory and Humanitarian Intervention." *Nomos* 47 (2006): 31–57.

Brunstetter, Daniel, and Megan Braun. "From *Jus Ad Bellum* to *Jus Ad Vim*: Recalibrating Our Understanding of the Moral Use of Force." *Ethics & International Affairs* 27, no. 1 (2013): 87–106.

Brunstetter, Daniel, and Megan Braun. "The Implications of Drones on the Just War Tradition." *Ethics & International Affairs* 25, no. 3 (2011): 337–358.

Brunstetter, Daniel R., and Cian O'Driscoll, eds. *Just War Thinkers: From Cicero to the 21st Century.* Routledge, 2017.

Brunstetter, Daniel R., and Dana Zartner. "Just War against Barbarians: Revisiting the Valladolid Debates between Sepúlveda and Las Casas." *Political Studies* 59, no. 3 (2011): 733–752.

Bull, Hedley. "The Grotian Conception of International Society." *Diplomatic Investigations: Essays in the Theory of International Politics* 3 (1966): 51–73.

Burke, Anthony. "Just War or Ethical Peace? Moral Discourses of Strategic Violence after 9/11." *International Affairs* 80, no. 2 (2004): 329–353.

Bush, George W. "Second Inaugural Address." January 20, 2005. www.npr.org /templates/story/story.php?storyId=4460172

Chandler, David C. *Empire in Denial: The Politics of State-Building.* Pluto, 2006.

Chesterman, Simon. *Just War or Just Peace? Humanitarian Intervention and International Law.* Oxford University Press, 2001.

Cicero, Marcus Tullius. *On Duties* [De Officiis]. Trans. Walter Miller. Loeb edition. Harvard University Press, 1913.

Cicero, Marcus Tullius. *Political Works of Marcus Tullius Cicero.* Vol. II. Trans. Francis Barham. Edmund Spettigue, 1842.

Coady, Tony. "Terrorism, Just War and Right Response." *Ethics of Terrorism and Counter-Terrorism* 3 (2005): 135–150.

Coates, Anthony. "Humanitarian Intervention: A Conflict of Traditions." *Nomos* 47 (2006): 58–83.

Cole, Darrell. "Torture and Just War." *Journal of Religious Ethics* 40, no. 1 (2012): 26–51.

Coleman, Gabriella. *Anonymous in Context: The Politics and Power behind the Mask.* Internet Governance Papers, no. 3. Centre for International Governance Innovation, 2013.

Cook, James. "'Cyberation' and Just War Doctrine: A Response to Randall Dipert." *Journal of Military Ethics* 9, no. 4 (2010): 411–423.

Crawford, Neta C. "Just War Theory and the US Counterterror War." *Perspectives on Politics* 1, no. 1 (2003): 5–25.

Deane, Herbert A. *The Political and Social Ideas of St. Augustine.* Columbia University Press, 1966.

Department of the Army. *Counterinsurgency.* Field Manual 3–24. December 2006.

De Paulo, Craig J. N., Patrick A. Messina, and Daniel P. Tompkins, eds. *Augustinian Just War Theory and the Wars in Afghanistan and Iraq: Confessions, Contentions, and the Lust for Power.* Peter Lang, 2012.

Der Derian, James. *Virtuous War: Mapping the Military-Industrial-Media-Entertainment Network.* Routledge, 2009.

Dipert, Randall R. "The Ethics of Cyberwarfare." *Journal of Military Ethics* 9, no. 4 (2010): 384–410

Dorn, A. Walter. "The Just War Index: Comparing Warfighting and Counterinsurgency in Afghanistan." *Journal of Military Ethics* 10, no. 3 (2011): 242–262.

Dunn, John. "The Identity of the History of Ideas." *Philosophy* 43, no. 164 (1968): 85–104.

Eberle, Christopher J. "Just War and Cyberwar." *Journal of Military Ethics* 12, no. 1 (2013): 54–67.

Elshtain, Jean Bethke. *Just War against Terror: The Burden of American Power in a Violent World.* Basic Books, 2004.

Elshtain, Jean Bethke. *Sovereignty: God, State, and Self.* Basic Books, 2008.

Elshtain, Jean Bethke. "Terrorism, Regime Change, and Just War: Reflections on Michael Walzer." *Journal of Military Ethics* 6, no. 2 (2007): 131–137.

Elshtain, Jean Bethke. "Third Annual Grotius Lecture: Just War and Humanitarian Intervention." *American University International Law Review* 17, no. 1 (2001): 1–12.

Evans, Mark. "Moral Responsibilities and the Conflicting Demands of *Jus Post Bellum.*" *Ethics & International Affairs* 23, no. 2 (2009): 147–164.

Evans, Gareth, and Mohamed Sahnoun. "The Responsibility to Protect." *Foreign Affairs* 81, no. 6 (2002): 99–110.

Farwell, James P., and Rafal Rohozinski. "Stuxnet and the Future of Cyber War." *Survival* 53, no. 1 (2011): 23–40.

Fassbender, Bardo, Anne Peters, Simone Peter, and Daniel Högger, eds. *The Oxford Handbook of the History of International Law.* Oxford University Press, 2012.

Finlay, Christopher J. "Just War, Cyber War, and the Concept of Violence." *Philosophy & Technology* 31, no. 3 (2018): 357–377.

Finnemore, Martha. *The Purpose of Intervention: Changing Beliefs about the Use of Force.* Cornell University Press, 2004.

Fitzsimmons, Scott. "Just War Theory and Private Security Companies." *International Affairs* 91, no. 5 (2015): 1069–1084.

Fixdal, Mona, and Dan Smith. "Humanitarian Intervention and Just War." *Mershon International Studies Review* 42, no. 2 (1998): 283–312.

Flint, Colin, and Ghazi-Walid Falah. "How the United States Justified Its War on Terrorism: Prime Morality and the Construction of a 'Just War'." *Third World Quarterly* 25, no. 8 (2004): 1379–1399.

Frost, Mervyn. "The Ethics of Humanitarian Intervention: Protecting Civilians to Make Democratic Citizenship Possible." In *Ethics and Foreign Policy*, ed. K. Smith and M. Light, 33–54. Cambridge University Press, 2001.

Frowe, Helen. "On the Redundancy of *Jus Ad Vim*: A Response to Daniel Brunstetter and Megan Braun." *Ethics & International Affairs* 30, no. 1 (2016): 117.

Gentili, Alberico. *Three Books on the Law of War*. Carnegie Institute Classics of International Law, vol. 16, no. 2. Ed. James Brown Scott. Trans. John C. Rolfe. Clarendon Press, 1933.

Graburn, Nelson H. H. "What Is Tradition?" *Museum Anthropology* 24, no. 2–3 (2000): 6–11.

Griffiths, Paul J. "The Good Samaritan's Burden." *First Things*, February 2013.

Grotius, Hugo [Campbell]. *The Rights of War and Peace*. Trans. A. C. Campbell. M. Walter Dunne, 1901. Available through the Liberty Fund: https://oll .libertyfund.org/titles/553. Pagination taken from digital image of original hardcopy.

Grotius, Hugo [Kelsey/Neff]. *Hugo Grotius on the Law of War and Peace: Student Edition*. Ed. Stephen C. Neff. Trans. Francis W. Kelsey. Cambridge University Press, 2012.

Grotius, Hugo [Morrice/Tuck]. *The Rights of War and Peace*. Ed. Richard Tuck and Jean Barbeyrac. Trans. John Morrice. Liberty Fund, 2005. https://oll .libertyfund.org/titles/1877. Originally published 1734. Pagination taken from digital image of original hardcopy.

Guelff, Richard, and Adam Roberts, eds. *Documents on the Laws of War*. Oxford University Press, 2000.

Hazony, Yoram. *The Virtue of Nationalism*. Hachette UK, 2018.

Hehir, J. Bryan. "Just War Theory in a Post-Cold War World." *Journal of Religious Ethics* 20, no. 2 (1992): 237–257.

Henrie, Mark C. "War without End." *First Things*, February 2013.

Holmes, Arthur Frank. *War and Christian Ethics: Classic and Contemporary Readings on the Morality of War*. Baker Academic, 2005.

International Commission on Intervention and State Sovereignty. *The Responsibility to Protect: Report of the International Commission on Intervention and State Sovereignty*. IDRC, 2001.

Johnson, James Turner. *Ethics and the Use of Force: Just War in Historical Perspective*. Routledge, 2016.

Johnson, James Turner. "Humanitarian Intervention after Iraq: Just War and International Law Perspectives." *Journal of Military Ethics* 5, no. 2 (2006): 114–127.

Johnson, James Turner. *Ideology, Reason, and the Limitation of War: Religious and Secular Concepts, 1200–1740*. Princeton University Press, 1975.

Johnson, James Turner. "The Just War Idea: The State of the Question." *Social Philosophy and Policy* 23, no. 1 (2006): 167–195.

Johnson, James Turner. "Just War in the Thought of Paul Ramsey." *Journal of Religious Ethics* 19, no. 2 (1991): 183–207.

Johnson, James Turner. *Just War Tradition and the Restraint of War: A Moral and Historical Inquiry*. Princeton University Press, 1981.

Johnson, James Turner. *Sovereignty: Moral and Historical Perspectives*. Georgetown University Press, 2014.

Johnson, James Turner. "Thinking Historically about Just War." *Journal of Military Ethics* 8, no. 3 (2009): 246–259.

Johnson, James Turner. *The War to Oust Saddam Hussein: Just War and the New Face of Conflict*. Rowman & Littlefield, 2005.

Jones, Seth. *The Evolution of the Salafi-Jihadist Threat*. Center for Strategic and International Studies, 2018.

Jones, Seth. "The Rise of Afghanistan's Insurgency: State Failure and Jihad." *International Security* 32, no. 4 (2008): 7–40.

Kahl, Colin H. "Not Time to Attack Iran: Why War Should Be a Last Resort." *Foreign Affairs* 91, no. 2 (2012): 166–173.

Kello, Lucas. "The Meaning of the Cyber Revolution: Perils to Theory and Statecraft." *International Security* 38, no. 2 (2013): 7–40.

Kelsay, John. "Just War Thinking as a Social Practice." *Ethics & International Affairs* 27, no. 1 (2013): 67–86.

Kent, James. *Kent's Commentary on International Law*. 2nd edition. Ed. J. T. Abdy. Deighton, Bell, and Company, 1878.

Kingsbury, Benedict, and Benjamin Straumann, eds. *The Roman Foundations of the Law of Nations: Alberico Gentili and the Justice of Empire*. Oxford University Press, 2010.

Krepinevich, Andrew F., Jr. *The Army and Vietnam*. JHU Press, 1986.

Krishnan, Armin. *Killer Robots: Legality and Ethicality of Autonomous Weapons*. Routledge, 2016.

Kroenig, Matthew. "Time to Attack Iran: Why a Strike Is the Least Bad Option." *Foreign Affairs* 91 (2012): 76.

Lang, Anthony F., Jr, ed. *Just Intervention*. Georgetown University Press, 2003.

Lang, Anthony F., Jr. "The Just War Tradition and the Question of Authority." *Journal of Military Ethics* 8, no. 3 (2009): 202–216.

Lang, Anthony F., Jr, Cian O'Driscoll, and John Williams, eds. *Just War: Authority, Tradition, and Practice*. Georgetown University Press, 2013.

Leeman, Jonathan. "Not an Augustinian Liberal, but a Liberal Augustinian." *Providence Magazine*, Spring/Summer 2018.

Liaropoulos, Andrew. "War and Ethics in Cyberspace: Cyber-Conflict and Just War Theory." *Leading Issues in Information Warfare & Security Research* 1, no. 2 (2011).

Luban, David. "Just War and Human Rights." *Philosophy & Public Affairs* 9, no. 2 (1980): 160–181.

Luban, David. "The Romance of the Nation-State." *Philosophy & Public Affairs* (1980): 392–397.

MacIntyre, Alasdair. *After Virtue*. A&C Black, 2013.

MacIntyre, Alasdair C. *Whose Justice? Which Rationality?* Duckworth, 1988.

Markus, Robert A. "Saint Augustine's Views on the 'Just War'." *Studies in Church History* 20 (1983): 1–13.

Miller, Paul D. "Afghanistan, Justice, and War." *First Things*, February 2013.

Miller, Paul D. *American Power and Liberal Order: A Conservative Internationalist Grand Strategy*. Georgetown University Press, 2016.

Miller, Paul D. *Armed State Building: Confronting State Failure, 1898–2012*. Cornell University Press, 2013.

Miller, Paul D. "Augustine of Hippo: Christian Democrat." *Providence Magazine*, Spring/Summer 2018.

Miller, Paul D. "Augustinian Liberalism: A Symposium." *Providence Magazine*, Spring/Summer 2018.

Miller, Paul D. "How Does Jihadism End?" *War on the Rocks*, September 11, 2016.

Miller, Richard B. "Love, Intention, and Proportion: Paul Ramsey on the Morality of Nuclear Deterrence." *Journal of Religious Ethics* 16, no. 2 (Fall 1988): 201–221.

Murray, John Courtney. "Remarks on the Moral Problem of War." *Theological Studies* 20, no. 1 (1959): 40–61.

Nardin, Terry. "Humanitarian Imperialism." *Ethics & International Affairs* 19, no. 2 (2005): 21–26.

Nardin, Terry. "The Moral Basis of Humanitarian Intervention." *Ethics & International Affairs* 16, no. 1 (2002): 57–70.

New America Foundation, "America's Counterterrorism Wars." Dataset accessed July 11, 2019. www.newamerica.org/in-depth/americas-counterterrorism-wars

Niebuhr, Reinhold. *The Children of Light and the Children of Darkness: A Vindication of Democracy and a Critique of Its Traditional Defense.* University of Chicago Press, 2011.

Obama, Barack. "Nobel Lecture." Lecture delivered in Oslo, Norway, on December 10, 2009. www.nobelprize.org/prizes/peace/2009/obama/26183-nobel-lecture-2009

Obama, Barack. "Remarks by the President." Speech delivered at the National Defense University, Washington, DC, on May 23, 2013. https://obamawhite house.archives.gov/the-press-office/2013/05/23/remarks-president-national-defense-university

Obama, Barack. "Remarks by the President on a New Strategy for Afghanistan and Pakistan," March 27, 2009. https://obamawhitehouse.archives.gov/the-press-office/remarks-president-a-new-strategy-afghanistan-and-pakistan

O'Donovan, Oliver. *The Just War Revisited.* Cambridge University Press, 2003.

O'Driscoll, Cian. "Divisions within the Ranks? The Just War Tradition and the Use and Abuse of History." *Ethics & International Affairs* 27, no. 1 (2013): 47–65.

O'Driscoll, Cian. "Hedgehog or Fox? An Essay on James Turner Johnson's View of History." *Journal of Military Ethics* 8, no. 3 (2009): 165–178.

O'Driscoll, Cian. "James Turner Johnson's Just War Idea: Commanding the Headwaters of Tradition." *Journal of International Political Theory* 4, no. 2 (2008): 189–211.

O'Driscoll, Cian. "Keeping Tradition Alive: Just War and Historical Imagination." *Journal of Global Security Studies* 3, no. 2 (2018): 234–247.

O'Driscoll, Cian. *The Renegotiation of the Just War Tradition and the Right to War in the Twenty-First Century.* Springer, 2008.

Orend, Brian. "*Jus Post Bellum*: The Perspective of a Just-War Theorist." *Leiden Journal of International Law* 20, no. 3 (2007): 571–591.

Orend, Brian. "Justice after War." *Ethics & International Affairs* 16, no. 1 (2002): 43–56.

Orend, Brian. *Michael Walzer on War and Justice.* McGill-Queen's University Press, 2001.

Orend, Brian. *The Morality of War.* Broadview Press, 2013.

Orend, Brian. *War and International Justice: A Kantian Perspective.* Wilfrid Laurier University Press, 2006.

O'Sullivan, Niamh Maria. "The Moral Enigma of an Intervention in Syria: A Just War Analysis." Instituto Affair Internazionali, 2012.

Owen, John. "Retrieving Christian Liberalism." *Providence Magazine*, Spring/Summer 2018.

Patterson, Eric. "Bury the Bloody Hatchet: Secularism, Islam, and Reconciliation in Afghanistan." *Journal of Interreligious Studies* 5 (2011): 1–9.

Patterson, Eric D. *Ending Wars Well: Order, Justice, and Conciliation in Contemporary Post-Conflict*. Yale University Press, 2012.

Patterson, Eric. "Ethics and US Af-Pak Policy: Order, Justice, and Conciliation." *International Journal of Applied Philosophy* 24, no. 1 (2010): 31–46.

Patterson, Eric, ed. *Ethics beyond War's End*. Georgetown University Press, 2012.

Patterson, Eric. *Just American Wars: Ethical Dilemmas in US Military History*. Routledge, 2018.

Patterson, Eric. *Just War Thinking: Morality and Pragmatism in the Struggle against Contemporary Threats*. Lexington Books, 2009.

Pufendorf, Samuel. *Of the Law of Nature and Nations*. Carnegie Institute Classics of International Law, vol. 17, no. 2. Ed. James Brown Scott. Trans. C. H. Oldfather and W. A. Oldfather. Clarendon Press, 1934.

Ramsey, Paul. *The Just War: Force and Political Responsibility*. Charles Scribner's Sons, 1968.

Ramsey, Paul. *War and the Christian Conscience: How Shall Modern War Be Conducted Justly?* Literary Licensing, LLC, 2011.

Ramsey, Paul. "Some Rejoinders." *Journal of Religious Ethics* 4, no. 2 (Fall 1976): 185–237.

Rawls, John. *The Law of Peoples: With "The Idea of Public Reason Revisited."* Harvard University Press, 2001.

Reichberg, Gregory M., Henrik Syse, and Endre Begby, eds. *The Ethics of War: Classic and Contemporary Readings*. Wiley-Blackwell, 2008.

Rengger, Nicholas. *Just War and International Order: The Uncivil Condition in World Politics*. Cambridge University Press, 2013.

Rengger, Nicholas. "On the Just War Tradition in the Twenty-First Century." *International Affairs* 78, no. 2 (2002): 353–363.

Ricks, Thomas E. *Fiasco: The American Military Adventure in Iraq*. Penguin, 2006.

Rid, Thomas, and Ben Buchanan. "Attributing Cyber Attacks." *Journal of Strategic Studies* 38, no. 1–2 (2015): 4–37.

Rigstad, Mark. "*Jus Ad Bellum* after 9/11: A State of the Art Report." *International Political Theory Beacon*, 2007.

Roff, Heather M. "The Strategic Robot Problem: Lethal Autonomous Weapons in War." *Journal of Military Ethics* 13, no. 3 (2014): 211–227.

Rommen, Heinrich Albert. *The Natural Law: A Study in Legal and Social History and Philosophy*. Trans. Thomas R. Hanley. Liberty Fund, 1998.

Rosenzweig, Paul, Steven P. Bucci, and David Inserra. "Next Steps for US Cybersecurity in the Trump Administration: Active Cyber Defense." *Backgrounder* 3188 (2017): 11.

Rowe, Neil C. "The Ethics of Cyberweapons in Warfare." *International Journal of Technoethics* 1, no. 1 (2010): 20–31.

Russell, Frederick H. *The Just War in the Middle Ages*. Cambridge University Press, 1975.

Sanger, David E., and William J. Broad, "US and Allies Warn Iran over Nuclear 'Deception'." *New York Times*, September 25, 2009.

Schadlow, Nadia. *War and the Art of Governance: Consolidating Combat Success into Political Victory*. Georgetown University Press, 2017.

Schulzke, Marcus. "Autonomous Weapons and Distributed Responsibility." *Philosophy & Technology* 26, no. 2 (2013): 203–219.

Schulzke, Marcus. "Robots as Weapons in Just Wars." *Philosophy & Technology* 24, no. 3 (2011): 293.

Scupin, Hans-Ulrich. "History of International Law, 1815 to World War I." In *The Max Planck Encyclopedia of Public International Law*. Oxford University Press, 2012.

Sharma, Serena K. "The Legacy of *Jus Contra Bellum*: Echoes of Pacifism in Contemporary Just War Thought." *Journal of Military Ethics* 8, no. 3 (2009): 217–230.

Sherman, Gordon E. "*Jus Gentium* and International Law." *American Journal of International Law* 12, no.1 (1918): 56–63.

Sigmund, Paul E. *Natural Law in Political Thought*. Revised edition. UPA, 1981.

Simon, Yves René Marie. *The Tradition of Natural Law: A Philosopher's Reflections*. Fordham University Press, 1992.

Simpson, Thomas W., and Vincent C. Müller. "Just War and Robots' Killings." *Philosophical Quarterly* 66, no. 263 (2015): 302–322.

Sorley, Lewis. *A Better War: The Unexamined Victories and Final Tragedy of America's Last Years in Vietnam*. Harcourt, 1999.

Suárez, Francisco de. *Selections from Three Works of Francisco Suárez*. Trans. Gwladys L. Williams, Ammi Brown, and John Waldron. Liberty Fund, 2015.

Syse, Henrik. "Augustine and Just War: Between Virtue and Duties." In *Ethics, Nationalism, and Just War: Medieval and Contemporary Perspectives*, ed. Henrik Syse and Gregory M. Reichberg, 36–50. Catholic University Press of America, 2007.

Taddeo, Mariarosaria. "An Analysis for a Just Cyber Warfare." In *2012 4th International Conference on Cyber Conflict (CYCON 2012)*, 1–10. IEEE, 2012.

Tesón, Fernando R. "Ending Tyranny in Iraq." *Ethics & International Affairs* 19, no. 2 (2005): 1–20.

Totten, Mark. *First Strike: America, Terrorism, and Moral Tradition*. Yale University Press, 2010.

Tuck, Richard. *The Rights of War and Peace: Political Thought and the International Order from Grotius to Kant*. Oxford University Press, 2000.

UN General Assembly. Resolution A/RES/60/1. "2005 World Summit Outcome." October 24, 2005.

US National Conference of Catholic Bishops. *The Challenge of Peace: God's Promise and Our Response*. A pastoral letter on war and peace. 1983. www.usccb.org/upload/challenge-peace-gods-promise-our-response-1983.pdf

US National Conference of Catholic Bishops. *The Harvest of Justice Is Sown in Peace*. 1993. www.usccb.org/beliefs-and-teachings/what-we-believe/catholic-social-teaching/the-harvest-of-justice-is-sown-in-peace.cfm

Van Vollenhoven, Cornelis. *The Three Stages in the Evolution of the Law of Nations.* Martinus Nijhoff, 1919.

Vattel, Emer de. *The Law of Nations.* Ed. Bela Kapossy and Richard Whatmore. Liberty Fund, 2008.

Vitoria, Francisco de. *Political Writings.* Ed. Anthony Pagden and Jeremy Lawrence. Cambridge University Press, 1991.

Von Elbe, Joachim. "The Evolution of the Concept of the Just War in International Law." *American Journal of International Law* 33, no. 4 (1939): 665–688.

Vorobej, Mark. "Just War Theory and the Invasion of Afghanistan." *Peace Research* 41, no. 2 (2009): 29–58.

Walker, Andrew. "Eschatology and the Defects of Liberalism." *Providence Magazine*, Spring/Summer 2018.

Waltz, Kenneth N. "Why Iran Should Get the Bomb: Nuclear Balancing Would Mean Stability." *Foreign Affairs* 91, no. 4 (2012): 2–5.

Walzer, Michael. *Arguing about War.* Yale University Press, 2008.

Walzer, Michael. *Just and Unjust Wars: A Moral Argument with Historical Illustrations.* Basic Books, 1992 (2nd edition); 2000 (3rd edition); 2006 (4th edition); 2015 (5th edition).

Walzer, Michael. "The Moral Standing of States: A Response to Four Critics." *Philosophy & Public Affairs* 09, no.3 (1980): 209–229.

Wendt, Alexander. "Anarchy Is What States Make of It: The Social Construction of Power Politics." *International Organization* 46, no. 2 (1992): 391–425.

Wheaton, Henry. *Wheaton's Elements of International Law.* 5th English edition. Stevens and Sons, 1916.

Williams, John. "Distant Intimacy: Space, Drones, and Just War." *Ethics & International Affairs* 29, no. 1 (2015): 93–110.

Wolff, Christian von. *The Law of Nations Treated According to a Scientific Method.* Carnegie Institute Classics of International Law, vol. 13, no. 2. Ed. James Brown Scott. Trans. Joseph H. Drake. Clarendon Press, 1934.

Woodward, Bob. *Plan of Attack.* Simon and Schuster, 2004.

Woodward, Bob. *State of Denial.* Simon and Schuster, 2006.

Wynn, Phillip. *Augustine on War and Military Service.* Fortress Press, 2013.

Zehr, Nahed Artoul. "James Turner Johnson and the 'Classic' Just War Tradition." *Journal of Military Ethics* 8, no. 3 (2009): 190–201.

Zolo, Danilo. *Cosmopolis: Prospects for World Government.* John Wiley & Sons, 2013.

Index

For EU product safety concerns, contact us at Calle de José Abascal, 56–1°,
28003 Madrid, Spain or eugpsr@cambridge.org.